UNDERSTANDING THE USA LEGAL SYSTEM

Law for Everyday Life

RAJENDER KUMAR

For more information, contact: support@JambaAcademy.com.

Published by:
Jamba Academy

Printed in the United States of America

First Printing Edition, 2025

Found Typos & Broken Link

We apologize in advance for any typos or broken link that you may find in this book. We take pride in the quality of our content and strive to provide accurate and useful information to our readers. Please let us know where you found the typos and broken link (if any) so that we can fix them as soon as possible. Again, thank you very much in advance for bringing this to our attention and for your patience.

If you find any typos or broken links in this book, please feel free to email me.

support@JambaAcademy.com

Support

We would love to hear your thoughts and feedback! Could you please take a moment to write a review or share your thoughts on the book? Your feedback helps other readers discover the books and helps authors to improve their work. Thank you for your time and for sharing your thoughts with us!

If there is anything you want to discuss or you have a question about any topic of the book, you can always reach out to me, and I will try to help as much as I can.

support@JambaAcademy.com

This book is dedicated to all newcomers, families, and everyday individuals whose bravery in pursuing truth and justice fuels this work.

May these pages embolden you to stand with confidence and responsibility within the bounds of the law, safeguarding your rights, dignity, and aspirations.

Disclaimer

The content in *Understanding the USA Legal System: Law for Everyday Life* is provided for general informational purposes only, on an "as is" basis, without any warranties, express or implied, including but not limited to warranties of merchantability, fitness for a specific purpose, or non-infringement. The authors and publisher are not liable for any loss or damage, whether direct or indirect, arising from the use of or reliance on the information in this book. This book is not a comprehensive guide to all aspects of the U.S. legal system and should not be considered a substitute for professional legal advice or services. The authors and publisher strongly recommend consulting a qualified legal professional before taking any actions based on the information provided herein.

UNDERSTANDING THE USA LEGAL SYSTEM

Law for Everyday Life

Author: Rajender Kumar

Publisher: Jamba Academy, 2025

Table of Contents

Preface

When I first set foot in the United States over a decade ago, the world before me felt both exhilarating and daunting. Every street sign, official notice, and legal document seemed to carry a weight of meaning that I only partially understood. I recall vividly my first encounter with a traffic stop—my palms sweating not from any wrongdoing, but from a simple, overwhelming uncertainty: What was expected of me? What were my rights? What were my responsibilities? This single, seemingly mundane event sparked a lifelong fascination with the laws that shape everyday existence in America. It also revealed a profound gap—so much of what governs daily life here is unspoken, assumed, or hidden within layers of specialized language and tradition.

As my journey unfolded—both as an immigrant adjusting to a new country and later as a software professional and community advocate—my questions deepened. Why do certain laws exist? How does one's cultural background influence the way laws are perceived and followed? And perhaps most crucially, how can ordinary people, regardless of origin or education, confidently navigate the U.S. legal system to protect themselves and contribute meaningfully to their communities?

These are not simply academic questions. They are the very real challenges that millions face, whether newcomers or native-born citizens, young students or seasoned professionals. With these questions in mind, I wrote **Understanding the USA Legal System: Law for Everyday Life**—not just as a manual, but as a bridge across cultures, experiences, and generations.

Personal and Cultural Motivations

My personal journey is interwoven with the tapestry of this book. Growing up in India, I was surrounded by a legal culture quite distinct from America's. Even basic concepts—like the presumption of innocence or the division of powers—were often explained differently, if at all. Arriving in America, I encountered a rich, sometimes baffling legal tradition shaped by centuries of debate, struggle, and reform.

Yet, I soon realized that confusion about the law was not unique to immigrants. In my work with community organizations and universities, I met countless individuals—students, parents, entrepreneurs—who felt lost when it came to the practicalities of the U.S. legal system. Whether dealing with landlord disputes, understanding employment contracts, or navigating the intricacies of immigration paperwork, the sense of uncertainty was universal.

This book is, in many ways, my response to those experiences. It is an attempt to distill both the spirit and substance of American law into clear, accessible language—without sacrificing depth or complexity. I am motivated by a belief that informed citizens are empowered citizens, and that the law, at its best, is not a barrier but a foundation for justice and opportunity.

Intended Audience

- **Law for Everyday Life** is written for a wide spectrum of readers. It is for:

- **Newcomers to the United States** who want to understand the rules and rights that shape their new home.
- **Students and young adults** embarking on their first experiences of independence and responsibility.
- **Working professionals, business owners, and tenants** seeking clarity in their legal relationships.
- **History enthusiasts** interested in the evolution of law and its impact on society.
- **Anyone who has ever wondered what happens during a traffic stop, a police encounter, or a court case.**

No background in law is assumed. My goal is to make this book approachable, illuminating, and practical—a companion for everyday situations as well as deeper reflection.

Unique Narrative and Thematic Contributions

What sets this book apart is its commitment to storytelling and context. Rather than presenting the law as a static set of rules, I invite readers to explore its living, breathing reality. Each chapter is anchored by real-world examples, historical anecdotes, and the lived experiences of diverse Americans. The book draws not only from U.S. history, but also from global perspectives, comparing how everyday legal issues are addressed in countries like Canada, the United Kingdom, and India. This comparative lens enriches our understanding of what is unique—and what is universal—about the American legal experience.

We look at how the law has evolved through landmark cases and social movements, and how it continues to adapt to new challenges, from digital privacy to immigration reform. The book demystifies legal language, offering clear definitions and practical advice. It does not shy away from uncomfortable truths: the disparities in how laws are enforced, the histories of exclusion and struggle, and the ongoing debates about justice and reform.

Above all, **Law for Everyday Life** is rooted in the conviction that the law belongs to everyone—not just lawyers, judges, or politicians, but to every person who calls America home.

Addressing Key Themes and Societal Issues

This book addresses crucial themes: the importance of knowing your rights, the realities of legal inequality, and the ongoing need for reform. It shines a light on historical gaps—the underrepresentation of minority perspectives, the evolution of civil rights, and the challenges facing immigrants and marginalized groups. In a time of intense debate over justice and fairness, I hope this book offers clarity and hope.

Whether you are a curious reader, a concerned parent, or someone facing a pressing legal question, my hope is that **Law for Everyday Life** provides not only answers, but also the confidence to ask new questions and seek justice for yourself and your community.

The journey through the U.S. legal system is one we all share, whether by choice or by circumstance. I invite you to join me in exploring its history, challenges, and possibilities—and in building a society where the law truly serves us all.

Rajender Kumar

Acknowledgements

The journey to bring **Understanding the USA Legal System: Law for Everyday Life** to fruition has been both intellectually rewarding and personally transformative. This book is the result of countless hours of research, writing, review, and reflection, and it could not have been accomplished without the support and expertise of a remarkable group of individuals. I am deeply grateful for their contributions, each of which has shaped this work into a richer, more accessible, and more culturally resonant resource.

First and foremost, I wish to thank the team of researchers whose meticulous archival research laid the groundwork for this book's historical and legal accuracy. Their dogged pursuit of primary sources and contemporary case studies ensured that every chapter reflects not only the letter of the law but the lived realities of people navigating the U.S. legal system.

To the historians, **Dr. Angela Kim** and **Dr. Samuel Thompson**, your insights into the social evolution of American law added essential context, connecting the past to the present and illuminating the diverse pathways that have shaped our legal landscape. Your willingness to share your knowledge and to challenge my preconceptions made this narrative more nuanced and inclusive.

Special acknowledgment is due to my editorial team. Your keen editorial feedback refined my prose, clarified complex legal concepts, and strengthened the book's narrative flow. Jane, your unwavering commitment to clarity and accessibility ensured that every chapter would be approachable for readers of all backgrounds. Rashid, your sharp eye for detail and thoughtful suggestions were invaluable in making this text both reliable and engaging.

Cultural consultants **Ayesha Patel** and **Gabriel Torres** deserve heartfelt thanks for their critical role in enhancing the book's cultural sensitivity and relevance. Through their guidance, I learned to consider legal norms from a variety of cultural perspectives, and to recognize the unique challenges faced by newcomers, immigrants, and minority communities in the U.S. legal system. Their contributions helped ensure that this book speaks to a wide audience and respects the diverse experiences of all readers.

On a personal level, I am forever grateful to my family and friends, especially **my friend, Jam Aleem Nawaz Khan**, and my parents, whose emotional support and encouragement sustained me through the long months of writing and revision. Jam's empathy and patience, along with her candid feedback on early drafts, helped me stay focused on the book's mission: to make the law less intimidating and more empowering for everyday people.

Collaboration was the beating heart of this project. Working alongside such a varied and passionate group of individuals not only improved the factual and narrative quality of this book, but also reminded me of the importance of multiple perspectives in understanding the law's impact on real lives. Through open dialogue, respectful debate, and shared vision, we strove to create a resource that is as informative as it is inclusive—one that invites readers to engage with the U.S. legal system with curiosity, confidence, and a sense of shared responsibility.

To everyone who contributed their time, expertise, and support—thank you. This book is as much yours as it is mine.

Structure of the Book

The book is organized into twelve chapters, each focusing on a key aspect of the legal system as it intersects with daily life:

- **Foundations of the U.S. Legal System** – Exploring the Constitution, federalism, and the basic structure of government.
- **Understanding Legal Language** – Decoding terms like misdemeanor, felony, arrest, and due process.
- **Your Rights and Responsibilities** – Constitutional rights, civil liberties, and civic duties.
- **Interactions with Law Enforcement** – What to expect, your rights, and how to respond.
- **Traffic Laws and Public Safety** – Rules of the road and consequences of violations.
- **Property Rights and Housing** – Rentals, ownership, landlord-tenant law, and disputes.
- **Business and Employment Law** – Contracts, workplace rights, and starting a business.
- **Immigration Rules and Realities** – Visas, citizenship, and the rights of immigrants.
- **Family Law in Daily Life** – Marriage, divorce, child custody, and adoption.
- **Criminal Justice: From Arrest to Trial** – The process, the roles of lawyers and judges, and the burden of proof.
- **Evidence and the Courts** – What counts as evidence, who decides, and how judgments are made.
- **Staying Informed and Empowered** – Resources, self-advocacy, and ongoing legal education.

Each chapter concludes with practical reflections, resources for further learning, and, where appropriate, a comparative look at how similar issues are handled in other societies.

Introduction: The Invisible Handcuffs—And Keys—of Everyday Life

The Law in a Cup of Coffee

On a brisk morning in 1992, Stella Liebeck, a 79-year-old grandmother, ordered a cup of coffee from a McDonald's drive-thru in Albuquerque, New Mexico. As her grandson parked the car, Stella placed the cup between her knees and attempted to remove the lid to add cream and sugar. The coffee spilled, causing severe burns and sending her to the hospital for eight days. The lawsuit that followed—**Liebeck v. McDonald's Restaurants**—became a media sensation and sparked a nationwide debate about "frivolous lawsuits" and personal responsibility. But beneath the headlines lay a complex web of legal rights, duties, and procedures that few Americans had ever considered.

This single cup of coffee—served a few degrees too hot—illustrates how the law quietly shapes our daily lives. Whether you're buying breakfast, crossing a street, renting an apartment, starting a business, or interacting with the police, the legal system is always present: guiding, protecting, and, at times, restricting our choices. Yet for many, the law remains an invisible force, mysterious and intimidating—a labyrinth navigated only by lawyers and judges.

But what if understanding the law was as essential—and accessible—as knowing how to read a map or drive a car? What if, instead of fearing legal complexity, you could use it as a tool to safeguard your rights, fulfill your responsibilities, and make confident decisions every day?

Why Law Matters—Yesterday and Today

The United States legal system is both ancient and ever-changing. Its roots stretch back to English common law, the Constitution, and foundational moments like the **Brown v. Board of Education** Supreme Court decision of 1954, which ended racial segregation in public schools. Over centuries, laws have evolved alongside society's shifting values, economic realities, and growing diversity.

Consider the story of **Fred Korematsu**, a Japanese American who, during World War II, refused to comply with the forced internment of Japanese Americans ordered by Executive Order 9066. Korematsu's act of courage led to a landmark Supreme Court case. Decades later, it would serve as a cautionary tale about civil liberties and the dangers of unchecked governmental power. This case, like so many others, reveals how law is not just a set of rules—it is a living conversation about justice, identity, and the promise of equality.

Today, the law touches every aspect of our lives. Americans—citizens, immigrants, and visitors alike—navigate a complex landscape of local ordinances, state statutes, and federal regulations. From understanding your rights during a police stop to knowing who is responsible when a neighbor's tree damages your property, legal knowledge is no longer a luxury for the few. It's a necessity for all.

Law in a Global Context

While this book focuses on the U.S. legal system, law is a universal language—one that varies across borders but shapes daily life everywhere. In Germany, citizens must carry identification at all times; in Japan, business contracts often rely more on trust and custom than litigation. Meanwhile, in South Africa, the post-apartheid constitution enshrines unique protections for rights to housing, water, and health care—demonstrating law's power to transform societies.

By exploring American law through global stories and comparisons, this book highlights not only what makes the U.S. system unique, but also the shared human values and challenges that legal systems everywhere must navigate.

The Purpose and Promise of This Book

Law for Everyday Life is your practical, approachable guide to the U.S. legal system. It is not a textbook, nor a manual for aspiring attorneys. Instead, it is written for everyone: newcomers to the United States, students embarking on adulthood, small business owners, parents, renters, and anyone who wants to live responsibly and confidently, armed with essential legal knowledge.

This book aims to:

- **Demystify** the structure and workings of the U.S. legal system, from local courts to the Supreme Court.
- **Clarify** your rights and responsibilities in common situations—at home, work, school, or in public.
- **Explain** key legal terms and procedures without jargon, making legal concepts accessible and relevant.
- **Empower** you to recognize when to seek help, how to interact with law enforcement, and what to do if you face legal trouble.
- **Illuminate** the broader social and historical context of American law, drawing lessons from landmark cases and real-world stories.

Above all, this book invites you to see the law not as a distant authority, but as something personal and participatory—a toolkit for protecting yourself, improving your community, and shaping the future.

Stories That Shape the Law

Throughout the book, you will meet people whose lives have been transformed by the law—sometimes for better, sometimes for worse. You'll read about:

- **Claudette Colvin**, a teenager who refused to give up her bus seat in Montgomery, Alabama, months before Rosa Parks' more famous protest. Her legal challenge laid the groundwork for the **Browder v. Gayle** case, which ended bus segregation.
- **A recent immigrant family** navigating the path to citizenship, confronting both the promise of opportunity and the maze of paperwork and regulations.
- **A small business owner** learning the hard way about zoning laws and business licenses—discovering that a missed permit can mean the difference between success and closure.

By grounding legal concepts in real experiences, this book aims to make the law tangible, relatable, and—above all—human.

A Living Conversation

Law is not static. It reflects the changing values, struggles, and aspirations of society. When the Supreme Court ruled in **Obergefell v. Hodges** (2015) that same-sex marriage is a fundamental right, it didn't just change legal paperwork for couples—it transformed families, communities, and the nation's understanding of love and equality.

Similarly, the law adapts in response to technological innovation, global migration, and evolving notions of justice. The smartphone in your pocket, the ride-share you hail, the online contract you sign—all are governed by laws that must be continually re-examined and reformed.

By learning about the law, you become part of this living conversation. You gain the power to advocate for yourself, to help others, and to participate meaningfully in civic life.

A Global Perspective on Everyday Law

No legal system exists in a vacuum. Throughout this book, we will draw comparisons to other countries' legal traditions—highlighting how different societies balance order, freedom, and justice.

In **Sweden**, restorative justice emphasizes repairing harm rather than punishing offenders, offering a model for alternatives to incarceration.
In **India**, the world's largest democracy, access to legal aid remains a pressing challenge, but recent innovations in mobile legal clinics are bridging the gap for rural communities.
In the **United States**, the right to a jury trial is enshrined in the Constitution, reflecting a belief in participatory justice—though not without its own complexities and controversies.

These global examples remind us that the U.S. legal system is part of a broader human effort to create fair, responsive, and inclusive societies. By understanding our own laws, we are better equipped to appreciate, critique, and improve them.

Your Journey Begins Here

Whether you are facing a simple traffic ticket, considering a new job, renting your first apartment, or simply seeking to be a more informed citizen, this book is for you. The law might seem daunting, but it is not beyond your reach. With each chapter, you will gain practical knowledge, confidence, and a sense of agency.

As you turn the page, remember: every right comes with a responsibility. Every rule has a reason. And every one of us—regardless of background, education, or experience—has a stake in the laws that shape our daily lives.

So, let's begin this journey together. Let's unlock the mysteries of the legal system, learn from the stories of those who came before us, and equip ourselves to make better, safer, and more just choices.

Ready to discover the law's hidden presence in your everyday world? The keys are in your hands.

About the Author

Rajender Kumar is a seasoned data professional whose analytical acumen and passion for social understanding have shaped a distinguished career spanning more than a decade. With a robust educational foundation in computer science and statistics, Rajender has contributed to several Fortune 500 companies and non-profit organizations, leveraging the power of data to illuminate complex societal trends and inform critical decision-making. His expertise lies at the intersection of data analytics, public policy, and civic education—a unique vantage point that brings clarity and practical insight to the intricate workings of the U.S. legal system.

Rajender's journey toward demystifying the law for everyday citizens began long before his foray into publishing. Raised in a multicultural household where conversations about rights, responsibilities, and the rule of law were common, he developed an early appreciation for how legal frameworks shape daily life. His move to the United States as a young adult deepened this awareness, as he navigated a new country's legal landscape not just as a professional, but as a resident and a community member. He vividly recalls his initial challenges deciphering the language of legal documents—rental agreements, workplace contracts, and municipal codes—and how these experiences underscored the critical need for accessible, practical legal knowledge.

Throughout his career, Rajender has been a passionate advocate for bridging the gap between technical expertise and public understanding. He has designed educational workshops on data-driven policy analysis, mentored students in civic technology initiatives, and contributed to community outreach programs aimed at empowering immigrants and newcomers. His work frequently explores how seemingly abstract laws and regulations manifest in the lived experiences of individuals, whether in disputes over property rights, interactions with law enforcement, or the pursuit of small business dreams.

What sets Rajender's approach apart is his ability to distill complex legal and regulatory concepts into clear, actionable guidance, using storytelling and real-world examples that resonate across cultures. Drawing from his own experiences—as well as those of his diverse friends, colleagues, and neighbors—he brings a global perspective to the narrative, highlighting both the universality of legal challenges and the unique features of the American system. His writing reflects a deep respect for the historical evolution of law and its power to promote justice, protect freedoms, and foster social cohesion.

Rajender's commitment to legal education is rooted in the belief that knowledge is both a shield and a tool for empowerment. He views Understanding the USA Legal System: Law for Everyday Life not merely as a guidebook, but as an invitation for readers to engage with the legal foundations of their communities, ask informed questions, and advocate for themselves and others. By making the U.S. legal system accessible and relevant to everyone—regardless of background or prior experience—he aims to inspire a new generation of informed, responsible, and confident citizens.

Through his work, Rajender Kumar affirms that understanding the law is not the exclusive province of lawyers or policymakers; it is a vital part of everyday life. He is honored to share his knowledge, experiences, and insights with readers, and remains dedicated to fostering a culture of legal literacy and civic engagement in an ever-changing world.

"The law is not a distant code, but a living presence that shapes every choice we make — protecting our freedoms, defining our responsibilities, and guiding us through the complexities of daily life."

— Justice Sandra Day O'Connor

Prologue

Crossing the Street, Crossing the Line

On a brisk autumn morning in New York City, the world's most hurried pedestrians crammed the corners of 42nd Street and Lexington Avenue. With coffee cups in hand and earbuds pressed tight, the crowd waited for the signal to change. And then, as if choreographed, a handful of New Yorkers darted into the crosswalk—well before the light flashed green. A sharp whistle cut through the city's hum. "Hey! That's jaywalking," barked a police officer, gesturing for the violators to step aside. The rest of the crowd watched, some amused, some annoyed, but most unfazed. After all, it was "just" jaywalking.

But in that moment—so ordinary it's almost invisible—lies the heart of our everyday relationship with the law. The U.S. legal system, vast and sometimes intimidating, shapes the smallest acts of daily life: crossing a street, renting an apartment, buying groceries, posting on social media. For most people, the law isn't experienced in a courtroom or lawyer's office—it's felt in the routines, rights, and responsibilities that quietly govern our days.

The Law in Unexpected Places

Consider another scene, this one in a quiet suburb outside Los Angeles. Maria Hernandez, a first-generation immigrant, saved for years to open a small bakery. She dreamed of passing her grandmother's recipes to a new generation. But before Maria could unlock her doors, she encountered a maze of permits, health inspections, and zoning laws. One overlooked form, and her opening day was delayed by weeks. "I thought baking was the hard part," Maria later joked, "but understanding the rules was a whole new recipe."

Maria's story is echoed in towns and cities across the country. Whether you're starting a business, driving to work, or signing a lease, the legal system is there—often unnoticed, sometimes misunderstood, but always present. The law isn't just for lawyers or judges; it's woven into the fabric of community life.

History's Everyday Lessons

The influence of law on ordinary people is not a modern invention. In 1776, as the ink dried on the Declaration of Independence, the founding generation debated what rights would define the new nation. Many of their concerns were practical: How would property be protected? Who could participate in government? What freedoms would be guaranteed to the people? These questions weren't just theoretical—they affected how families farmed their land, worshipped, traveled, and spoke their minds.

One of the earliest legal battles involved a Massachusetts farmer, Peter Oliver, who refused to pay a new tax imposed by the colonial government. His protest—seemingly small—helped ignite a movement that would eventually topple an empire. The law, it turned out, was not some distant edict from on high; it was a living, breathing thing that individuals could challenge, change, and use to protect their livelihoods.

This dynamic continues today. From the Civil Rights Movement's lunch counter sit-ins to contemporary debates over privacy on the internet, ordinary people have shaped and been shaped by the law. Sometimes, the rules change because enough people demand it. Other times, the law changes us—nudging, guiding, or, at times, restraining our actions.

The Invisible Guide

Yet, for all its influence, the legal system often feels impenetrable. Legal language is dense, procedures are complex, and consequences can be severe. When does a mistake become a crime? What rights do you have during a traffic stop? How do you resolve a dispute with a neighbor? These aren't just questions for law school—they're dilemmas that can confront anyone at any time.

Globally, the everyday impact of law is felt in different ways. In Japan, for instance, a culture of harmony and consensus shapes how laws are enforced—minor disputes are often resolved through mediation rather than lawsuits. In Sweden, robust consumer protections mean that buying a faulty product is rarely a legal nightmare for the customer. These examples remind us that while the U.S. legal system is unique, the quest for justice and order is universal. Understanding the rules is key to participating fully in society, no matter where you call home.

Why Understanding Matters

Imagine the consequences of not knowing the law: a teenager detained for a prank that crossed a legal line; a tenant evicted for violating a lease clause they never understood; a driver facing heavy fines for a misunderstood traffic rule. Beyond embarrassment or inconvenience, lack of legal knowledge can threaten livelihoods, freedom, and even safety.

But knowledge is power. The more you understand what the law requires—and what it protects—the better equipped you are to navigate life's uncertainties. You don't have to be a legal scholar to ask the right questions, make informed choices, or stand up for your rights. You just need a guide that translates the complex into the practical, the abstract into the everyday.

A Journey Through Everyday Law

This book is that guide. It's built not just for those who want to know the law, but for anyone who wants to live with confidence and clarity in a world shaped by rules. From traffic stops to tenant rights, immigration paperwork to business licenses, we'll explore how the U.S. legal system operates—and how you can make it work for you.

Along the way, you'll meet real people—immigrants building new lives, entrepreneurs chasing dreams, families resolving disputes—whose experiences illustrate the living, breathing nature of American law. You'll learn the difference between a misdemeanor and a felony, what "burden of proof" means in plain English, and how laws evolve alongside society's changing needs.

Most importantly, you'll discover that the law isn't just a set of prohibitions and penalties—it's a tool for building safer, fairer, and more vibrant communities. Whether you're a lifelong resident or a newcomer, a student or a seasoned professional, understanding the law is essential to protecting yourself and contributing to the common good.

Looking Ahead

As you turn these pages, keep in mind the everyday moments—like crossing a busy street or opening a small bakery—where law quietly shapes the choices before you. Each chapter will break down complex ideas into clear, actionable knowledge, empowering you to move through life with greater understanding and assurance.

The journey begins now: together, we'll step into the world of everyday law, uncovering its hidden influence and practical wisdom. Welcome to a guide that promises not just to inform, but to empower—because in the United States, the law belongs to all of us.

Prerequisites

Before diving into the intricacies of the U.S. legal system and its influence on everyday life, it's helpful to establish a shared foundation of knowledge. While this book is designed to be accessible to readers from all backgrounds, a basic understanding of certain historical, cultural, and legal concepts will make your journey through its pages smoother and more rewarding. This prerequisites section will outline the essential context, recommend resources for further exploration, illustrate with real-world scenarios, and address common barriers to engaging with legal concepts.

Foundational Concepts and Historical Context

The Roots of the U.S. Legal System

To fully understand how law shapes daily life in the United States, it's important to recognize that the American legal system did not develop in a vacuum. Instead, it grew from a rich tapestry of historical and cultural influences, most notably the **English common law** tradition. Under common law, judicial decisions from past cases (precedents) play a significant role in shaping future rulings. This concept, often described as **"stare decisis"** (Latin for "to stand by things decided"), remains central to how American courts interpret laws today.

The **U.S. Constitution**—adopted in 1787—serves as the supreme law of the land. It not only establishes the framework for the federal government but also outlines fundamental rights and liberties, such as freedom of speech, due process, and equal protection under the law. Understanding the Constitution's structure (including the **Bill of Rights** and subsequent amendments) will help you recognize how legal protections apply to everyday scenarios.

Federalism and the Separation of Powers

Another cornerstone is the concept of **federalism**: the division of authority between federal and state governments. This means that laws can sometimes differ significantly from one state to another, especially in areas like property law, criminal offenses, or business regulations.

Additionally, the **separation of powers** among the legislative (Congress), executive (President), and judicial (courts) branches prevents any single branch from dominating the government. This system of checks and balances ensures that laws are not only created thoughtfully but also interpreted and enforced fairly.

Everyday Relevance

Many people encounter the law in subtle ways each day—crossing the street, signing a lease, starting a business, or interacting with police officers. A working knowledge of **civil law** (rights and responsibilities between individuals), **criminal law** (offenses against society), and **administrative law** (rules governing government agencies) will help you navigate real-life situations with confidence and awareness.

Recommended Resources

To deepen your understanding before or alongside reading this book, the following resources—chosen for their clarity and accessibility—provide valuable perspectives on U.S. law and its historical underpinnings:

- **"A People's History of the United States" by Howard Zinn**

Zinn's narrative approach offers a vibrant, people-centered look at American history, including the development of its legal system and the struggles for rights and justice.

- **"The U.S. Constitution: A Very Short Introduction" by David J. Bodenhamer**

This concise book breaks down the Constitution's structure, history, and ongoing relevance in clear, straightforward language.

- **Khan Academy: "U.S. Government and Civics"**

[Khan Academy's free online course] (https://www.khanacademy.org/humanities/us-government-and-civics) provides short, engaging videos on topics like federalism, civil liberties, and the court system.

- **"Gideon's Trumpet" (book and film adaptation)**

Anthony Lewis's account of a landmark Supreme Court case makes legal history accessible and illustrates the real-life stakes of legal rights.

- **National Constitution Center Website**

[constitutioncenter.org] (https://constitutioncenter.org) includes interactive resources and explanations suitable for learners at all levels.

These materials will reinforce your grasp of the legal concepts and historical periods referenced throughout this book.

Illustrative Scenarios: Why Background Knowledge Matters

Scenario 1: Navigating a Traffic Stop

Imagine you are pulled over by a police officer for a minor traffic violation. Understanding your rights—such as the right to remain silent, the right to refuse a search without probable cause, and the requirement to provide identification—empowers you to interact with law enforcement respectfully and safely. Knowledge of relevant laws and procedures not only protects your rights but also helps you avoid unnecessary conflict or escalation.

Scenario 2: Renting Your First Apartment

Suppose you're signing a lease for your first apartment in the U.S. If you're unfamiliar with legal terms like "security deposit," "tenant's rights," or "eviction notice," you might inadvertently agree to unfavorable terms or miss out on protections guaranteed by state and local laws. A foundational understanding of property law and contract basics can prevent costly mistakes and ensure you make informed decisions.

These scenarios highlight the real-life value of having even a modest grasp of legal history, vocabulary, and principles.

Addressing Barriers to Engagement

Demystifying Legal Language

Legal writing is sometimes criticized for being dense and filled with **"legalese"**—specialized terminology that can feel intimidating. Terms like **"affidavit," "tort,"** or **"habeas corpus"** may appear daunting, but this book is committed to defining such terms in plain language and providing context for their use. Our goal is to make the law understandable, not impenetrable.

Cultural and Historical Differences

Readers from outside the United States, or those unfamiliar with American government, may find some concepts—like the prominence of individual rights or the adversarial nature of U.S. courts—different from legal systems in other countries. For example, in many European nations, civil law systems rely more on written codes and less on judicial precedent. Recognizing these differences enriches your perspective and fosters appreciation for the diversity of global legal traditions.

Encouraging All Readers

No prior legal education is required to benefit from this book. Whether you are a newcomer to the United States, a lifelong resident, or simply curious about the legal forces shaping your daily life, be assured that curiosity, an open mind, and a willingness to learn are the only prerequisites you truly need.

Summary and Reflection

A firm grounding in U.S. history, government structure, and basic legal concepts will help you make the most of this book's practical insights. By familiarizing yourself with the Constitution, the division of powers, and the essential vocabulary of law, you'll find the material more accessible and relevant. Remember: the law is not just a subject for lawyers and judges—it's a living force that touches everyone. With the right foundation, you'll be better equipped to understand, engage with, and, when necessary, challenge the legal systems that shape our everyday lives.

Getting Ready: Essential Resources, Mindset, and Preparation

Before embarking on the journey through the U.S. legal landscape, it's important to pause and consider how best to approach this book. The law, often seen as an intimidating or mysterious field, is woven into the very fabric of daily life. This section aims to demystify the learning process, break down barriers to understanding, and empower you—regardless of background—to engage with confidence and curiosity.

What You Don't Need: Dispelling Common Myths

Let's begin by clearing away a few misconceptions:

No Law Degree Required: You do not need a background in legal studies or a law degree to benefit from this book. The material is written for everyone—students, newcomers, parents, professionals, and community members alike.
No Legal Jargon Mastery Needed: While legal terms will appear, each important term will be clearly defined and explained in plain language. There's no expectation that you come in knowing the difference between a misdemeanor and a felony, or what "burden of proof" means.
No Special Tools or Software: All you need is this book, an open mind, and perhaps a notebook for jotting down questions or thoughts. You won't need any special technology, paid subscription, or access to legal databases.

By removing these barriers, the path to understanding the legal system becomes not only accessible but inviting.

The Mindset: Curiosity, Empathy, and Openness

Curiosity as Your Guide

Approach this book not as a test, but as an exploration. The legal system is full of stories—of individuals, communities, and even entire nations grappling with questions of right and wrong, fairness and justice. By maintaining a sense of curiosity, you'll find that even complex concepts become more approachable.

Empathy and Perspective-Taking

Laws affect people differently, depending on where they live, their background, and their experiences. As you read, try to put yourself in others' shoes. How might a traffic stop feel for someone new to the country? What challenges might a small business owner face when navigating regulations? Empathy not only enriches your understanding but also deepens your appreciation for the law's role in society.

Openness to Learning

Be prepared for moments when what you read challenges your assumptions or introduces unfamiliar perspectives. The U.S. legal system has evolved through conflict, compromise, and change. An open mind allows you to appreciate this complexity, see patterns, and connect ideas across chapters.

Practical Resources to Support Your Journey

While this book is designed to be self-contained, there are a few accessible resources and habits that can enhance your engagement:

1. Local Library and Community Centers

Your public library is a treasure trove of legal information. Most libraries offer not only books but also free workshops, pamphlets, and even occasional talks by local attorneys or advocates. If a particular chapter piques your interest—say, on tenant rights or consumer protection—your library can help you find additional, easy-to-understand resources.

Example:

After reading the property rights section, you visit your library and discover a free workshop on renters' rights in your city. By attending, you gain practical advice tailored to your local laws and make connections with knowledgeable community members.

2. Reputable Online Legal Information

The internet can be overwhelming, but several trusted websites break down legal concepts for everyday readers. These include:

- **USA.gov:** The U.S. government's official web portal, which links to resources on laws, regulations, and government services.
- **Legal Aid Societies:** Many states and cities have legal aid websites that explain rights and responsibilities in plain language.
- **LawHelp.org:** A gateway to free legal aid programs and information across the country.

Example:

You're unsure about your rights during a police stop. After reading the relevant chapter, you visit LawHelp.org to find a printable wallet card that summarizes your rights, giving you confidence and peace of mind.

3. Discussion and Reflection

Learning is deepened when shared. Consider discussing what you've learned with friends, family, or in online forums dedicated to civic education. If English is not your first language, many immigrant and community organizations offer workshops or translated materials to help you engage more fully.

Example:

A recent immigrant reads the section on immigration rules and, at a community center event, shares questions with others in a similar situation. A staff member helps clarify specific points, turning abstract rules into actionable knowledge.

How These Resources and Mindsets Enhance Your Journey

Let's see how these approaches come together to transform your learning experience:

Breaking Down Barriers:

By recognizing that you don't need a legal background, you're free to ask questions without fear of "not knowing enough." This openness invites a richer and more honest engagement with the material.

Deepening Understanding Through Real-World Connection:

When you take part in a local workshop or explore trustworthy websites, you see how the law operates in real life—not just on the page. This practical connection makes the information more memorable and useful.

Building a Supportive Learning Community:

Whether through family conversations, online discussion groups, or community events, sharing what you learn fosters a sense of empowerment. You realize that legal knowledge isn't just for lawyers—it's a tool available to all.

Encouragement for the Road Ahead

As you prepare to read further, remember: the law belongs to everyone. Its language may sometimes seem complicated, but its purpose is to serve and protect the people. By approaching this book with curiosity, empathy, and openness—and by drawing on accessible resources—you'll discover not only how the legal system works, but how it shapes and reflects the values of a diverse nation.

Along the way, you may recognize similarities with legal systems in other countries, or appreciate the unique features of the U.S. approach. For example, while many European nations have centralized legal codes, the U.S. system is marked by a blend of federal and state laws, reflecting its history and diversity. In Japan, legal reforms after World War II created a hybrid system influenced by both Western and traditional principles, demonstrating how cultural context shapes the law. By staying open to these global perspectives, you enrich your understanding of how law evolves to meet the needs of different societies.

In summary, no prior expertise is needed—just a willingness to learn, reflect, and engage. The journey ahead promises to be both practical and enlightening, equipping you with the knowledge and confidence to navigate the U.S. legal system in your everyday life. Let's begin.

What You Will Gain from This Book

Understanding the Journey Ahead

Imagine standing at a crossroads, each path representing a different aspect of your daily life—driving to work, signing a lease, starting a small business, or simply walking in your neighborhood. At every turn, the law quietly shapes your choices, offering both protection and boundaries. Yet, for many, the U.S. legal system appears as a maze: complex, intimidating, and shrouded in jargon. **Understanding the USA Legal System: Law for Everyday Life** is designed to be your map and compass, guiding you through the landscape of American law with clarity, context, and practical wisdom.

In these pages, you will not just learn *what* the law says—you will discover *why* the law exists, *how* it evolved, and *what* it means for you, your loved ones, and your community. Whether you are a newcomer to the United States, a lifelong resident seeking clarity, or a curious student of society, this book will empower you to navigate everyday legal situations with confidence and insight.

Specific Insights, Perspectives, and Knowledge

By engaging with this book, you will gain:

A Working Knowledge of Key U.S. Laws:

You will become familiar with essential rules governing traffic, property, business, immigration, and interpersonal conduct. For example, you will learn the difference between a **misdemeanor** (like running a stop sign) and a **felony** (such as grand theft), and understand why these distinctions matter for your record and rights.

An Understanding of Legal Rights and Responsibilities:

When should you show identification to a police officer? What are your rights if you are stopped, questioned, or detained? This book will break down scenarios you might face—such as a routine traffic stop or an encounter in a public space—so you know how to respond respectfully and assertively.

Clarity on Legal Terminology and Procedures:

Legal language can be daunting. Here, terms like **arrest**, **detainment**, **burden of proof**, and **admissible evidence** are explained with real-world examples and simple analogies. Instead of feeling lost in translation, you'll recognize these concepts when they appear in news headlines or daily conversation.

Awareness of Legal Consequences:

Every action has potential legal implications. Whether it's neglecting to pay a parking ticket or inadvertently violating a lease agreement, you'll learn about possible penalties, fines, or even jail time—and, more importantly, how to avoid common pitfalls.

A Sense of Legal Empowerment:

You'll come away with strategies for protecting yourself, your property, and your loved ones. From understanding your rights as a tenant to knowing what to do if you're involved in a car accident, this book offers both preventative advice and guidance for when things go wrong.

Applying Insights in Everyday Life

To bring these concepts to life, let's consider a few real-world scenarios and historical moments:

1. A Routine Traffic Stop: Knowing Your Rights and Duties

Emily, a new driver, is pulled over for a broken taillight. She is nervous—what should she say? What documents should she provide? Through this book, Emily learns that she must present her driver's license and registration, remain calm, and politely ask why she was stopped. She also discovers her right to remain silent if questioned beyond the basics. By understanding both her responsibilities and her rights, Emily avoids escalation and resolves the situation smoothly.

2. The Story of Miranda v. Arizona (1966): The Right to Remain Silent

This landmark U.S. Supreme Court case transformed legal practice by requiring police to inform individuals of their rights upon arrest—the now-famous "Miranda rights." Before this ruling, many people, especially those with limited English or education, unknowingly waived their rights. By learning about this pivotal moment, readers see how legal principles evolve to protect vulnerable individuals and why knowing your rights is essential in any society.

3. Comparing Tenant Protections: U.S. and Germany

In the United States, tenant rights vary widely by state, but renters are generally protected from unlawful eviction and have rights to safe, habitable housing. By contrast, Germany's tenant laws are among the world's strongest, providing long-term security and capping rent increases. By exploring such global examples, readers gain a broader perspective on how cultural values shape legal protections, sparking ideas for advocacy and reform at home.

Relevance to Today's Society

In an era of rapid change—driven by technology, shifting demographics, and evolving social norms—the law is both a stabilizing force and a work in progress. Consider the ongoing debates over privacy rights in the digital age, immigration reform, or criminal justice policies. **Law for Everyday Life** situates these issues within a historical and cultural context, helping you distinguish between enduring legal principles and those in flux.

For instance, the recent national conversations about police encounters and the rights of protestors echo earlier civil rights struggles, reminding us that the law is not static but responsive to public demand and moral progress. By tracing these threads, the book invites readers to engage critically with the legal system—not only as subjects of the law, but as its potential shapers.

Transformative Potential: From Confusion to Confidence

At its core, this book is about transformation: turning the intimidating and opaque into the understandable and actionable. By demystifying the U.S. legal system, you gain not just knowledge, but agency. Imagine the peace of mind that comes from knowing where you stand in a legal dispute, or the power to advocate for yourself and others in moments of uncertainty.

As you journey through these pages, you'll find more than facts—you'll find stories, analogies, and lessons that resonate across backgrounds and borders. You'll emerge not only as a more informed citizen, but as an empowered participant in the legal life of your community.

With every chapter, you will unlock the tools to navigate daily challenges, contribute to a more just society, and ensure that the law serves you—never just the other way around.

Rajender Kumar

UNDERSTANDING THE USA LEGAL SYSTEM

LAW FOR EVERYDAY LIFE

1 Foundations of Law—Why Rules Matter

1.1 The Purpose of Law in Society

From the earliest days of human civilization, people have created rules to guide their interactions and resolve disputes. Whether carved in stone, memorized as oral traditions, or written into vast legal codes, these laws form the backbone of any organized society. But what, fundamentally, is the purpose of law? Why do we need it, and how does it shape our daily lives in the United States and beyond?

Law as the Framework for Order

At its core, **law** serves as the invisible architecture of society. Imagine a bustling city intersection without traffic lights or road signs—chaos would quickly erupt. In much the same way, laws provide order, predictability, and stability, giving people confidence in how they can act and what they can expect from others.

Protecting individuals and property: Laws guard our physical safety, our possessions, and our rights.
Setting expectations: Laws outline acceptable behavior, helping people anticipate consequences and make informed choices.
Resolving conflicts: When disputes arise, legal systems offer structured ways to settle them fairly—without resorting to violence or intimidation.

Justice and Fairness: Aspirations and Realities

The ideal of **justice**—that everyone should be treated fairly under the law—has inspired countless legal reforms. The U.S. legal system, for instance, is grounded in the principle that all are equal before the law. Yet, the journey towards justice is ongoing, and history offers many lessons.

A Historical Anecdote: The March Toward Equality

Consider the story of **Brown v. Board of Education** (1954). For decades, American schools were segregated by race, enforced by laws that claimed to be "separate but equal." But in this landmark case, the Supreme Court declared these laws unconstitutional, stating that "separate educational facilities are inherently unequal." This decision didn't just change schools—it was a catalyst for the broader Civil Rights Movement, showing how law can be a powerful tool for social change.

Protection and Security in Everyday Life

Laws aren't just lofty ideals or dramatic courtroom battles; they touch our daily routines in countless ways.

Traffic laws keep roads safe for everyone, regardless of whether you're a driver, cyclist, or pedestrian.
Consumer protection laws ensure the products we buy are safe and that we aren't deceived by false advertising.
Tenant and landlord laws spell out rights and obligations in housing, safeguarding both parties.

A Real-World Example: Knowing Your Rights

Imagine you're pulled over for a minor traffic violation. The officer explains the reason, asks for your license, and issues a citation. This scenario, while routine, is governed by a web of laws designed to protect both you and the officer:

- You have the right to remain silent and not incriminate yourself.
- The officer is required to follow proper procedures, ensuring your rights aren't violated.

Understanding these legal basics can prevent misunderstandings and protect your interests.

Law as a Social Contract

The concept of law as a **social contract**—an unwritten agreement among members of a society—helps explain why people generally obey laws, even when no one is watching. We comply not just out of fear of punishment, but because we recognize that laws benefit everyone, creating a safer, more predictable world.

Global Perspective: Law in Diverse Societies

While the U.S. legal system is uniquely shaped by its history and Constitution, the underlying purposes of law are shared worldwide. In Japan, for example, consensus and harmony play a central role in legal processes, emphasizing mediation over confrontation. In Sweden, laws are designed to promote social welfare and equality. These varied approaches highlight how cultural values influence the way laws are developed and enforced.

The Evolution of Law

Laws are not static—they evolve as societies change. New technologies, shifting values, and emerging challenges require constant adaptation. The COVID-19 pandemic, for instance, saw rapid legal changes around public health, business closures, and individual freedoms. Early societies relied on unwritten customs. Modern legal systems, like the U.S., draw on centuries of legal tradition and ongoing legislative action.

```
Fact: In the United States, the principle of "rule of law" means that no one-not even government officials-is above the law.
```

The purpose of law in society is both practical and aspirational: it keeps order, protects rights, and strives for fairness. By understanding these foundations, we prepare ourselves not only to follow the rules but to engage thoughtfully with the legal system when challenges or questions arise.

As we move forward, we'll explore the structure of the U.S. legal system—how it's built, who makes the laws, and what roles courts, legislatures, and agencies play in shaping the rules that govern our everyday lives.

1.2 The Origins of the U.S. Legal System

From the moment the United States first began to take shape, the question of how to create fair and just laws lay at the heart of its founding. The legal system we rely on today is a product of centuries of evolution, drawing from both ancient traditions and revolutionary ideals. Understanding where these rules come from—and why they matter—is crucial for anyone living under their influence.

Roots in English Common Law

The single most significant influence on the U.S. legal system is **English Common Law**. When the first English colonists arrived on North American shores, they brought with them not only their language and customs, but also a legal tradition based on precedent, or **stare decisis**—the idea that past judicial decisions should guide future ones. This approach emphasized consistency, fairness, and adaptability, allowing judges to interpret the law based on previous cases rather than following a rigid code.

Common Law is built largely on case decisions rather than written statutes.
Judges play a central role in interpreting and shaping the law over time.
Legal principles such as the right to a fair trial and the presumption of innocence have their origins in this tradition.

Real-World Example: The Case of John Peter Zenger

A pivotal moment in early American legal history occurred in 1735, when **John Peter Zenger**, a printer in New York, was put on trial for publishing criticisms of the colonial governor. British law at the time treated such speech as a crime, but the jury found Zenger not guilty, establishing the principle of **freedom of the press**. This case set a precedent that still influences First Amendment rights today.

The Influence of Civil Law

While common law forms the backbone of most U.S. states' legal systems, there are notable exceptions—most famously, **Louisiana**, whose legal code is rooted in the **Napoleonic Code**. This civil law tradition, common in continental Europe and Latin America, relies more on comprehensive written statutes than on judicial decisions.

Civil Law systems prioritize written codes and statutes.
Judges have less discretion to interpret the law compared to common law systems.

Global Perspective: Comparing Legal Traditions

- Many countries blend both traditions, or choose one over the other. For example:

- **France** and **Japan** have legal systems based on civil law, emphasizing legislative codes.
- The **United Kingdom**, **Canada** (outside of Quebec), and **Australia** follow the common law tradition, like most of the U.S.

This diversity highlights the adaptability of legal systems to different cultures and histories, reminding us that the rules we live by are shaped by both local conditions and global influences.

The Constitution: A Revolutionary Blueprint

The **U.S. Constitution**, adopted in 1787, solidified a uniquely American legal framework. It established:

- The separation of powers between the **legislative**, **executive**, and **judicial** branches.
- The principle of **federalism**, dividing authority between state and national governments.
- Fundamental rights, later expanded by the **Bill of Rights**, such as freedom of speech, due process, and equal protection.

Historical Anecdote: The Bill of Rights

When the Constitution was first drafted, many Americans feared it granted too much power to the federal government. In response, the first ten amendments—the **Bill of Rights**—were added, guaranteeing essential freedoms and limiting government authority. These amendments continue to protect citizens in everyday situations, from expressing opinions online to expecting fair treatment during police encounters.

A Living System: Change and Adaptation

The U.S. legal system is not static. Over time, it has adapted to new challenges, technologies, and social changes. Landmark Supreme Court cases like **Brown v. Board of Education** (1954), which struck down racial segregation in schools, and more recent debates over digital privacy, show how the legal system evolves to meet society's needs.

```
The U.S. Constitution is the supreme law of the land—no law can override its
principles. Every person in the U.S., citizen or not, is protected by the
Constitution's core rights and freedoms.')
```

As we trace the origins of the U.S. legal system, it becomes clear that our laws are not just arbitrary rules—they are the product of centuries of debate, adaptation, and aspiration for justice. Understanding these foundations equips us to navigate the legal landscape with confidence and responsibility.

In the next section, we'll break down the structure of today's U.S. legal system, exploring how laws are made, interpreted, and enforced—laying the groundwork for understanding your rights and responsibilities in everyday life.

1.3 Key Principles of American Law

The Rule of Law: The Bedrock of Justice

At the heart of the U.S. legal system lies a powerful concept: **the rule of law**. This principle means that everyone—citizens, government officials, and even the president—must follow the same laws. No individual or group is above the law. The rule of law ensures fairness and predictability, creating a society where rights are protected and obligations are clear.

This idea traces back to the founding of the United States. The **Declaration of Independence** proclaimed that all people are endowed with certain unalienable rights, and the **U.S. Constitution** set forth a government limited by checks and balances. By entrusting power to laws instead of individuals, the rule of law has shaped American society for centuries.

Due Process: Fairness in Legal Proceedings

One of the most significant protections within American law is **due process**. The Fifth and Fourteenth Amendments to the Constitution guarantee that no one may be deprived of "life, liberty, or property, without due process of law." But what does this mean in practice?

Due process requires the government to act fairly and follow established procedures before taking away a person's rights. This includes:

Notice: You must be informed of legal actions against you.
Hearing: You have the right to a fair hearing before an impartial judge.
Representation: You are entitled to legal representation in many proceedings.

Consider the story of **Miranda v. Arizona (1966)**. Ernesto Miranda was arrested and interrogated by police without being told his rights. The Supreme Court ruled this violated due process, leading to the now-famous **Miranda warnings**: the right to remain silent and the right to an attorney. Today, these are recited to anyone taken into police custody, ensuring fairness and clarity in the justice system.

Equal Protection: Justice for All

Another cornerstone is the **equal protection clause** of the Fourteenth Amendment, which requires states to treat individuals in similar situations equally under the law. This principle has been central to major social changes in American history.

For example, the Supreme Court's decision in **Brown v. Board of Education (1954)** declared racial segregation in public schools unconstitutional, recognizing that "separate but equal" was inherently unequal. This landmark case propelled the civil rights movement and reinforced the idea that justice must not discriminate.

Presumption of Innocence: Proving Guilt Beyond Doubt

In U.S. law, everyone is presumed innocent until proven guilty. The **burden of proof** in criminal cases falls on the prosecution, which must convince the judge or jury of the defendant's guilt "beyond a reasonable doubt." This high standard protects individuals from wrongful conviction and upholds the integrity of the justice system.

Separation of Powers and Checks and Balances

To prevent the abuse of power, the U.S. legal system divides government responsibilities among three branches:

Legislative: Makes laws (Congress)
Executive: Enforces laws (President and agencies)
Judicial: Interprets laws (Courts)

This **separation of powers** ensures no single branch becomes too powerful. **Checks and balances**—like the president's veto, Congress's power to override vetoes, and judicial review—maintain equilibrium and accountability.

Flexibility and Change: Amending the Law

American law is not static. The **Constitution** can be amended, and statutes can be updated to address new challenges. Over time, amendments have abolished slavery, extended voting rights, and adapted to the evolving needs of society.

Global Perspective: Comparing Legal Traditions

While the U.S. legal system is rooted in English common law, other countries take different approaches. For instance, **France** and many European nations use a **civil law** system, relying on comprehensive legal codes rather than precedent. In Japan, the post-World War II constitution adopted many American legal principles, reinforcing rights and due process.

```
The right to remain silent and the right to legal counsel are fundamental
protections when interacting with law enforcement in the U.S. Violating these
rights can render evidence inadmissible in court.
```

Reflection and Transition

The key principles of American law—rule of law, due process, equal protection, presumption of innocence, and the separation of powers—form the foundation of justice and liberty in daily life. By understanding these ideas, you gain the tools to recognize your rights and responsibilities. Next, we'll examine how these principles come alive in the practical structure of courts, police, and the legislative process—revealing how the legal system truly operates in everyday situations.

1.4 Global Legal Systems: A Comparative View

Legal Systems Around the World: An Introduction

To truly appreciate the unique features of the U.S. legal system, it's essential to recognize that there is no single global model of law. Around the world, societies have developed distinct legal frameworks shaped by history, culture, religion, and politics. By comparing these systems, we gain a deeper understanding of why certain rules exist—and how they serve the needs of their communities.

The Three Main Legal Traditions

Most countries' laws fall into one of three major traditions:

- **Common Law**: Originating in England, this system relies heavily on court decisions and judicial precedent. The United States, Canada, India, and many former British colonies use common law, which allows judges' interpretations in past cases to guide current decisions.
- **Civil Law**: Rooted in Roman law and codified in the Napoleonic Code, civil law is based on comprehensive, written statutes. Countries like France, Germany, Japan, and much of Latin America follow this system. Judges interpret the law but have less flexibility than in common law systems.
- **Religious Law**: In some nations, law is largely derived from religious texts. For example, **Sharia law** in Saudi Arabia and parts of Nigeria is based on Islamic principles, while **Jewish Halakha** and **Hindu law** influence personal matters in Israel and India, respectively.

Key Differences

Flexibility: Common law evolves through judicial decisions, adapting to new situations. Civil law relies on legislative change.

Role of Judges: In civil law, judges act more like investigators, while in common law, they function as arbiters and interpreters of precedent.

Sources of Law: Religious systems prioritize sacred texts; common and civil law emphasize human-made statutes and constitutions.

Real-World Example: Traffic Laws Across Borders

Consider the experience of **Maria**, a Brazilian student who moved to the United States. In Brazil, a civil law country, traffic rules are strictly codified, and police have little discretion when issuing tickets. When Maria received a speeding citation in the U.S., she was surprised to learn she could contest the ticket in court, and that the outcome might depend on the judge's interpretation of the circumstances—a hallmark of common law's flexibility.

This small incident reveals much about the differences in how laws are enforced and interpreted worldwide. For newcomers to the U.S., understanding that legal outcomes can depend on precedent and individual circumstances is crucial for navigating daily life.

Historical Anecdote: Magna Carta and the Birth of Common Law

The roots of the U.S. legal system can be traced back to **1215**, when English barons forced King John to sign the **Magna Carta**. This "Great Charter" limited royal power and established the idea that even rulers are subject to the law. The principles of due process and the right to a fair trial, enshrined in Magna Carta, later crossed the

Atlantic and became foundational in American law. In contrast, many civil law countries developed their systems from different sources, emphasizing the supremacy of written codes over judicial interpretation.

Global Perspectives: Why Diversity Matters

Comparing legal systems isn't just an academic exercise—it has practical, everyday implications:

- **Travel and Immigration**: Understanding differences helps travelers and immigrants avoid unintentional legal trouble.
- **Business**: Companies operating internationally must navigate varied contract laws, property rights, and dispute resolution mechanisms.
- **Human Rights**: Some systems prioritize individual rights, while others emphasize collective harmony or religious principles. This can influence everything from freedom of speech to family law.

```
The U.S. legal system is based on common law, meaning that court decisions and
past rulings shape how laws are applied today—unlike many other countries,
where written statutes are supreme.
Civil law systems, like those in France and Japan, rely on detailed written
codes, offering less flexibility for judges than in the U.S.
```

Reflection and Transition

By exploring the world's diverse legal systems, we see that laws are living reflections of the societies they govern. Whether rooted in precedent, code, or faith, every legal tradition seeks to balance order, justice, and cultural values. As we turn our focus back to the United States, we'll delve into the practical structure of courts, police, and legislation—unpacking how these institutions bring legal principles to life in our everyday experiences. Understanding these global perspectives offers valuable context for appreciating the strengths and challenges of the U.S. legal system as we encounter it daily.

1.5 Why Legal Awareness Matters

Legal awareness is more than a set of facts memorized for a civics test—it is a vital compass that helps individuals navigate the complexities of everyday life in the United States. When people understand their rights, responsibilities, and the broad framework of laws that govern society, they are empowered to make informed decisions, protect themselves, and contribute meaningfully to their communities.

The Power of Knowing the Law

Imagine standing at a busy intersection, unsure whether you have the right of way. Now, consider a landlord-tenant dispute, where one party lacks knowledge of basic rental laws. In both scenarios, legal awareness can make the difference between peaceful resolution and costly conflict. The law is not just about courts and judges—it shapes our daily routines, from how we drive to how we resolve disagreements.

- **Personal Empowerment**: Knowing the law means you can advocate for yourself, avoid common pitfalls, and recognize when your rights may be violated.
- **Civic Engagement**: An informed citizenry is the backbone of a functioning democracy. Understanding legal processes encourages participation in local, state, and federal government.
- **Community Well-being**: Legal awareness contributes to safer neighborhoods, more equitable workplaces, and fairer marketplaces.

Historical Anecdote: The Miranda Warning

The famous **Miranda v. Arizona** (1966) Supreme Court decision illustrates the impact of legal awareness on individual rights. Ernesto Miranda, unaware of his right to remain silent, confessed to a crime during police interrogation. The Court ruled that suspects must be informed of their rights—a practice now known as the **Miranda warning**. This decision not only changed law enforcement procedures nationwide but also underscored the principle that knowing your rights is essential to protecting them.

Global Perspective: Legal Literacy Around the World

Legal awareness is not just a U.S. concern. In India, a movement called **Legal Literacy Camps** helps rural citizens understand their rights regarding land, marriage, and employment, reducing exploitation and injustice. Similarly, in Sweden, schoolchildren are taught the basics of their legal system, fostering a culture of respect for the law from an early age. These examples remind us that legal literacy is a universal safeguard against abuse and misunderstanding.

Everyday Consequences of Legal Ignorance

Failing to understand the law does not exempt anyone from its consequences. Whether it's missing a court date, violating a lease, or misunderstanding tax obligations, ignorance can lead to:

Fines or penalties

Loss of property or employment

Criminal charges
Erosion of trust in institutions

Understanding even the basics—what constitutes a contract, how to respond to law enforcement, or when to seek legal advice—can prevent many of these issues.

```
Ignorance of the law is not a defense.
The Miranda warning exists because every person in the U.S. has the right to
remain silent and to an attorney when detained by police.
```

Reflection and Transition

Legal awareness is the first line of defense in safeguarding your rights and fulfilling your responsibilities as a member of society. It builds confidence, fosters respect, and enables better choices in interactions both big and small. As we move forward, we will explore how these principles take shape in the everyday legal situations you are most likely to encounter—from traffic stops to rental agreements to workplace disputes—ensuring you're not just living under the law, but living informed within it.

1.6 Law in the Lives of Immigrants and Newcomers

For many immigrants and newcomers, entering the United States is not just about crossing a border—it's about stepping into a complex web of laws, rights, and responsibilities that can shape nearly every aspect of daily life. While the legal system is designed to protect all residents, understanding its rules is especially crucial for those unfamiliar with its foundations. Rules and regulations, after all, don't simply serve as barriers; they can also be lifelines, empowering newcomers to build secure, dignified lives.

Navigating New Legal Terrain

Arriving in the U.S. with dreams of opportunity, many newcomers quickly realize that everyday activities—finding a job, leasing an apartment, or sending children to school—involve a series of legal considerations. Unlike in some countries where verbal agreements might suffice, the U.S. legal system relies heavily on written documentation and clear records.

Employment: Laws protect workers, regardless of origin, from discrimination and unsafe conditions. The Fair Labor Standards Act (FLSA) guarantees minimum wage and overtime pay, while the Equal Employment Opportunity Commission (EEOC) enforces anti-discrimination laws.

Housing: The Fair Housing Act prohibits discrimination based on race, color, national origin, religion, sex, familial status, or disability. However, newcomers may not know their rights or how to assert them.
Education: Children, regardless of immigration status, have a right to attend public school—a principle established by the landmark Supreme Court case **Plyler v. Doe (1982)**.

The Role of Legal Status

Legal status—whether someone is a citizen, permanent resident, visa holder, or undocumented—affects which rights and responsibilities apply. For example, while all people in the U.S. are protected by the Constitution's due process and equal protection clauses, only citizens can vote in federal elections.

A helpful way to understand the timeline of how legal status can evolve:

Arrival: Entry may be as a visitor, student, refugee, or undocumented migrant.
Adjustment: Some individuals apply for permanent residency (a "green card") through family, employment, or humanitarian programs.
Naturalization: After a period of lawful residency, eligible individuals may apply for citizenship, gaining full participation in civic life.

This path is not always straightforward. Each stage involves a maze of paperwork, deadlines, and legal criteria—making legal literacy essential.

Real-World Example: The Story of Maria

Consider the story of **Maria**, who arrived from El Salvador seeking safety and a better future for her children. At first, Maria hesitated to report unsafe working conditions at her job, fearing repercussions due to her limited English and uncertain immigration status. However, after attending a community legal clinic, she learned that labor laws protect all workers—regardless of status. With guidance, she was able to file a complaint, leading to safer conditions for herself and her coworkers.

Maria's experience illustrates how understanding the law can transform vulnerability into empowerment, helping newcomers assert their rights and contribute to their communities.

Cultural and Global Perspectives

Not all legal systems operate like the U.S.'s. In some countries, informal negotiations or community elders resolve disputes, and written contracts are less common. This contrast can lead to misunderstandings in the U.S., where:

The default is "if it isn't written, it didn't happen."
Failing to comply with formal legal requirements—such as registering a business or reporting income—can result in serious consequences.

Globally, countries like **Canada** and **Australia** have similar legal protections for newcomers but may differ in processes for legal status or social services. Learning how the U.S. system fits into this broader context helps newcomers adapt more quickly.

Key Legal Rights for Immigrants

All residents, regardless of status, have certain fundamental rights:

- The right to remain silent when questioned by law enforcement.
- Protection from unreasonable searches and seizures.
- Access to emergency medical care.

However, there are limits—such as eligibility for public benefits or risks of deportation for certain violations—that make knowing the law even more important.

Did you know?
All individuals in the U.S.–regardless of immigration status–have constitutional rights to due process and equal protection under the law. Even undocumented immigrants cannot be summarily deported without a legal process.

Laws are not just abstract rules—they're the framework that allows newcomers to move from uncertainty to security, from fear to participation. By understanding the legal system's basics, immigrants are better equipped to navigate daily life, protect their families, and pursue their goals. As we continue, we'll explore how these foundational principles apply in specific, everyday situations—like driving, renting, and working—ensuring everyone is prepared to live confidently within the law.

2 The Structure of the U.S. Legal System

2.1 Three Branches of Government

The Foundation of Checks and Balances

When the United States declared its independence and began crafting a new government, the Founders faced a crucial dilemma: how to create a system powerful enough to govern effectively, yet restrained enough to prevent tyranny. To solve this, they divided the government into three distinct branches—**Legislative**, **Executive**, and **Judicial**—each with its own unique powers and responsibilities. This separation is the backbone of the U.S. legal system and is often referred to as the **system of checks and balances**.

The Legislative Branch: Making the Laws

The **Legislative Branch** is established by Article I of the U.S. Constitution and is composed of the **U.S. Congress**, which consists of two chambers:

The Senate (100 members; two from each state)
The House of Representatives (435 members, apportioned by population)

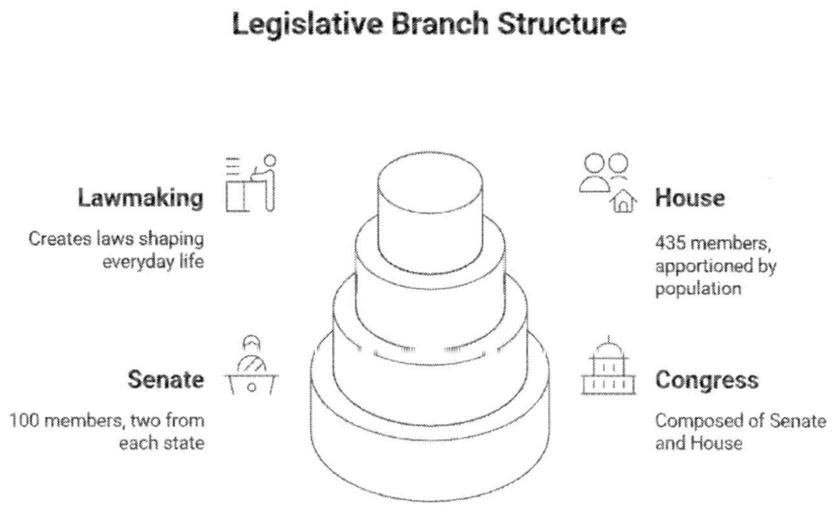

Their primary job is to create, debate, and pass laws that shape everyday life. For instance, Congress passes laws that determine how taxes are collected, how public funds are spent, and which activities are considered federal crimes.

Real-World Example: The Americans with Disabilities Act

In 1990, Congress passed the **Americans with Disabilities Act (ADA)**, a landmark piece of legislation that prohibits discrimination against individuals with disabilities in all areas of public life. This law, crafted and enacted by the legislative branch, has had profound effects on building accessibility, employment, and transportation, illustrating how Congress directly influences day-to-day experiences for millions of Americans.

The Executive Branch: Enforcing the Laws

The **Executive Branch**, outlined in Article II of the Constitution, is headed by the **President of the United States**. This branch is responsible for enforcing and administering the laws passed by Congress. It includes:

The President and Vice President
The President's Cabinet (e.g., Secretaries of State, Defense, Education)
Numerous federal agencies and departments (e.g., FBI, EPA, Department of Homeland Security)

Structure of the Executive Branch

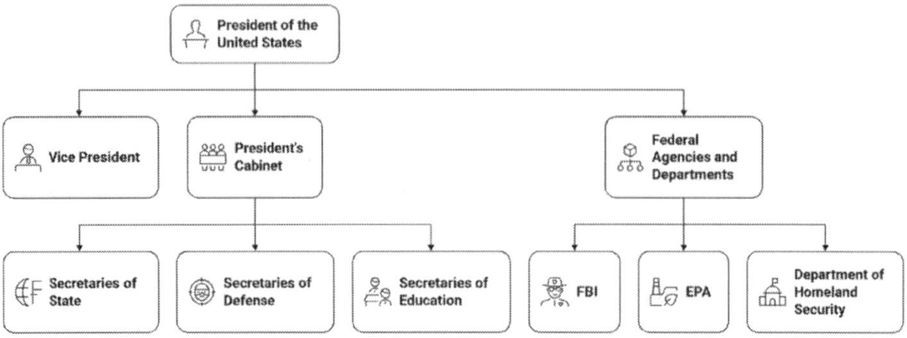

The President also serves as the Commander-in-Chief of the armed forces, negotiates treaties (with Senate approval), and can issue executive orders to direct the activities of the federal government.

Historical Anecdote: Executive Orders in Action

During the 1960s, President Lyndon B. Johnson signed **Executive Order 11246**, which required government contractors to take affirmative action in hiring practices. This executive action played a vital role in promoting workplace equality and demonstrates how the executive branch can impact social policy without waiting for new legislation.

The Judicial Branch: Interpreting the Laws

Article III of the Constitution establishes the **Judicial Branch**, with the **Supreme Court of the United States** at its apex. This branch interprets laws, resolves disputes, and determines whether laws or executive actions violate the Constitution. The federal court system includes:

The Supreme Court (9 justices)
Courts of Appeals (circuit courts)
District Courts (trial courts)

Through **judicial review**, courts can strike down laws or policies that conflict with the Constitution, ensuring that neither Congress nor the President can overstep their bounds.

Structure of the Judicial Branch

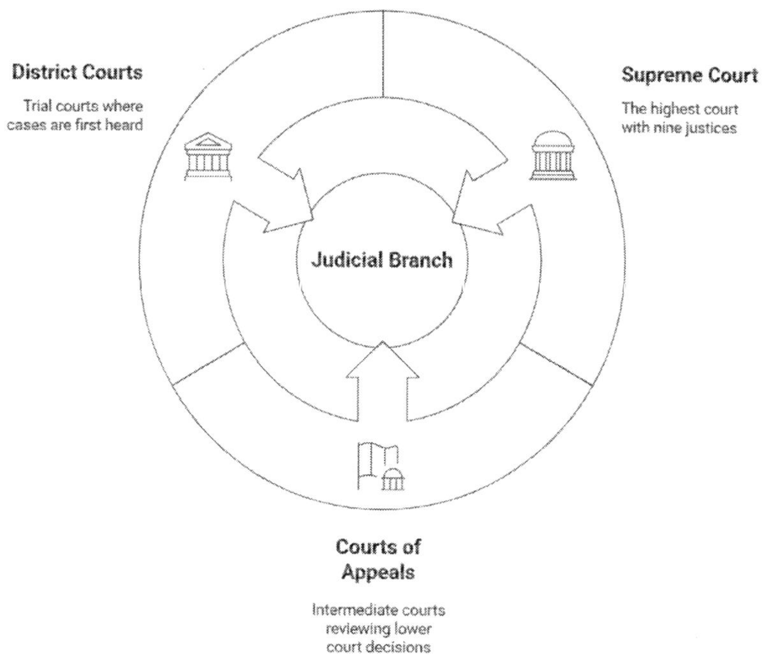

Personal Story: A Local Court Experience

Consider Maria, a small business owner who faced a zoning dispute with her city. When city officials attempted to shut down her shop, Maria challenged the action in court. The judge reviewed the city's ordinance and found that it conflicted with state law, ruling in Maria's favor. This real-life scenario highlights how the judicial branch safeguards individual rights and maintains rule of law, even in local matters.

How the Branches Work Together—and Apart

The genius of America's three-branch system is its balance. Each branch can check the others:

The President can veto laws from Congress.
Congress can override a veto or impeach the President.
The Supreme Court can declare laws or executive actions unconstitutional.

This ongoing interplay ensures that power is not concentrated in one person or group, protecting citizens' freedoms.

```
Did you know? The Supreme Court's power of judicial review was established in
1803 with Marbury v. Madison, setting a precedent for courts to strike down
unconstitutional laws.
```

2.2 The Court System: Federal and State

One of the most distinctive aspects of the U.S. legal framework is its **dual court system**, which consists of both federal and state courts. This structure is a direct result of the Constitution's commitment to federalism—a balance between a strong national government and the rights of individual states. While this may sound abstract, it shapes everything from where you pay a traffic ticket to how landmark civil rights cases are decided.

The Federal Courts: Guardians of the Constitution

The **federal court system** hears cases that involve federal laws, the U.S. Constitution, or disputes between states or citizens from different states. Federal courts are established under Article III of the U.S. Constitution, and their authority extends across the entire country. The federal judiciary is structured in three main tiers:

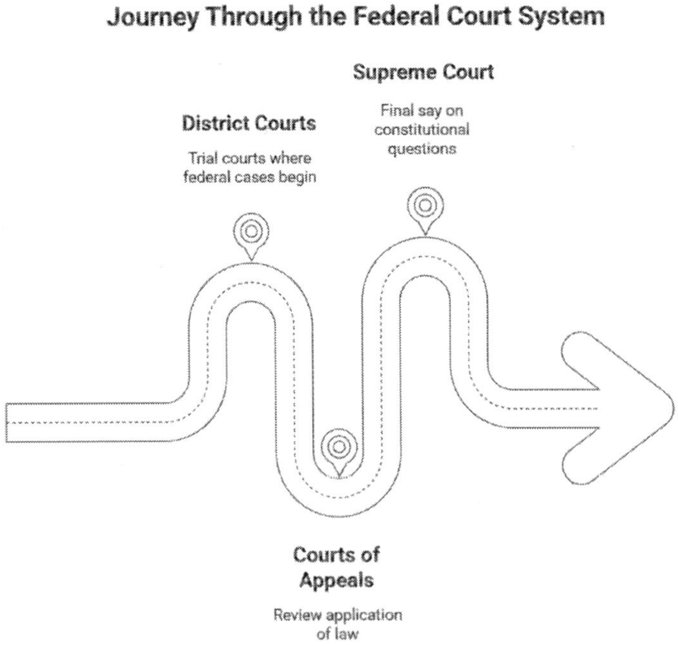

District Courts – These are trial courts where most federal cases begin. There are 94 district courts across the United States. If someone were accused of violating a federal law, such as mail fraud or immigration offenses, their case would start here.

Courts of Appeals (Circuit Courts) – If a party loses in a district court and believes legal errors affected the outcome, they can appeal to one of 13 circuit courts. These courts review the application of law rather than re-examining the facts.

The Supreme Court of the United States – As the nation's highest court, the Supreme Court has the final say on constitutional questions and federal law. Its decisions set binding precedents for all other courts.

Real-World Example: Federal Court in Action

Consider the famous case of **Brown v. Board of Education** (1954). The plaintiffs challenged racial segregation in public schools, arguing it violated the U.S. Constitution. The case traveled through lower federal courts before the Supreme Court issued its historic ruling, declaring segregation unconstitutional. This example underscores how federal courts can shape the fabric of American society.

The State Courts: Everyday Justice

Every state in the U.S. operates its own court system, handling the vast majority of legal matters that affect people's daily lives—including family law, property disputes, criminal cases, and more. State courts are typically structured in three levels:

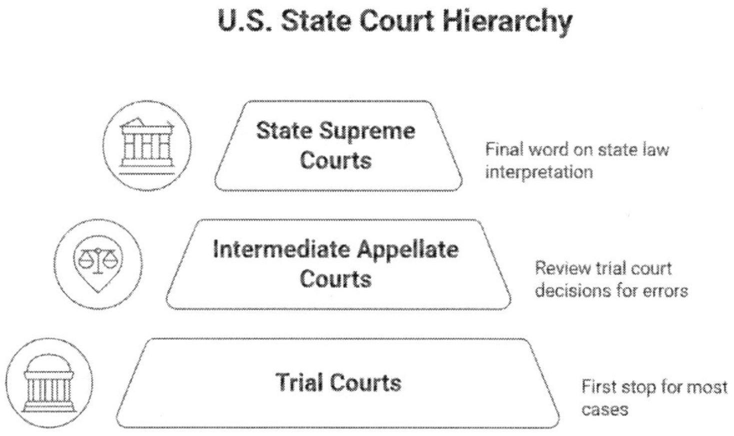

Trial Courts – Sometimes called superior, municipal, or circuit courts, these are the first stop for most cases, from small claims to serious felonies.

Intermediate Appellate Courts – Not all states have these, but where they exist, they review decisions made by trial courts for legal errors.

State Supreme Courts – The highest court within a state, these justices have the final word on interpreting state law.

Personal Story: A Day in Traffic Court

Imagine Maria, a recent immigrant to California, who receives a speeding ticket. Unsure of her rights, she chooses to contest the ticket in a local trial court. The judge listens to both sides and makes a ruling. Maria's case is handled entirely within the state system, showing how most legal issues—especially those involving traffic laws or property—are resolved close to home.

How Do Federal and State Courts Interact?

Most legal matters stay within their respective systems, but sometimes cases can move from state to federal court. For instance, if a state law is believed to violate a federal constitutional right, the case might eventually reach federal courts. Conversely, federal courts may sometimes interpret state law, especially when hearing cases involving parties from different states.

Jurisdiction is key: Federal courts hear cases involving federal law; state courts handle state law.

Some cases can be tried in both systems (known as "concurrent jurisdiction"), but this is relatively rare.

Global Perspective: Comparing Legal Systems

Unlike the U.S., some countries—like France or Japan—have unified national court systems, with no separate state-level judiciary. The U.S. approach allows states significant autonomy, reflecting its unique historical and cultural context.

```
Memorable Fact:
The vast majority of legal cases in the U.S.—over 90%—are resolved in state
courts, not federal courts.
```

The dual court system is a hallmark of American legal life, balancing national standards with local needs. Whether dealing with a constitutional crisis or a minor dispute, understanding which court to turn to is essential. As we move forward, we'll explore how laws are made and changed within this system, revealing the dynamic process that keeps our legal framework responsive to society's evolving needs.

2.3 Federal vs. State Law

At the heart of the U.S. legal structure lies a unique feature: the division of authority between **federal law** and **state law**. This dual system is rooted in the U.S. Constitution, which grants certain powers to the federal government while reserving others for the states. Such a system ensures both unity and diversity in how laws are created, interpreted, and enforced across the country.

What Is Federal Law?

Federal law is established by the U.S. Congress, interpreted by federal courts, and enforced by national agencies. It covers issues that affect the country as a whole—think of matters like immigration, interstate commerce, national defense, and civil rights.

Sources: U.S. Constitution, acts of Congress, federal regulations, and treaties.
Jurisdiction: Applies in all 50 states and U.S. territories.
Examples: The Civil Rights Act, federal income tax laws, immigration statutes.

What Is State Law?

State law is created by individual state legislatures, interpreted by state courts, and enforced by state and local agencies. These laws address issues not specifically reserved for the federal government and can vary widely from state to state.

Sources: State constitutions, laws passed by state legislatures, state regulations.
Jurisdiction: Applies only within that specific state.
Examples: Marriage and divorce laws, property rules, most criminal offenses like theft or assault, and traffic laws.

How Do Federal and State Laws Interact?

The relationship between federal and state law is sometimes straightforward, but can also be a source of complexity or even conflict. The **Supremacy Clause** of the U.S. Constitution declares that federal law is the "supreme law of the land." If a state law conflicts with a federal law, the federal law prevails.

Example: Marijuana Legislation

A compelling real-world example is the status of marijuana. **Federal law** still classifies marijuana as an illegal substance. Yet, many states—including California and Colorado—have legalized it for medicinal or recreational use. This creates a legal gray area: while state authorities may not prosecute for marijuana possession, federal agencies technically retain the authority to do so. This tension highlights the ongoing negotiation and balance of power between state and federal systems.

When Do Federal and State Courts Have Authority?

Which court system handles a case depends on the nature of the law involved and sometimes the specifics of the case itself.

Federal courts generally hear cases involving:

- Violations of federal law

- Disputes between citizens of different states (if the amount exceeds a certain threshold)

- Constitutional issues

State courts handle:

- Violations of state laws

- Most family law, probate, and contract cases

- Issues arising under state constitutions

Historical Anecdote: The Case of Loving v. Virginia (1967)

The story of **Mildred and Richard Loving**—an interracial couple sentenced to a year in prison by the state of Virginia for marrying—shows the interplay between federal and state law. Their case eventually reached the Supreme Court, which struck down state laws banning interracial marriage. This landmark decision reinforced the idea that federal constitutional rights override conflicting state laws.

Why the Division Matters in Daily Life

Understanding whether a law is federal or state is crucial. For example, traffic tickets are usually state matters, but transporting certain goods across state lines might trigger federal regulations. Similarly, knowing whether a legal issue falls under state or federal jurisdiction can determine which court you'll appear in and which set of rules will apply.

Global Perspective: Federal vs. Unitary Systems

The U.S. model of dividing powers is known as a **federal system**. By contrast, countries like France or Japan have **unitary systems**, where most legal power is centralized in the national government. In Canada and Germany—also federal systems—there are similar divisions of authority, though the balance and specifics may differ.

```
The Supremacy Clause ensures that federal law always takes precedence over
conflicting state law, shaping many landmark Supreme Court decisions and
everyday legal outcomes.
```

Reflection and Transition

The interplay between federal and state law creates a dynamic legal landscape that can be both empowering and confusing for citizens. By grasping these distinctions, you'll be better prepared to navigate your rights and responsibilities in any jurisdiction. Next, we'll turn our attention to how laws are made, exploring the legislative processes that bring new rules into the world and change old ones—an essential step in understanding your role in the evolving fabric of American law.

2.4 Local Laws and Ordinances

While federal and state laws often command headlines, much of the law that shapes daily life in the United States is crafted at the local level. **Local laws and ordinances** are the rules established by cities, counties, townships, and other municipal entities. These regulations affect everything from where you can park your car, to how loud your music can be at night, to the types of businesses allowed in your neighborhood.

Local governments derive their authority from state constitutions and statutes. While their powers are not unlimited, local agencies are granted significant flexibility to address the specific needs of their communities. This "home rule" approach reflects a fundamental principle of American governance: that those closest to the people often know best how to regulate their own affairs.

Understanding Ordinances: What Are They?

An **ordinance** is essentially a law enacted by a local government. Ordinances can address a wide array of matters, including:

Zoning and land use (where homes, businesses, and factories can be located)
Building codes (standards for construction and safety)
Health and sanitation (garbage disposal, pest control, restaurant inspections)
Noise restrictions
Animal control
Curfews for minors

Some ordinances are minor and enforced with fines, while others—such as zoning laws—can have a profound impact on property values, neighborhood character, and quality of life.

How Local Laws Are Made

The process for creating local ordinances typically mirrors the legislative process on a smaller scale:

Proposal: A city council member, county commissioner, or even a local citizen proposes a new rule.

Review: Committees or boards review the proposal, sometimes holding public hearings to gather input from residents.

Debate: The governing body discusses the merits and potential impacts.

Vote: Council members or commissioners vote on adoption.

Enactment: If passed, the ordinance becomes law, usually after a waiting period or public posting.

Real-World Examples: Local Laws in Action

To truly understand the impact of local law, consider two real-life stories:

The Sidewalk Café: In New Orleans, city ordinances regulate whether restaurants can place tables on the sidewalk. After Hurricane Katrina, many eateries lobbied for relaxed rules. The city responded by amending ordinances to encourage outdoor dining, helping revitalize neighborhoods and foster a sense of community.

Noise and Neighborhood Harmony: In many college towns, ordinances set limits on late-night noise. In Boulder, Colorado, repeated complaints from long-time residents led to stricter noise ordinances and stepped-up enforcement. Students learned the hard way that breaking these local rules could mean hefty fines or even eviction from rental properties.

The Patchwork of Local Regulations

One of the great challenges—and charms—of the U.S. legal system is its diversity. A behavior that is perfectly legal in one city may be illegal just a few miles down the road. For instance:

Fireworks Laws: Some counties allow backyard fireworks on July 4th; others ban them outright due to fire hazards.

Plastic Bag Bans: While several California cities prohibit single-use plastic bags, neighboring towns may not.

Such variation reflects local priorities and concerns, but it can also create confusion for residents and visitors alike. That's why it's crucial to check local ordinances, especially when moving to a new area or starting a business.

The Importance of Compliance

Violating a local ordinance may seem trivial, but consequences can be significant. Penalties may include:

Fines
Community service
Revocation of business licenses
Even short-term detention for repeat or serious infractions

Moreover, some local offenses can escalate into state or federal matters if they involve public safety, discrimination, or environmental harm.

```
Remember: Ignorance of the law is not a defense. Even if you are unaware of a
local ordinance, you can still be held accountable for violating it.
```

Looking Beyond: How Local Laws Connect to the Broader System

Local laws and ordinances are the threads that weave together the fabric of everyday life in the United States. They demonstrate how the legal system adapts to community values and evolving needs. As we move forward, we'll explore how these local rules interact with state and federal laws, and how conflicts between them are resolved—a vital step in understanding the full architecture of American legal life.

In the next section, we'll examine the critical differences between civil and criminal law, setting the stage for a deeper exploration of your rights and responsibilities in both everyday and extraordinary circumstances.

2.5 How a Case Moves Through the Courts

When legal disputes or alleged crimes arise, they set in motion a series of well-established steps that guide cases through the U.S. court system. Whether the matter is civil or criminal, understanding this journey can help demystify what can otherwise seem like an intimidating or confusing process.

The Life Cycle of a Legal Case

At its core, a case's path through the courts follows a logical sequence, ensuring that every party has an opportunity to present their side and that justice is pursued fairly.

1. The Beginning: Filing and Initiation

Civil Cases: These often start when an individual or organization (the **plaintiff**) files a **complaint** against another party (the **defendant**) alleging harm or violation of rights. For example, if your neighbor builds a fence on your property, you might bring a civil lawsuit seeking to resolve the dispute.

Criminal Cases: Here, the government (local, state, or federal) initiates prosecution. After law enforcement investigates and gathers evidence, a prosecutor decides whether to file charges against a suspect.

2. Pre-Trial Steps: Pleadings, Discovery, and Motions

Pleadings: Both parties exchange legal documents outlining their positions.
Discovery: Each side gathers evidence. This can include requesting documents, taking depositions (sworn statements), and interviewing witnesses.
Motions: Before trial, lawyers may ask the judge to rule on certain issues—such as dismissing parts of the case or excluding evidence.

3. The Trial Process

Jury Selection: In most criminal and many civil cases, a jury is chosen to hear the case. Sometimes, the judge alone decides (a **bench trial**).
Opening Statements: Both sides outline their cases for the judge or jury.
Presentation of Evidence: Witnesses testify, and documents are introduced. Each side can cross-examine the other's witnesses.
Closing Arguments: Lawyers summarize their positions, highlighting the evidence that supports their claims.

4. Verdict and Judgment

Criminal Cases: The jury (or judge) must decide if the defendant is guilty "beyond a reasonable doubt." If found guilty, the judge imposes a sentence.
Civil Cases: The standard is usually **"preponderance of the evidence"**—meaning it's more likely than not that the claim is true. The court then issues a judgment, which may include financial compensation or other remedies.

5. Appeals and Higher Courts

If a party believes a mistake was made during the trial—such as the improper admission of evidence or incorrect instructions to the jury—they may appeal to a higher court.

Appellate Courts: These courts review the trial record but do not hear new evidence. If the appellate court finds significant errors, it can overturn the verdict, order a new trial, or remand the case for further proceedings.
Supreme Court: In rare cases, parties can further appeal to the state supreme court or the U.S. Supreme Court, but these courts select only a small number of cases to review each year.

Comparative Perspective: The U.S. and Other Legal Systems

In contrast to the U.S., many countries use the **civil law system**—such as France or Japan—where judges play a more active role in investigating facts. In the U.S., the **adversarial system** puts the burden of building a case on the parties, with judges acting as neutral referees. Understanding these differences can clarify why American courts operate as they do.

A crucial fact: Most U.S. legal cases—over 90%—are resolved not by trial, but by settlement (in civil cases) or plea bargain (in criminal cases).

In summary, each case's journey—while sometimes long and complex—reflects a commitment to due process, accountability, and fairness. Recognizing these steps helps empower individuals to navigate or understand the system more confidently. Next, we'll explore the key roles of judges, juries, lawyers, and other courtroom participants, shedding light on who does what in the pursuit of justice.

2.6 Global Perspectives: Decentralization in Other Countries

When examining the architecture of the U.S. legal system, one striking feature is its **decentralization**—the division of legal authority among federal, state, and local governments. But how unique is this approach? To truly appreciate the American system, it's valuable to compare it with the structures of other nations. Around the globe, countries balance central and regional power in different ways, each with its own rationale, advantages, and challenges.

Contrasting Legal Structures: Federalism vs. Centralization

Many countries organize their legal systems as either **federal** or **unitary**. In a **federal** system, like that of the United States, power is constitutionally divided between a central government and subnational entities (states or provinces), each with its own laws and courts. Conversely, a **unitary** system vests legal authority primarily in the central government, with local entities administering—but not making—law.

Federal Model: Germany

Germany provides a vivid example of federalism outside the U.S. The German **Grundgesetz** (Basic Law) distributes authority between the national government and sixteen **Länder** (states). Each Land has its own parliament and judiciary, and can pass laws in certain areas such as education and police powers. However, the German system emphasizes national standards and coordination, especially in criminal and civil law. For instance, while police practices may vary, the **Strafgesetzbuch** (Criminal Code) applies uniformly across the country.

A historical anecdote illustrates the strengths and occasional tensions of this model. In the 1970s, Bavaria introduced stricter regulations on public demonstrations than other Länder, leading to legal challenges that reached the **Federal Constitutional Court**. The Court's role as an arbiter ensured that fundamental rights were uniformly protected, even amidst regional diversity.

Unitary Model: France

In contrast, **France** operates under a highly **unitary** system. The French government, based in Paris, creates laws that apply nationwide. Local governments mostly implement these laws and have limited legislative power. While there are administrative courts at the local level, their authority is tightly circumscribed.

Consider the case of traffic regulations: In France, national laws govern everything from speed limits to licensing requirements. A Parisian and a resident of Marseille are subject to the same driving rules—even though the character of their cities is vastly different. This centralization is thought to promote equality and uniformity, but can sometimes lead to inflexibility when local issues arise.

Mixed Approaches: Lessons from Around the World

Some countries blend federal and unitary principles, adapting decentralization to their unique histories and cultures.

Canada: Like the U.S., Canada divides power between the federal government and provinces. However, Canadian provinces have exclusive authority over some areas, like health and education. This has led to notable regional variations, such as Quebec's distinctive civil law system (in contrast to the common law used in other provinces).

India: India's constitution creates a federal structure, but with "unitary features." In periods of national emergency, the central government can override state laws, reflecting the country's vast diversity and the need for unity in crisis.

Personal Story: Discovering Differences

Maria, a Brazilian attorney who moved to the U.S., recalls her astonishment upon first encountering California's unique traffic laws—especially differences in right-of-way rules and carpool lane requirements. In Brazil, a federal country, traffic laws are almost entirely set at the national level, so drivers experience consistency across states. Maria's experience highlights how the U.S. system, for all its flexibility, can be bewildering for newcomers.

Why Decentralization Matters in Everyday Life

For residents and citizens, understanding whether laws are made locally or nationally is crucial. In decentralized systems like the U.S., it means:

Laws can vary significantly from state to state or city to city.
Local culture and priorities can shape legal outcomes.
Moving between jurisdictions may require learning new rules or procedures.

France's unitary system, meanwhile, offers consistency at the cost of local adaptation.

Comparing the U.S. legal structure with those of other countries shows how decentralization shapes not just legal theory but daily experience. Americans benefit from local control but must stay alert to varying rules. Next, we'll step into the courtroom itself, exploring the key roles of judges, juries, lawyers, and other participants who bring the legal system to life in every community.

3 Understanding Legal Language—Key Terms Demystified

3.1 Misdemeanors and Felonies

Understanding the distinction between **misdemeanors** and **felonies** is essential for anyone navigating the U.S. legal system. These two categories shape not only the potential penalties for breaking the law but also influence everything from employment opportunities to immigration status and voting rights. Let's demystify these key terms, exploring their definitions, consequences, and significance in everyday life.

What Are Misdemeanors?

A **misdemeanor** is generally considered a less serious crime compared to a felony. These offenses are punishable by fines, community service, probation, or incarceration in a local or county jail—typically for less than one year. Common examples include:

Petty theft (such as shoplifting)
Simple assault (without serious injury)
Driving under the influence (first offense, in many states)
Disorderly conduct
Trespassing

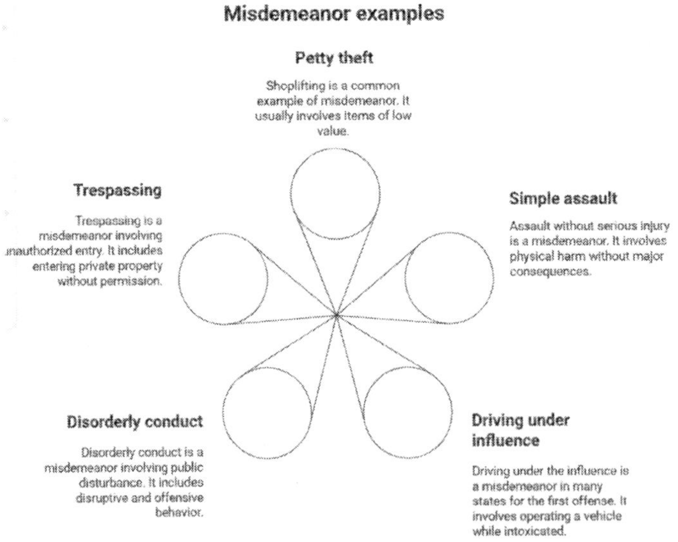

Despite being "less serious," misdemeanors can still carry lasting consequences. For instance, a person convicted of a misdemeanor may face difficulties in securing certain jobs or professional licenses.

What Are Felonies?

A **felony** is a more serious crime, punishable by imprisonment for more than one year, often served in a state or federal prison rather than a local jail. Felonies can also result in hefty fines, long-term probation, and the loss of fundamental civil rights such as voting, serving on a jury, or possessing firearms.

Common examples of felonies include:

Burglary
Aggravated assault
Arson
Drug trafficking
Murder

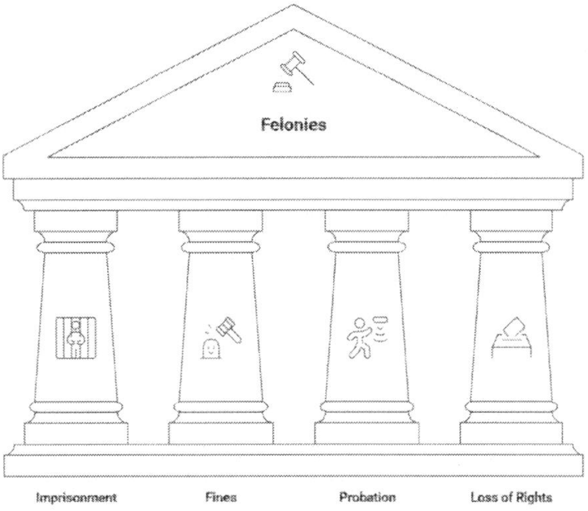

The gravity of a felony conviction extends far beyond the courtroom. It can impact housing opportunities, employment, immigration status, and even one's right to parent.

Degrees of Crimes

Both misdemeanors and felonies are often divided into **degrees** or **classes**, depending on the severity of the offense. For example:

First-degree felony: The most serious, such as intentional homicide.

Third-degree felony: Less severe, like certain types of fraud.
Class A misdemeanor: More serious, such as a first-time DUI.
Class C misdemeanor: Least severe, like some traffic infractions.

Each state defines these categories differently, but the underlying principle is consistent: the higher the degree or class, the more severe the potential penalties.

Real-World Example: The Case of College Pranks Gone Wrong

Consider a group of college students who break into a school building as a prank. If they simply trespass, they may be charged with a misdemeanor. However, if they steal property or cause significant damage, they could face felony charges. This distinction can turn a youthful mistake into a life-altering event.

Historical Anecdote: The Three Strikes Law

In the 1990s, some states, like California, implemented **"three strikes" laws** that imposed life sentences on individuals convicted of three or more felonies. These laws were intended to curb repeat offenses but sparked debate about fairness—especially for non-violent crimes. The controversy highlighted the profound impact felony classification can have on an individual's future.

```
Felony convictions can result in the permanent loss of voting rights in some
states, and even a single misdemeanor can remain on your record for life
unless expunged.
```

Compare crime severity and consequences.

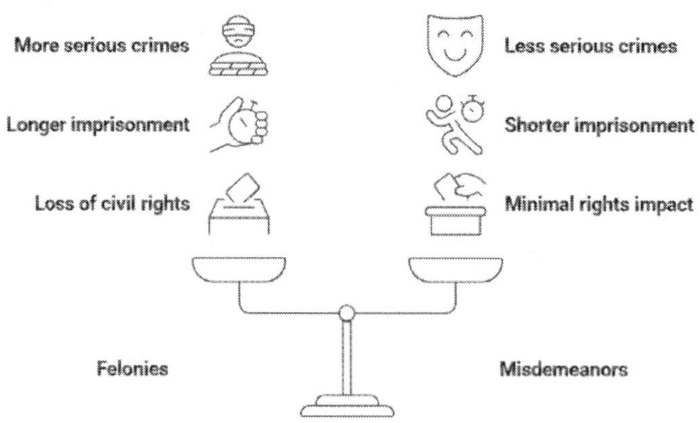

The labels **misdemeanor** and **felony** are more than just legal jargon—they define the seriousness of an offense and shape a person's future in profound ways. Understanding these terms helps us appreciate both the weight of legal consequences and the importance of making informed decisions. In the next section, we'll explore the terms **arrest** and **detainment**, unraveling what happens when law enforcement intervenes and what rights you have in those critical moments.

3.2 Degrees of Crime

When we hear about crimes in everyday conversation, the differences between various offenses can seem confusing. The U.S. legal system uses a structured approach to categorize crimes by their seriousness—these are known as degrees of crime. Understanding these distinctions is crucial, as the degree of a crime affects everything from the procedures police follow to the potential penalties a person might face.

The Hierarchy of Crime: Felonies and Misdemeanors

At its most fundamental, American law divides crimes into two main categories:

- **Misdemeanor:** Less serious offenses, often punished by fines or short jail terms (usually less than one year), such as petty theft or minor traffic violations.
- **Felony:** More serious crimes, carrying harsher penalties, including long-term imprisonment, significant fines, or even capital punishment in some states—for example, armed robbery or homicide.

But these categories are only the beginning. Within each, offenses are further divided by "degree." This helps the courts tailor punishments and ensures the justice system responds proportionally to different types of wrongdoing.

Degrees Explained: First, Second, and Third

Many states use a system of **degrees** to rank the severity of a particular crime. Here's how it typically works:

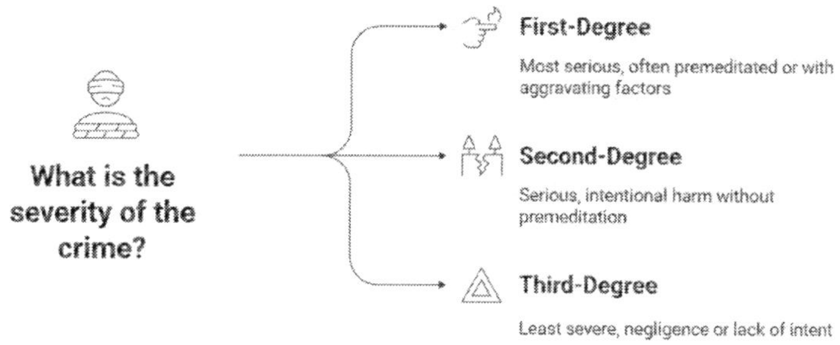

First-Degree: The most serious form of a crime. First-degree offenses are often deliberate, planned, or carried out with aggravating factors. For example, **first-degree murder** usually means the act was premeditated.

Second-Degree: Less severe than first-degree but more serious than third. Second-degree crimes typically involve intentional harm without premeditation, or a reckless disregard for human life.

Third-Degree (and beyond): The least severe form. Third-degree offenses might involve negligence or a lack of intent to cause serious harm.

Not all crimes have all three degrees; the use and definition of degrees can vary by state and by the nature of the crime.

Real-World Example: The Case of Theft

Consider **theft**, a crime familiar to many. In some states:

First-degree theft might involve stealing property worth more than $10,000 or from a vulnerable victim (like an elderly person).
Second-degree theft could be stealing property valued between $1,000 and $10,000.
Third-degree theft may cover property worth less than $1,000.

By assigning degrees, the law acknowledges that stealing a loaf of bread and embezzling millions from a corporation are not equally serious.

Historical Anecdote: The Evolution of Degrees

The concept of degrees can be traced back to English common law, which heavily influenced America's early legal system. In the 18th century, British courts began distinguishing murder by degrees to separate planned killings from those committed in the heat of passion. This practice crossed the Atlantic, where the first U.S. state to formally adopt degrees of murder was Pennsylvania in 1794, aiming to make punishments more just and less arbitrary.

Personal Story: A Lesson in Proportionality

Imagine Maria, a college student, who shoplifts a $20 item on a dare. She's caught and charged with third-degree theft—a misdemeanor in her state. Her friend, however, is involved in a larger, organized retail theft ring and faces first-degree theft charges, a felony. The outcomes for Maria and her friend are dramatically different because the law considers not just what was taken, but the context and intent.

```
In most states, a first-degree crime carries the harshest penalties, often
including lengthy prison sentences or, in rare cases, life imprisonment. A
```

```
third-degree crime, by contrast, may result in probation or short-term
incarceration.
```

Understanding degrees of crime helps demystify headlines and court cases, giving us clearer insight into the workings of justice. As we move forward, remember that these distinctions shape not just punishments, but also the rights and procedures that protect all of us. Next, we'll build on this foundation by examining what happens during an **arrest** or **detainment**, so you know what to expect—and what rights you can assert—if you ever find yourself in such a situation.

3.3 Arrest, Detainment, and Bail

What Is an Arrest?

An **arrest** is a formal act by law enforcement that takes away a person's freedom of movement, usually because they are suspected of committing a crime. The moment an arrest is made, important legal protections and procedures are triggered. In the United States, these protections are rooted in the Constitution, specifically the Fourth Amendment, which guards against unreasonable searches and seizures.

To make a lawful arrest, officers typically must have **probable cause**—a reasonable belief, based on facts, that a person has committed or is committing a crime. Sometimes, a warrant signed by a judge is required, but there are exceptions where officers may arrest without a warrant, such as when they witness a crime in progress.

Example:

Imagine a police officer sees someone breaking into a car. The officer can arrest the individual on the spot, without needing a warrant, because there is probable cause based on direct observation.

Detainment: Temporary and Distinct

Detainment is different from an arrest. When someone is detained, they are temporarily held by law enforcement for questioning or investigation, but not formally charged or taken into custody. Detainments are generally short and must be justified by **reasonable suspicion**—a lower standard than probable cause.

- During a detainment, you are not free to leave, but you have not been officially arrested.
- Police can perform a brief search (a "stop and frisk") if they believe you may be armed and dangerous.
- You have the right to remain silent and ask if you are free to go.

Personal Story:

Maria, a college student, was stopped by police while walking home late at night because she matched the description of someone seen near a recent theft. The officers detained her briefly, asked questions, and checked her identification. Once they determined she was not involved, they let her go. Maria was never arrested—her rights during this detainment were still important.

Bail: Securing Temporary Freedom

After an arrest, the next key step is often **bail**—a financial guarantee that allows a person accused of a crime to be released from jail while awaiting trial. Bail is intended to ensure the accused returns to court, not as a punishment.

- The amount and conditions of bail are set by a judge.
- In some cases, people may be released on their own recognizance, meaning no money is required; they simply promise to appear in court.
- If the accused cannot afford bail, they may remain in jail until their case is resolved.

Historical Anecdote:

The concept of bail dates back to medieval England, where it was used to prevent the overcrowding of jails and ensure accused individuals appeared for trial. The United States inherited this principle, but debates continue today about fairness and access, since high bail can disproportionately affect those with limited resources.

The Timeline: What to Expect

- **Detainment**: Temporary stop and questioning, based on reasonable suspicion.
- **Arrest**: Loss of freedom, based on probable cause; rights are read (Miranda rights).
- **Booking**: Personal information recorded, fingerprints and photographs taken.
- **Bail Hearing**: Judge determines if bail is set, and under what conditions.

Your Rights at Each Stage

- The right to remain silent.
- The right to an attorney.
- The right to know the charges against you.

```
If you are arrested, always ask to speak with a lawyer before answering
questions. This protects your rights and ensures you do not inadvertently
incriminate yourself.
```

3.4 Evidence and Its Role in Court

What Is Evidence?

At its core, **evidence** is any information presented in court to persuade the judge or jury about the facts of a case. Evidence forms the backbone of every legal dispute—whether it's a criminal trial, a civil lawsuit, or a small-claims matter. Without evidence, even the most compelling story is just an allegation.

Evidence comes in many forms, including:

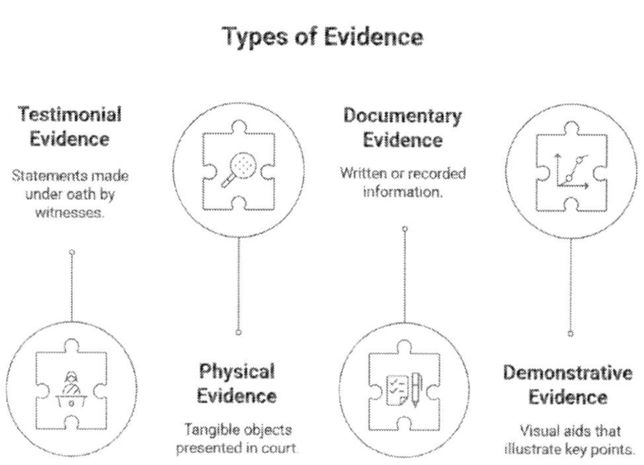

- **Testimonial evidence**: Statements made under oath by witnesses, including the parties involved, experts, or bystanders.
- **Physical evidence**: Tangible objects presented in court, such as a weapon, a document, or a photograph.
- **Documentary evidence**: Written or recorded information, including contracts, emails, or medical records.
- **Demonstrative evidence**: Visual aids like maps, charts, or models that help illustrate key points.

Admissibility: What Makes Evidence Acceptable?

Not all evidence can be shown in court. Judges act as gatekeepers, deciding what is **admissible**—that is, legally permissible to consider. The rules of evidence are designed to ensure fairness, accuracy, and reliability. For example, evidence must be:

Relevant: It must pertain directly to the case.
Reliable: It must be trustworthy and not based on speculation.
Not unduly prejudicial: It should not unfairly sway the jury against one side.

Certain types of evidence, like hearsay (an out-of-court statement presented to prove the truth of the matter asserted), are generally inadmissible unless a specific exception applies.

Example: The O.J. Simpson Trial

One of the most famous examples of evidence in a U.S. courtroom was the glove presented during the 1995 **O.J. Simpson trial**. Prosecutors believed the glove linked Simpson to the crime. However, when Simpson struggled to put it on in front of the jury, the defense used this as evidence that it did not belong to him. This dramatic moment underscored the power of physical and demonstrative evidence—and how its presentation can sway a case.

Types of Evidence and Their Impact

Understanding the types of evidence helps clarify how facts are established in court:

Direct evidence: Directly proves a fact (e.g., a witness saw the defendant at the scene).
Circumstantial evidence: Suggests a fact by implication (e.g., fingerprints at the scene suggest presence, but don't prove it outright).

Both types are valuable, and neither is inherently better—sometimes, a web of circumstantial evidence can be more persuasive than a single direct account.

Story: The Power of Video Evidence

In many modern cases, video footage has played a decisive role. For instance, the 2020 conviction of former police officer Derek Chauvin for the murder of George Floyd relied heavily on cellphone video captured by a bystander. This powerful documentary evidence was pivotal in shaping public understanding and the jury's perception.

The Importance of Proper Handling

Chain of custody—a record of who handled the evidence and when—is crucial. If evidence is mishandled, tampered with, or lost, its reliability is compromised, and it may be excluded from the trial.

```
Remember: Evidence must be handled, preserved, and presented according to
strict legal standards. Mishandled evidence can be thrown out, potentially
weakening a case or leading to a mistrial.
```

Evidence is the foundation of justice in the U.S. legal system. Understanding its types, rules for admissibility, and the critical role of proper handling empowers us as citizens—whether serving as jurors, witnesses, or parties to a dispute. In the next section, we'll unravel the concept of **burden of proof**—the legal responsibility for proving or disproving claims—which shapes every courtroom battle and protects the presumption of innocence.

3.5 Burden of Proof

What Is the Burden of Proof?

In every legal dispute, someone must take on the task of convincing the judge or jury that their version of events is true. This is known as the **burden of proof**—the legal obligation to prove one's claim to a certain standard. The burden of proof determines not just who must prove what, but also how convincing that proof must be.

At its core, the burden of proof is a safeguard for fairness. In the U.S. legal system, it ensures that no one is punished or held liable without adequate evidence. This concept underpins the celebrated principle: **"innocent until proven guilty."**

Types of Burden of Proof

There are two main aspects to this concept:

Burden of Production: The duty to present enough evidence to support your claim.
Burden of Persuasion: The duty to convince the judge or jury that your claim is more likely true than not, or, in criminal cases, true beyond a reasonable doubt.

Let's break down how these types of burdens play out in different legal settings.

Criminal Cases: Beyond a Reasonable Doubt

In criminal trials, prosecution carries the burden of proving the defendant's guilt **beyond a reasonable doubt**. This is the highest standard in law, reflecting the serious consequences—such as loss of liberty or even life—that a conviction can bring. The defense does not have to prove innocence; rather, the prosecution must convince the jury that there is no reasonable doubt regarding guilt.

Example:

Imagine a high-profile robbery case. The prosecutor presents eyewitness testimony, surveillance footage, and fingerprint analysis. If the defense can show inconsistencies or gaps—such as an alibi or a flaw in the fingerprint process—the jury must acquit if any reasonable doubt remains. The presumption of innocence stands unless the state's case is airtight.

Civil Cases: Preponderance of the Evidence

Civil cases, such as disputes over contracts or property, use a lower standard called **preponderance of the evidence**. Here, the party bringing the lawsuit (the plaintiff) must show that it is more likely than not—just over 50%—that their version is true.

Example:

Consider a landlord suing a tenant for unpaid rent. The landlord provides lease agreements, bank statements, and correspondence. If the tenant cannot offer convincing evidence to the contrary, the judge will likely rule for the landlord. The standard is not absolute certainty, but simply tipping the scales.

Shifting the Burden

Sometimes, the **burden of proof** can shift during a trial. For example, once the prosecution in a criminal case establishes a prima facie case (enough evidence to proceed), the defense might have to provide evidence of an affirmative defense, like self-defense or insanity.

Global Perspective

Other countries have different standards. In some civil law traditions, the judge plays a more active role in gathering evidence, and the burden may be less sharply defined. For example, in France, the inquisitorial system allows judges to direct investigations, whereas the U.S. adversarial system relies on parties to present their cases.

In U.S. criminal trials, the burden of proof is always on the prosecution—it never shifts to the defendant to prove innocence.

Understanding the burden of proof is crucial, sets the stage for every legal contest, ensuring fairness and protecting rights. Whether you're a defendant, plaintiff, or witness, knowing who must prove what (and how strongly) is vital to navigating the legal system. Next, we'll explore the rules of legal evidence—what can and cannot be presented in court—to see how these standards come alive in practice.

3.6 Key Legal Documents

What Are Legal Documents and Why Do They Matter?

Legal documents serve as the backbone of the U.S. legal system. They are the written records, agreements, and notices that formalize rights, responsibilities, and obligations in the eyes of the law. Whether you are renting an apartment, buying a car, starting a business, or simply proving your identity, understanding key legal documents is essential for protecting yourself and effectively communicating with authorities, businesses, or other individuals.

Common Types of Legal Documents

Some legal documents are so integral to daily life that most Americans will encounter them multiple times. Let's demystify a few of the most important:

- **Contracts:** Agreements between two or more parties that create mutual legal obligations. These can be as simple as a lease for an apartment or as complex as a multi-million-dollar business deal.
- **Wills and Trusts:** Documents that dictate how a person's assets will be distributed after their death.
- **Deeds and Titles:** Proofs of ownership for property, vehicles, or other significant assets.
- **Power of Attorney:** A document granting one person the legal authority to act on another's behalf in financial or medical matters.

- **Court Summons and Complaints:** Official notifications that a legal action has been initiated and that you are required to respond.
- **Affidavits:** Written statements of fact, sworn to be true, often used as evidence in court.
- **Birth Certificates, Passports, and Social Security Cards:** Foundational documents for establishing identity and citizenship.

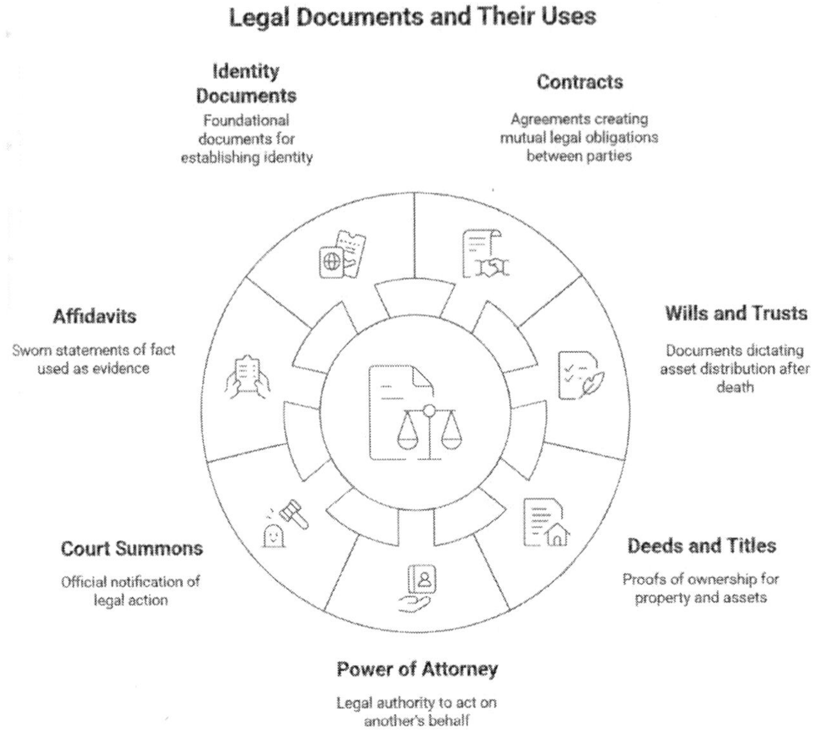

Real-World Example: The Lease Agreement

Consider Maria, a recent immigrant who moved into her first U.S. apartment. She signed a **lease agreement** with her landlord. Several months later, the landlord tried to evict her without notice, claiming she had violated the lease. Because Maria had a copy of her signed lease, she could prove in court that the landlord was required to provide written notice and a valid reason for eviction. The document protected her rights and gave her the confidence to stand up for herself.

Historical Anecdote: The Power of a Will

In the early 20th century, the famous American industrialist **Andrew Carnegie** ensured his vast fortune would benefit libraries and educational institutions by drafting a detailed will. This legal document ensured his wishes were honored long after his death, shaping U.S. public libraries for generations.

Breaking Down Legal Language in Documents

Legal documents can be intimidating, often filled with dense language or unfamiliar terms. Here are a few tips for understanding them:

- Read every word; don't assume standard forms are always fair or accurate.
- Look for **key terms** like "party," "consideration," "liability," and "jurisdiction."
- When in doubt, seek clarification from a trusted source—attorneys, government agencies, or consumer advocacy groups.
- Never sign anything under pressure or without understanding the consequences.

The Importance of Keeping Legal Documents Safe

Legal documents should be stored in a secure but accessible place. Losing them can create significant hardships, from delays in receiving benefits to legal disputes over property or identity.

```
Fact: A signed contract does not always require a lawyer's involvement, but it
is legally binding as long as all parties understand and agree to its terms.
```

Legal documents are more than just paperwork—they are powerful tools that shape our rights, responsibilities, and future opportunities. By understanding and respecting these documents, you place yourself in a stronger legal position and can avoid common pitfalls. Next, we will turn our attention to the practical side: how to interact with law enforcement and navigate everyday legal situations, ensuring you are prepared for whatever life throws your way.

3.7 Everyday Terms You Should Know

The Language of the Law: Words You Encounter Every Day

Legal language can often feel like a maze, filled with unfamiliar words and phrases that can intimidate even the most confident individuals. Yet, many of these terms shape our daily experiences—whether you're signing a lease, driving to work, or interacting with local authorities. Understanding some of the most commonly used legal terms is your first step to navigating the U.S. legal system with confidence.

Let's break down several terms you are likely to encounter in everyday life, demystifying their meanings and providing relatable context.

- **Misdemeanor**: This refers to a criminal offense that is less serious than a felony but more serious than an infraction. Misdemeanors often carry penalties such as fines, community service, or jail time of less than a year, typically served in local or county jails.

- **Felony**: A felony is a more serious criminal offense, often involving violence or significant harm to people or property. Conviction can result in imprisonment for more than a year, typically in a state or federal prison.
- **Infraction**: These are minor violations, such as traffic offenses or jaywalking, usually punishable by a fine and not considered criminal offenses.
- **Plaintiff**: The person or party who brings a lawsuit to court, alleging harm or seeking remedy.
- **Defendant**: The individual, company, or institution being accused or sued in a court of law.
- **Arrest**: The act of detaining someone suspected of breaking the law. An arrest is usually followed by the person being taken into police custody.
- **Detainment**: When a person is temporarily held by authorities for questioning or investigation but not formally charged with a crime—distinct from an arrest.
- **First-degree and Third-degree Crimes**: These terms describe the severity of a crime. A first-degree crime is the most serious, often involving premeditation or significant harm, while a third-degree crime is less severe.
- **Burden of Proof**: This is the obligation to prove one's assertion in a legal case. In criminal cases, the prosecution bears this burden and must prove guilt "beyond a reasonable doubt."

Real-World Example: Traffic Stop Terminology

Imagine you are pulled over for running a red light. The officer might inform you that you have committed a minor violation of traffic law. If you argue or resist, the situation could escalate, and the officer might decide to **detain** you for questioning. If the officer has reason to believe you were driving under the influence, you could be **arrested** and charged with a **misdemeanor** or even a **felony** if aggravating circumstances are present.

Historical Anecdote: Miranda Rights

In 1966, the U.S. Supreme Court decided the case of **Miranda v. Arizona**, establishing that detained suspects must be informed of their rights—such as the right to remain silent and the right to an attorney—before interrogation. This ruling is why officers today recite the **Miranda warning** during arrests, ensuring that suspects understand their legal protections. This case highlights the importance of legal terminology in everyday encounters with law enforcement.

```
In the U.S., a person is presumed innocent until proven guilty. This principle
applies to all criminal cases, placing the burden of proof on the prosecution.
```

By gaining familiarity with these everyday legal terms, you're better prepared to understand your rights and responsibilities in a wide range of situations—from routine traffic stops to more serious legal matters. Remember, knowledge of these terms isn't just useful in courtrooms; it's vital for daily life. Next, we'll explore what you should do—and what you should avoid—when interacting with law enforcement, empowering you to protect your interests and stay on the right side of the law.

4 Your Rights and Responsibilities

4.1 Constitutional Rights in Everyday Life

Every resident of the United States, whether a citizen or not, is protected by a set of fundamental rights enshrined in the **U.S. Constitution**. These rights, particularly those found in the **Bill of Rights** (the first ten amendments), shape everyday interactions with government, law enforcement, and even fellow citizens. They are not just abstract principles—they have practical effects on daily life, affecting everything from speech and assembly to privacy and due process.

Key Constitutional Protections

Some of the most significant constitutional rights that come into play in daily life include:

- **Freedom of Speech and Expression (First Amendment):** Allows individuals to express themselves without government interference, within certain limits (such as threats or incitement to violence).
- **Freedom of Religion (First Amendment):** Protects the right to practice any religion—or none at all—without government coercion.
- **Right to Privacy (Fourth Amendment):** Shields people from unreasonable searches and seizures by the government, requiring warrants in most cases.
- **Right to Remain Silent (Fifth Amendment):** Guarantees that individuals do not have to incriminate themselves when questioned by law enforcement.
- **Right to Legal Counsel (Sixth Amendment):** Ensures that anyone accused of a crime can have a lawyer, even if they cannot afford one.

These rights are not unlimited, but they are deeply woven into the fabric of American society.

How Rights Play Out in Daily Life

Consider the simple act of posting a comment on a social media platform. The **First Amendment** protects your right to express your opinion—even if it is critical of the government. However, private companies can set their own rules, and speech that incites violence or constitutes a true threat is not protected. Knowing where your rights begin and end is essential.

Another common scenario is a traffic stop. If a police officer pulls you over, the **Fourth Amendment** protects you from unreasonable searches of your car. The officer typically needs a good reason—called "probable cause"—to search your vehicle without your consent. If you're arrested, the **Fifth Amendment** allows you to remain silent, and the **Sixth Amendment** ensures you can have an attorney present if you are questioned.

Everyday Responsibilities

With rights come responsibilities. For example, while you have the right to free speech, you are also responsible for not spreading false information that could harm others (**defamation**). The right to assemble peacefully does not allow for riots or destruction of property. Understanding this balance is key to being an informed, respectful member of society.

Global and Comparative Perspectives

Other democracies, such as Canada and Germany, offer similar constitutional protections, though the specifics may differ. For instance, Canada's **Charter of Rights and Freedoms** protects freedom of expression but permits more restrictions in the name of public order. By contrast, some countries have fewer legal protections for free speech or privacy, reminding us that these rights are neither universal nor guaranteed everywhere.

When Rights Are Challenged

Sometimes, constitutional rights are tested during national emergencies or times of social unrest. After the September 11 attacks, new laws increased government surveillance in the name of security—a move that sparked ongoing debates about how to balance safety and privacy. Courts often play a crucial role in interpreting these boundaries, ensuring that fundamental rights are not eroded over time.

> The "Miranda warning" you hear on TV—"You have the right to remain silent..."—originates from a real Supreme Court case, Miranda v. Arizona (1966). Every law enforcement officer must give this warning before questioning a suspect in custody, or their statements may be inadmissible in court.

4.2 Rights During Police Encounters

Every interaction between individuals and law enforcement is governed by both rights and responsibilities—an intricate dance shaped by centuries of legal tradition, constitutional amendments, and hard-earned lessons from history. When the blue lights flash in your rearview mirror or a police officer approaches you on the street, it's crucial to know not only what the law says, but also how to assert your rights respectfully and safely.

Constitutional Protections

The **Fourth Amendment** protects against unreasonable searches and seizures, while the **Fifth Amendment** ensures the right to remain silent to avoid self-incrimination. The **Sixth Amendment** guarantees the right to counsel if you are charged with a crime. These foundational rights apply to every resident, regardless of citizenship status, and form the backbone of lawful police conduct.

Key Rights During Police Encounters

- **Right to Remain Silent:** You are not required to answer incriminating questions. Politely stating, "I am exercising my right to remain silent," is sufficient.
- **Right to Refuse Consent to a Search:** Unless police have a warrant, probable cause, or exigent circumstances, you may refuse a search of your person, vehicle, or home.
- **Right to an Attorney:** If detained or arrested, you have the right to speak with a lawyer before answering questions.
- **Right to Know Why You're Being Stopped:** Officers must provide a reason for detaining you.

Responsibilities

- **Provide Identification:** In many states, you are required to give your name if asked during a lawful stop.
- **Remain Calm and Courteous:** Interactions are less likely to escalate when approached with respect.
- **Do Not Resist Physically:** Even if you believe your rights are being violated, physical resistance can lead to arrest or injury.

What to Do During a Traffic Stop

- **Pull Over Safely:** Use your turn signal, stop at a safe location, and turn off your engine.
- **Keep Your Hands Visible:** Place them on the steering wheel.
- **Wait for Instructions:** Do not reach for documents until asked.
- **Comply with Lawful Orders:** Provide license, registration, and proof of insurance when requested.

You may ask, "Am I free to go?" If you are not being detained, you have the right to leave. If detained, you may assert your right to remain silent.

Global Perspectives: Comparing Police Encounters

In the United Kingdom, police stops are governed by the **PACE Code of Practice**, requiring officers to provide their name, station, and the reason for the stop. In Germany, police must inform individuals of their rights in a language they understand. While procedures vary, the underlying principle—balancing public safety with individual liberty—is a shared value in democratic societies.

When Things Go Wrong

Unfortunately, not all police encounters unfold smoothly. There have been instances—such as the 2015 incident involving Sandra Bland in Texas—where confusion, fear, or disagreement escalated a routine stop into tragedy. These stories underscore the importance of understanding both your rights and the safest ways to exercise them.

```
Always ask if you are free to leave during a police encounter. If you are not,
you may be detained or under arrest, and different rights apply.
Never physically resist a police officer, even if you believe your rights are
being violated. Use legal channels to challenge improper conduct.
```

Understanding your rights during police encounters is not just about protecting yourself—it's about participating in a society where law, order, and fairness coexist. By learning how to assert these rights calmly and respectfully, you can help ensure your own safety and contribute to healthier community-police relations.

As we move forward, the next section will explore what happens when legal issues escalate—how to navigate the court system, what to expect during legal proceedings, and how the pursuit of justice continues in America's courts.

4.3 Responsibilities as a Resident or Citizen

While much attention is often given to rights in the U.S. legal system, an equally important pillar is **responsibility**. Living in the United States—whether as a citizen, a permanent resident, or even as a long-term visitor—comes with certain legal and civic duties. These responsibilities ensure not just personal compliance with the law, but also contribute to the wider social fabric and the effective functioning of communities.

Everyday Legal Duties

Some responsibilities are universal, forming the backbone of civic life. Others may vary depending on your status—citizen, permanent resident, or temporary visitor. Understanding these obligations is crucial for legal safety and social harmony.

- **Obeying the Law:** Everyone, regardless of status, is required to follow federal, state, and local laws. This extends from fundamental rules—like not stealing or committing violence—to more specific regulations such as zoning codes or littering ordinances.
- **Paying Taxes:** The obligation to pay taxes applies to most people earning income in the U.S., not just citizens. This helps fund essential public services such as roads, schools, and emergency services.

- **Jury Duty:** U.S. citizens may be summoned for jury service, a fundamental facet of the justice system. Serving on a jury is both a privilege and a civic duty, contributing directly to the pursuit of justice.
- **Selective Service Registration:** Male citizens and certain immigrants aged 18-25 must register with the Selective Service System, ensuring preparedness for national defense if ever needed.
- **Respecting the Rights of Others:** Responsibilities extend beyond formal laws to include respecting the freedoms and property of neighbors, coworkers, and the broader public.

Case Study: The Power of Jury Duty

Consider the story of **Mary Perez**, a naturalized citizen living in Texas. Called for jury duty, Mary initially saw it as an inconvenience. However, during a real-life civil trial, she realized her unique perspective as an immigrant helped the jury better understand cultural nuances in the case. Her participation reinforced the system's inclusiveness and the vital role everyday people play in justice. Jury duty, often overlooked, is a powerful reminder that the law is shaped not only by officials and experts but also by ordinary citizens.

Legal Consequences of Neglecting Responsibilities

Failing to fulfill these obligations can carry real consequences:

Legal Penalties: Ignoring tax payments can result in fines or even criminal charges. Skipping jury duty may lead to court summons or penalties.
Status Implications: For non-citizens, breaking certain laws or failing to meet responsibilities (like registering for Selective Service) can jeopardize residency status or eligibility for citizenship.
Community Impact: Disregarding responsibilities undermines trust, public safety, and the overall effectiveness of the legal system.

Historical Anecdote: Taxation and Civic Trust

In the early 20th century, the U.S. government introduced the federal income tax to fund public projects and services. While initially met with resistance, widespread compliance eventually fostered a sense of shared investment in national growth. This historical shift underscored how fulfilling civic duties isn't just about legal compliance—it's about building a nation together.

Responsibilities Unique to Citizenship

While many responsibilities are shared, some are specific to U.S. citizens:

- **Voting:** Only citizens can vote in federal elections, shaping government policies and leadership.
- **Running for Public Office:** U.S. citizenship is generally required to hold most elected positions.
- **Applying for a U.S. Passport:** Only citizens can receive this document, which provides international protection and mobility.

Global Perspective: Civic Duties Around the World

Other countries approach civic responsibility differently. For example, in Australia, voting is compulsory for citizens, and failure to vote can result in fines. In Germany, civic integration courses are mandatory for new residents, emphasizing not just rights but also community responsibilities. These global examples highlight the diversity of civic expectations, illustrating that legal responsibilities are universal concepts, though their specifics may differ.

```
Did you know?
In the U.S., not registering for Selective Service as required can affect your eligibility for federal student aid, government jobs, and even citizenship for some immigrants.
```

Fulfilling legal responsibilities is not only a matter of avoiding penalties but also an act of participation in the country's democratic and social systems. By understanding and meeting these obligations, residents and citizens alike help uphold the rule of law and foster mutual trust. In the next section, we will follow what happens when legal issues escalate, guiding you through the U.S. court system—its structure, key processes, and what to expect if you ever find yourself navigating its halls.

4.4 When Rights and Responsibilities Clash

In every society, **rights** and **responsibilities** are often viewed as two sides of the same coin—each necessary to uphold a fair and functional social order. In the United States, this balance is foundational, but it is not always easy or straightforward. Sometimes, one person's exercise of their rights may conflict with the responsibilities or rights of another. When such clashes occur, the law steps in to mediate, aiming to strike a balance that protects everyone's interests as equitably as possible.

Common Areas of Conflict

The U.S. legal system is filled with examples where rights and responsibilities intersect—and sometimes collide. Key areas where these conflicts often arise include:

Freedom of Speech vs. Public Order: The First Amendment protects free speech, but this right is not absolute. Speech that incites violence or panic, such as shouting "fire" in a crowded theater, can be legally restricted to maintain public safety.

Property Rights vs. Community Needs: Homeowners have significant property rights, but these may be limited by zoning laws, environmental regulations, or eminent domain when the broader community's needs take precedence.

Individual Privacy vs. Law Enforcement: The right to privacy is protected, but law enforcement agencies may lawfully intrude on this right with a warrant or under certain exceptions for public safety.

Case Study: The Right to Protest

One of the most vivid illustrations of rights and responsibilities clashing occurs during **public protests**. Citizens have the right to assemble and speak freely, but these actions often intersect with the public's right to safety and order.

Consider the 2017 events in Charlottesville, Virginia, where conflicting groups gathered to express their views. Law enforcement faced the challenge of upholding the right to protest while also ensuring the safety of the public and preventing violence. When tensions escalated into violence, authorities intervened, resulting in arrests and legal proceedings. This incident highlights the difficult decisions officials must make when rights are exercised in ways that threaten public safety.

Personal Story: The Noise Complaint

Let's turn to a more everyday example. Imagine a tenant, Maria, who loves playing piano in her apartment. She sees this as an expression of her right to enjoy her property. However, her neighbor, James, works night shifts and needs quiet during the day to rest. Maria's right to play music clashes with James's right to peaceful enjoyment of his own home.

Maria receives a noise complaint and learns that local ordinances limit "excessive noise" during certain hours. She now faces the responsibility of respecting these rules, even though she feels her rights are being curtailed. If she ignores the ordinance, she could face fines or even eviction. This scenario illustrates how the law tries to balance individual freedoms with community responsibilities.

How Courts Resolve Clashes

When disputes like these arise, courts play a pivotal role in interpreting laws and weighing competing interests. Judges often ask:

- Whose right is being exercised, and to what extent?

- What responsibilities or limits exist under the law?
- Would unrestricted exercise of this right harm others or the community?

Courts may apply legal standards such as the **"reasonableness" test**, balancing the interests at stake. Sometimes, the law favors the individual; other times, it sides with the community or another party whose rights are at risk.

Timeline: Resolving a Rights-Responsibility Conflict

- **Incident Occurs:** Two parties' rights/responsibilities conflict (e.g., noise complaint).
- **Complaint Filed:** Affected party notifies authorities or files a complaint.
- **Investigation:** Authorities assess whether a law, ordinance, or regulation has been violated.
- **Mediation or Hearing:** Parties may be encouraged to resolve the issue amicably, or a hearing may be scheduled.
- **Legal Decision:** A judge or mediator decides based on statutes, ordinances, and precedents.
- **Enforcement:** The decision is enforced, sometimes with penalties or required actions.

Global Perspectives

Conflicts between rights and responsibilities aren't unique to the U.S. In Germany, for example, freedom of speech is protected but strictly limited when it comes to hate speech, reflecting a national history and social responsibility to prevent extremism. In Japan, harmony and respect for community often outweigh individual expression, influencing everything from noise regulations to public protests. These examples show that while rights are cherished worldwide, each culture negotiates the balance differently.

```
Remember: The exercise of your rights always comes with the responsibility to respect the rights and safety of others. Ignoring this balance can have legal—and personal—consequences.
```

4.5 Protecting Your Rights

Every person living in the United States—citizen or not—benefits from a range of rights protected by the Constitution and federal law. These fundamental rights serve as the backbone of a fair and just society, ensuring that the power of the government is balanced by the liberties of the individual. Understanding these rights is the first step to protecting them in everyday life.

Some of the most important constitutional protections include:

- **Freedom of Speech and Expression** (First Amendment): The right to express your opinions publicly, with certain limits related to safety and public order.
- **Right to Privacy** (Fourth Amendment): Protection against unreasonable searches and seizures by the government.
- **Right to Due Process** (Fifth and Fourteenth Amendments): Guarantees fair procedures before you can be deprived of life, liberty, or property.
- **Right to Legal Counsel** (Sixth Amendment): The right to have a lawyer if you are facing criminal charges.
- **Right Against Self-Incrimination** (Fifth Amendment): You cannot be forced to testify against yourself.

These rights are not just theoretical—they shape the way people interact with law enforcement and the legal system every day.

Exercising Your Rights in Practice

Knowing your rights is important, but knowing how to assert them in real-life situations is equally critical. Here's how you can protect yourself during key encounters:

During Interactions with Law Enforcement

If you are stopped by the police, remember:

- You have the right to remain silent. You do not have to answer questions about where you are going, where you live, or what you are doing.
- You can ask, "Am I free to go?" If the answer is yes, calmly walk away.
- If you are being detained or arrested, you have the right to know why.
- You have the right to refuse consent to a search of yourself, your car, or your home unless the officer has a warrant or probable cause.

When Facing Legal Action

If you are sued, accused of a crime, or called as a witness:

Seek legal advice as soon as possible. A qualified attorney can help you navigate the complexities of the legal system.
Respond to all court documents and deadlines promptly—ignoring legal notices can result in default judgments or additional penalties.

Maintain thorough records of your interactions, agreements, and evidence related to the matter.

Personal Story:

Ana, a recent immigrant, received a notice from her landlord threatening eviction. Unsure of her rights, she visited a local legal aid clinic. With guidance, she learned that she could not be evicted without due process. The experience empowered her to negotiate with her landlord and ultimately keep her home.

Recognizing and Reporting Violations

Sometimes, rights are violated. If you believe your rights have been infringed:

Document the incident—write down details, gather witnesses, and save any related communications.

File a complaint with the appropriate agency, such as a local police oversight board, civil rights office, or housing authority.

Consult with a legal professional or advocacy group for advice on further action.

Global Perspectives: Rights in Context

The U.S. legal system's approach to individual rights is rooted in its unique constitutional framework. For example, in the United Kingdom, police can stop and search individuals under broader circumstances, and the right to silence operates differently. In contrast, some countries, like Germany, offer even stronger privacy protections, especially regarding digital information. Recognizing these differences underscores the importance of understanding your rights within the U.S. context.

```
If you are arrested, you have the right to remain silent and to an attorney.
Anything you say can be used against you in court. Always invoke these rights
clearly and respectfully.
```

4.6 Comparative Insight: Rights Around the World

While the U.S. legal system stands on a unique foundation of constitutional rights and common law traditions, individual rights and responsibilities are not exclusive to America. Around the world, societies have developed varying approaches to balancing personal freedoms with social order. Understanding these differences not only helps us appreciate the strengths and limitations of the U.S. system but also deepens our awareness of universal human rights and the challenges of protecting them.

Civil Liberties: A Shared, Yet Varied Principle

Many countries recognize civil liberties—such as freedom of speech, religion, and due process—but the scope and enforcement of these rights can differ drastically:

In the **United States**, the First Amendment robustly protects free expression, allowing citizens to criticize the government and voice dissent without fear of prosecution.

In **Germany**, freedom of speech is also enshrined, but with legal limits on hate speech and symbols associated with Nazism—a response to the country's historical context.

In **China**, the constitution promises freedom of speech, but in practice, government censorship and legal restrictions limit public dissent and criticism.

This diversity reflects each nation's history, culture, and political structure. For example, Germany's restrictions are a direct response to its experience with extremism, while the U.S. tradition prioritizes broad protections even for controversial or unpopular speech.

Due Process and Legal Protections

The right to a fair trial is another cornerstone of legal systems worldwide, but what constitutes "fairness" varies:

United States: The Constitution guarantees due process, including the right to remain silent, access to legal counsel, and trial by jury in criminal cases.

United Kingdom: While sharing many protections with the U.S. due to common law heritage, the U.K. legal system relies more on judge-led trials and does not have a written constitution with a Bill of Rights.

Japan: The postwar constitution, influenced by American legal ideals, ensures rights to legal counsel and fair trials, but the system is renowned for its high conviction rates and heavy reliance on confessions.

A real-world example highlights these differences: In the U.S., Miranda v. Arizona (1966) established that individuals must be informed of their rights during police interrogation (the famous "Miranda warning"). In contrast, other countries may not require police to advise suspects of their rights in the same manner, potentially affecting the fairness of legal proceedings.

Responsibilities: Civic Duties Across Borders

With rights come responsibilities, and every society sets expectations for lawful behavior:

Jury Duty: Unique to countries like the U.S. and Australia, ordinary citizens are called to serve on juries, participating directly in the administration of justice.

Voting: Many nations, including Australia and Belgium, mandate compulsory voting—a civic duty that contrasts with the voluntary nature of voting in the U.S.

Obeying Laws and Paying Taxes: Universal responsibilities, though enforcement mechanisms and penalties for noncompliance can vary dramatically.

Personal Story: Navigating Rights as a Newcomer

Consider Maria, who emigrated from Brazil to the United States. In Brazil, interacting with police often meant keeping quiet and avoiding confrontation, as legal protections were less predictable. In the U.S., Maria learned—after an initial traffic stop—that she could ask for clarification, assert her rights politely, and expect due process. This experience underscored the importance of understanding not just rights, but also how cultural expectations and local laws shape daily interactions with authority.

Universal Rights: The Global Movement

International agreements, such as the **Universal Declaration of Human Rights** (UDHR), aspire to set minimum standards for human dignity worldwide. While the UDHR is not legally binding, it has influenced constitutions and laws across the globe, including the U.S. Bill of Rights and later amendments.

Examining rights and responsibilities through a global lens reveals both the universality and diversity of legal protections. By recognizing these differences, we better understand the privileges and duties we hold as residents of the United States. As we move forward, let's delve into how these rights are put into practice in American courtrooms—unpacking the procedures, key participants, and expectations that define the U.S. judicial experience.

5 Traffic Laws and Road Safety

5.1 Basics of Traffic Law

Every day, millions of Americans travel by car, bicycle, or on foot, sharing the public roads that weave through cities and towns across the country. To ensure order and safety, the United States has developed a comprehensive system of **traffic laws**—rules designed to protect everyone on the road. These laws govern everything from speed limits to right-of-way, and understanding them is not just a matter of convenience; it can mean the difference between safety and disaster, legality and liability.

Key Components of U.S. Traffic Law

Traffic laws in the U.S. are primarily set at the **state** and **local** levels, though some federal regulations influence broader transportation safety standards. While specifics vary between jurisdictions, several foundational rules are consistent throughout the nation:

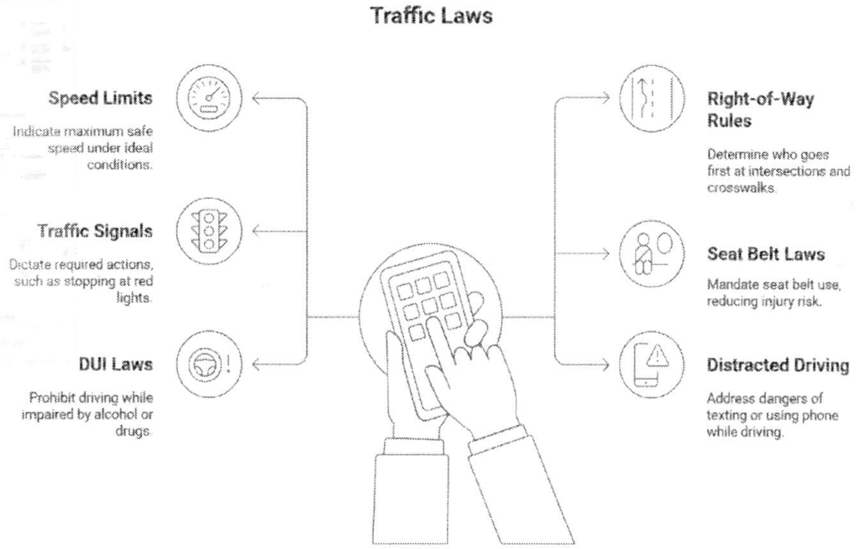

- **Speed Limits:** Posted to indicate the maximum safe speed under ideal conditions.
- **Right-of-Way Rules:** Determine who goes first at intersections, crosswalks, and when merging.

- **Traffic Signals and Signs:** Dictate required actions, such as stopping at red lights or yielding to pedestrians.
- **Seat Belt Laws:** Mandate that drivers and passengers use seat belts, greatly reducing injury risk.
- **DUI (Driving Under the Influence) Laws:** Prohibit operating a vehicle while impaired by alcohol or drugs.
- **Distracted Driving Prohibitions:** Address the dangers of texting or using a phone while driving.

These laws are enforced by local police, state troopers, and, in some cases, federal agencies for interstate highways. Violating these regulations can result in fines, points on your driver's license, increased insurance premiums, or even jail time for serious offenses.

A Story from the Road: The Impact of Speed

Consider the true story of **Sarah Chen**, a college student in California. One rainy night, Sarah decided to drive home after a late study session. Though the speed limit was 35 mph, she felt rushed and accelerated to 50 mph. Rounding a curve, she lost control and crashed into a guardrail. Fortunately, she survived with minor injuries, but the accident left a lasting impression. Police cited Sarah for **exceeding the speed limit and unsafe driving for conditions**—an important distinction, as in many states, drivers are expected to adjust their speed to match road and weather conditions, not just posted limits.

Sarah's experience underscores a vital aspect of U.S. traffic law: safety is about more than just following the numbers on a sign. Drivers are legally—and morally—responsible for making wise decisions based on the realities of the road.

Noteworthy Historical Context

The evolution of traffic laws in the U.S. mirrors the rise of the automobile itself. In the early 1900s, cars were a novelty, and roads were shared with horses, bicycles, and pedestrians—with little regulation. The first recorded **traffic ticket** in America was issued in 1904 to a New York City taxi driver for speeding at 12 mph. As cars became ubiquitous, so did the need for comprehensive rules, leading to the creation of driver's licenses, standardized signage, and the national adoption of the **Uniform Vehicle Code**.

Common Consequences of Violating Traffic Laws

Breaking traffic laws can have immediate and long-term effects:

Fines and Penalties: Monetary costs for violations such as speeding, running red lights, or illegal parking.

Points System: Many states use a point system—accumulating too many points can lead to license suspension.

Criminal Charges: Severe offenses like reckless driving or DUI may result in arrest, court appearances, or jail time.

Civil Liability: Causing an accident while breaking the law can make you responsible for damages or injuries.

```
Most traffic violations are categorized as infractions, not crimes, but
serious offenses (like DUI or reckless driving) can result in criminal
charges. Always check your state's specific laws.
```

Understanding the basics of traffic laws is essential for every resident, whether you're behind the wheel, on a bicycle, or simply crossing the street. These rules are not arbitrary—they exist to safeguard lives and uphold public order. As we move forward, we will explore the responsibilities and rights individuals have when interacting with law enforcement on the road, ensuring you are prepared for any situation that may arise during your daily travels.

5.2 Common Violations and Their Consequences

Every day, millions of Americans get behind the wheel, trusting that everyone else will follow the rules of the road. Yet, even minor lapses can lead to significant legal consequences. Understanding the most frequent traffic violations—and their associated penalties—can help you avoid costly mistakes and keep yourself and others safe.

Some of the most common traffic violations include:

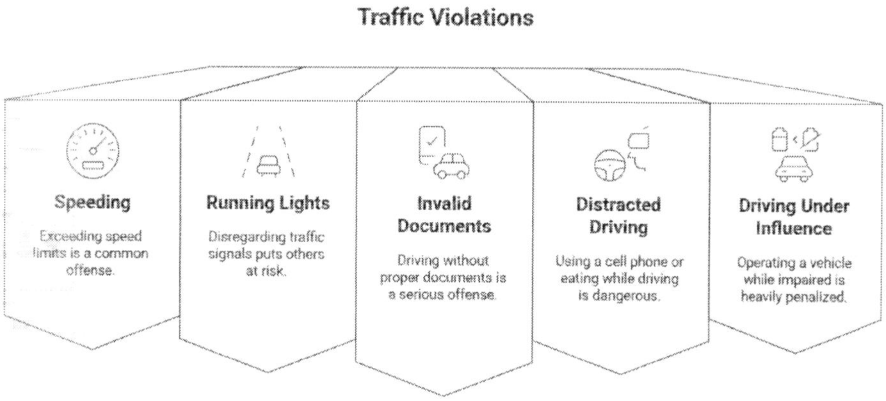

- **Speeding:** Exceeding posted speed limits is the most frequently cited traffic offense in the United States. Even going a few miles per hour over the limit can result in a ticket.
- **Running Red Lights or Stop Signs:** Disregarding traffic signals or signs not only puts others at risk but also carries steep fines and, in some cases, points on your driver's license.
- **Driving Without a Valid License or Insurance:** Operating a vehicle without the proper documentation is a serious offense and may result in arrest, fines, or vehicle impoundment.
- **Distracted Driving:** Using a cell phone, eating, or engaging in any activity that diverts attention from the road can result in citations in many states.
- **Driving Under the Influence (DUI):** Operating a vehicle while impaired by alcohol or drugs is among the most heavily penalized violations, with severe legal and personal consequences.

Legal Consequences of Violations

Penalties for traffic violations vary depending on the offense and the jurisdiction, but consequences can include:

- **Fines:** The most immediate penalty is usually a monetary fine, which can range from $50 for minor infractions to several thousand dollars for more serious offenses like DUI.
- **Points on Your License:** Many states use a point system. Accumulating too many points can result in license suspension or increased insurance premiums.
- **Court Appearance:** Certain violations require a mandatory court appearance, particularly if the offense involved injury, property damage, or reckless behavior.
- **Jail Time:** Serious offenses such as DUI, reckless driving, or driving with a suspended license can result in jail sentences, even for first-time offenders.
- **Community Service or Traffic School:** Courts may order offenders to attend traffic school or perform community service as part of their sentence.

Real-World Example: The Cost of Speeding

Consider the story of Maria, a college student in California. Running late for class, she was clocked going 15 mph over the speed limit in a school zone. Not only did she receive a hefty fine, but the violation added points to her license, resulting in higher insurance premiums for the next three years. Maria's experience is a common one, demonstrating how a moment's haste can have lasting financial impact.

Historical Anecdote: The First Traffic Ticket

The first recorded traffic violation in the United States dates back to 1899, when a New York City taxi driver named Jacob German was arrested for speeding at 12 miles per hour. The incident made headlines and set the precedent for modern traffic enforcement, highlighting society's early recognition of the need for road safety.

The Role of Law Enforcement

Officers are tasked with not only enforcing traffic laws but also educating the public about the importance of road safety. They may issue warnings for minor infractions or citations for repeat or serious offenses. In all cases, their goal is to deter dangerous behavior and protect the community.

```
Did you know? Accumulating too many points on your driving record can result
in license suspension—even for non-criminal offenses. Always check your
state's point system to understand the risks.
```

Traffic violations, whether minor or severe, carry consequences that extend beyond the driver to impact families and communities. By understanding common violations and their penalties, you can make informed choices every time you get behind the wheel. In the next section, we will explore your rights and obligations when interacting with law enforcement during a traffic stop—equipping you with knowledge to navigate these encounters with confidence and respect.

5.3 Traffic Stops: Know Your Rights

When the blue and red lights flash in your rearview mirror, your heart might race, but such moments are a common part of life for drivers in the United States. Understanding your rights and responsibilities during a traffic stop not only protects you but also contributes to safer, more respectful interactions with law enforcement.

What Happens During a Traffic Stop?

A traffic stop typically begins when a law enforcement officer signals for you to pull over. This can happen for a variety of reasons—speeding, a broken taillight, expired registration, or even a random check. The sequence usually follows these steps:

- **The Signal**: The officer activates their lights (and sometimes a siren) to signal you to stop.

- **Pulling Over**: You should safely pull to the right side of the road and stop your vehicle.
- **Initial Contact**: The officer approaches your vehicle, usually on the driver's side.
- **Request for Documents**: You'll be asked for your driver's license, vehicle registration, and proof of insurance.
- **Conversation and Assessment**: The officer may ask questions or explain the reason for the stop.
- **Resolution**: The encounter concludes with a warning, citation, or, in rare cases, arrest.

Your Rights During a Traffic Stop

Even as you cooperate with law enforcement, you retain certain constitutional rights. Knowing these can help you make informed decisions:

- **Right to Remain Silent**: You are not required to answer questions about where you are going, where you are coming from, or what you are doing. Politely state, "I am exercising my right to remain silent," if you choose not to answer.
- **Protection from Unreasonable Search**: Officers may not search your car without your consent unless they have probable cause, see evidence of a crime in plain view, or have another legal justification.
- **Right to Refuse Consent**: You may say, "I do not consent to a search," if asked.
- **Right to Know Why You Were Stopped**: You can politely ask the officer for the reason for the stop.

What Should You Do?

Stay calm and keep your hands visible, preferably on the steering wheel.
Comply with requests for identification and documents.
Avoid sudden movements or arguing with the officer.
Remember the details of the encounter for your records.

Real-World Example: The Sandra Bland Case

In 2015, Sandra Bland was pulled over in Texas for failing to signal a lane change. The interaction escalated after she questioned the officer's authority and refused to exit her vehicle. The stop ended in her arrest, and her subsequent death in custody sparked nationwide conversations about traffic stops, individual rights, and law enforcement accountability. This case underscores the importance of understanding both your rights and the safest ways to exercise them.

A Global Perspective: Traffic Stops in Germany

In Germany, police also conduct roadside checks, but the process can differ. Officers are required to identify themselves and explain the reason for the stop. German law strictly limits vehicle searches, reflecting a strong cultural emphasis on personal privacy. Comparing these systems highlights how legal rights—and expectations—vary across societies.

```
If you are issued a citation during a traffic stop, signing it is not an
admission of guilt. It is simply a promise to appear in court or pay the fine.

Recording police officers during a stop is generally legal in most states,
provided you do not interfere with their duties.
```

5.4 Accidents and Liability

When traffic laws are violated or accidents occur, questions of **liability**—who is legally responsible for damages or injuries—come to the forefront. Understanding how liability is determined and what steps should be taken after an accident is essential, not just for legal compliance but also for protecting your own interests and safety.

What to Do After an Accident

The moments immediately following a car accident can be chaotic and stressful. However, your actions during this period have significant legal implications. Here's what you should do:

- **Ensure Safety** – Move vehicles out of traffic if possible and check for injuries.
- **Call for Help** – Contact law enforcement and emergency services if anyone is injured or if there is significant property damage.
- **Exchange Information** – Legally, all involved parties must exchange names, addresses, driver's license numbers, and insurance information.
- **Document the Scene** – Take photos, note the time, weather, and any other relevant details.
- **File a Report** – In some states, you are required to file a police report, especially if there are injuries or substantial property damage.

Failing to follow these steps could result in legal penalties or complications with insurance claims.

Determining Liability

Liability in traffic accidents is typically based on **negligence**—the failure to exercise reasonable care on the road. The person found at fault is usually responsible for damages, including vehicle repairs, medical bills, and sometimes pain and suffering.

Comparative and Contributory Negligence

The United States employs two main systems for determining liability:

Comparative negligence: Fault is apportioned among all parties. If you are 20% responsible for an accident, you may only recover 80% of your damages.

Contributory negligence: If you are even slightly at fault (as little as 1%), you may be barred from recovering any damages. Only a few states follow this strict rule.

Real-World Example

Consider the case of **Smith v. Jones** in a suburban Texas community. Smith, distracted by a phone call, failed to stop at a red light and collided with Jones's vehicle. Although Jones was speeding, the court determined Smith was 70% responsible, while Jones bore 30% of the fault. Under comparative negligence, Jones's compensation for damages was reduced by 30%, reflecting his share of responsibility.

Insurance and Legal Consequences

Most drivers carry **liability insurance** to cover accidents they cause. However, if damages exceed policy limits, the at-fault driver may be personally liable. Additionally, serious accidents can lead to criminal charges, especially if reckless driving, intoxication, or leaving the scene (hit and run) are involved.

Global Perspective

Other countries approach accident liability differently. For example, in Japan, a strict liability system means drivers are almost always held responsible for injuries to pedestrians, regardless of fault. This contrasts with the U.S. emphasis on negligence and shared responsibility.

```
In most U.S. states, leaving the scene of an accident (hit and run) is a
criminal offense, often resulting in severe penalties including license
suspension, hefty fines, or imprisonment.
Your insurance rate may increase substantially after an at-fault accident—even
if no one is injured.
```

Next, we'll examine the consequences of traffic violations—exploring the range of penalties and how they can impact your daily life, legal record, and future opportunities. This knowledge will empower you to make informed choices and avoid unnecessary legal complications.

5.5 Special Rules for Cyclists and Pedestrians

While motorists make up the majority of road users, **cyclists** and **pedestrians** play an essential role in the U.S. transportation landscape. The law recognizes their unique vulnerabilities and sets out special rules to both protect and obligate them. Understanding these rules is crucial—not only for those who walk or cycle, but also for drivers who share the road.

Laws for Cyclists: More Than Two Wheels

Cyclists in the U.S. are generally considered vehicle operators, granting them both the rights and responsibilities of drivers. However, several important distinctions exist:

- **Bike Lanes and Road Positioning**: Many states require cyclists to use designated bike lanes where available. If no bike lane exists, riders are typically instructed to stay as far to the right as practicable, but may move left to avoid hazards or prepare for turns.
- **Obeying Traffic Signals**: Cyclists must follow all traffic control devices—stop signs, red lights, and yield signs—just like vehicles.
- **Helmet Laws**: While not uniformly required, many states and cities mandate helmets for children or all riders under a certain age.
- **Lighting and Visibility**: Most states require cyclists to use front white lights and rear red reflectors or lights when riding at night.
- **Signaling**: Hand signals are required to indicate turns or stops, ensuring that other road users can anticipate a cyclist's actions.

A Real-World Example: The Idaho Stop

In 1982, Idaho became the first state to allow cyclists to treat stop signs as yield signs and red lights as stop signs. This rule, now known as the **"Idaho Stop,"** acknowledges that cyclists can safely yield and proceed through intersections without coming to a complete stop, reducing collisions and improving traffic flow. The success of this law has led other states, like Delaware and Colorado, to adopt similar provisions.

Pedestrian Protections and Duties

Pedestrian safety is a cornerstone of traffic law. Rules are designed to safeguard those on foot while balancing their responsibilities to cross safely.

Right of Way in Crosswalks: Pedestrians generally have the right of way in marked or unmarked crosswalks. However, they must not suddenly leave a curb or place of safety into the path of an oncoming vehicle.

Obeying Signals: Pedestrians are legally required to follow walk/don't walk signals where present.

Jaywalking: Crossing outside a designated crosswalk or against a signal is illegal in most jurisdictions and may result in a fine.

Sidewalk Use: Where sidewalks are provided, pedestrians must use them; if none are available, walking on the left side of the road facing traffic is the norm for safety.

A Personal Story: A Life Changed in a Crosswalk

Consider the story of Angela, a college student in Boston. One rainy evening, she crossed a busy intersection with the walk signal. A driver, distracted by a phone, failed to yield. Angela suffered serious injuries. The resulting court case not only reinforced the driver's legal responsibility but also led to stricter enforcement of pedestrian right-of-way laws in the city. Angela's experience highlights the real-life stakes of these rules—for both pedestrians and drivers.

Global Perspectives

Different countries approach pedestrian and cyclist safety in unique ways. In the Netherlands, for instance, **strict liability** laws presume drivers are at fault in collisions with cyclists or pedestrians unless proven otherwise, resulting in a culture highly protective of vulnerable road users.

> Did you know?
>
> Pedestrian and cyclist fatalities make up nearly 20% of all traffic deaths in the U.S., highlighting the importance of knowing and following these special rules for everyone's safety.

5.6 Regional Variations and Global Road Rules

While the overarching goal of **traffic laws** across the United States is the same—ensuring safety and order on the roads—the specifics can vary dramatically from state to state, and even town to town. This regional diversity reflects the country's federal system, in which states and municipalities retain significant authority to set their own rules.

Take, for example, the issue of **right turn on red**. In most states, drivers are allowed to turn right at a red light after coming to a complete stop, unless posted otherwise. However, in New York City, this maneuver is generally prohibited unless a sign specifically allows it. Similarly, **speed limits** can differ not only between states but also between rural and urban areas within the same state.

Key Regional Differences

- **Distracted driving laws:** Some states ban all handheld device use while driving, while others only prohibit texting.
- **Seatbelt requirements:** All states except New Hampshire require adults to wear seatbelts, but enforcement varies between primary (officers can stop you for not wearing a seatbelt) and secondary (can only ticket if stopped for another offense) laws.
- **School bus rules:** In some states, all traffic must stop when a school bus displays its stop sign, even on divided highways; in others, only the traffic traveling in the same direction must stop.

Real-World Example: Florida vs. California

Consider **bicycle law** as an illustration. In Florida, cyclists are required to use bike lanes if provided, while in California, cyclists may choose whether to use a bike lane or ride in the general lane under certain conditions. These nuanced differences can pose challenges for travelers and newcomers.

Learning from Global Road Rules

The United States is not alone in its regional variation. Around the world, countries tailor their **traffic laws** to fit local needs and customs. Comparing U.S. practices with those of other nations can offer valuable perspectives.

International Contrasts

Driving orientation: In the U.S., people drive on the right side of the road. In the United Kingdom, India, Australia, and Japan, driving is on the left.

Blood alcohol content (BAC) limits: The legal BAC limit for drivers in the U.S. is typically 0.08%. In Sweden, the limit is just 0.02%, reflecting a stricter approach to drinking and driving.

Pedestrian right-of-way: Many European countries give pedestrians greater priority, with harsh penalties for failing to yield at crosswalks.

Anecdote: The International License

In 2016, Maria, a recent immigrant from Brazil, was pulled over in Texas for failing to yield to a school bus—a law she was unfamiliar with. In Brazil, school buses are less common, and the rules differ. The officer explained the local law, and Maria was given a warning. Her experience underscores the importance of understanding

regional traffic laws—not just for legal compliance, but for the safety of everyone on the road.

```
All drivers in the U.S. are responsible for knowing and following local
traffic laws, regardless of where their license was issued; ignorance of the
law is not a valid defense.
Many U.S. states share information about traffic infractions, so violations in
one state may affect your driving record in another.
```

5.7 Preventing Trouble on the Road

The most effective way to avoid legal entanglements and physical danger on the road is to practice **defensive driving**. This means being vigilant, anticipating the actions of others, and knowing how to respond safely to sudden hazards. **Defensive drivers** are not only less likely to cause accidents but also less likely to be cited for traffic violations. The National Safety Council reports that defensive driving can reduce accident risk by over 50%.

Key defensive driving habits include:

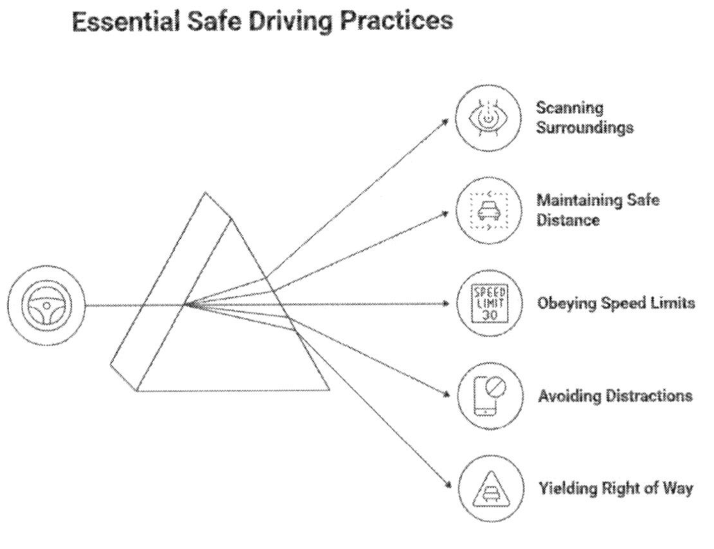

- Always scanning your surroundings and checking mirrors frequently.
- Maintaining a safe following distance—at least three seconds behind the vehicle ahead.
- Obeying all speed limits and adjusting speed for weather or traffic conditions.
- Avoiding distractions, such as texting or eating while driving.

- Yielding the right of way and never assuming other drivers will obey traffic rules.

Real-World Example: A Preventable Collision

Consider the story of **Maria Lopez**, a recent immigrant to the U.S. who was unfamiliar with four-way stop signs. One rainy evening, she approached an intersection, mistakenly thinking she had the right of way. A local driver, expecting Maria to stop, proceeded through—and the two cars collided. Thankfully, no one was seriously injured, but Maria received a citation for failing to yield. This incident could have been avoided with greater familiarity with local traffic rules and by both drivers practicing defensive caution.

The Role of Routine Vehicle Maintenance

Preventing trouble on the road isn't just about how you drive—it's also about the condition of your vehicle. Many states require **regular inspections** to ensure basic safety features like brakes, lights, and tires are functioning. Failing to maintain your car can lead to unexpected breakdowns, accidents, or citations.

Simple steps to keep your vehicle road-legal and safe include:

- Checking tire pressure and tread regularly.
- Ensuring headlights, brake lights, and turn signals work.
- Keeping windshield wipers in good condition for clear visibility.
- Scheduling regular oil changes and brake checks.

Understanding Local and State Laws

Traffic laws can vary widely from state to state, and even city to city. For example, some states allow **right turns on red** after a full stop, while others prohibit it. Similarly, speed limits may differ on rural highways versus city streets. Knowing these local nuances is essential, especially for new residents or travelers.

Historical Anecdote: When the United States first implemented the **55 mph national speed limit** in the 1970s due to the oil crisis, compliance and enforcement varied dramatically across the nation. Some states resisted, creating a patchwork of enforcement that highlighted the importance of understanding regional laws.

Encounters with Law Enforcement

If you are pulled over, staying calm and respectful is crucial. Keep your hands visible, follow the officer's instructions, and provide requested documents (license, registration, proof of insurance). Remember, you have the right to **remain silent** and to ask why you were stopped.

Steps to Follow When Pulled Over:

- Pull over safely and promptly.
- Turn off your engine and lower your window.
- Wait for instructions; do not reach for items until asked.
- Respond politely and honestly.

```
Did you know? Even minor traffic violations, like rolling through a stop sign,
can lead to increased insurance rates and points on your license, impacting
your driving privileges.
Important: Failure to appear in court or pay a traffic ticket can result in a
warrant for your arrest in some jurisdictions.
```

Preventing trouble on the road involves more than just following the rules; it's a mindset of caution, respect, and responsibility for yourself and others. By staying informed, maintaining your vehicle, and approaching every drive with care, you help keep your community safe—and avoid unnecessary legal complications. In the next section, we'll explore what to do if you find yourself facing a traffic violation, including your rights and responsibilities when dealing with citations and the court system.

6 Property Rights—Home, Rent, and Beyond

6.1 Owning Real Estate

Owning real estate is more than just having a place to live or work—it's a cornerstone of financial security, personal freedom, and, in many ways, the American Dream. In the United States, property ownership carries significant legal rights and responsibilities. Whether you're buying your first home, investing in rental properties, or inheriting land, understanding these principles can help you protect your investment and ensure your rights are respected.

Key Rights Associated with Ownership

When you own real estate in the U.S., you gain what is known as **"fee simple"** ownership, which is the most complete form of property ownership. This bundle of rights typically includes:

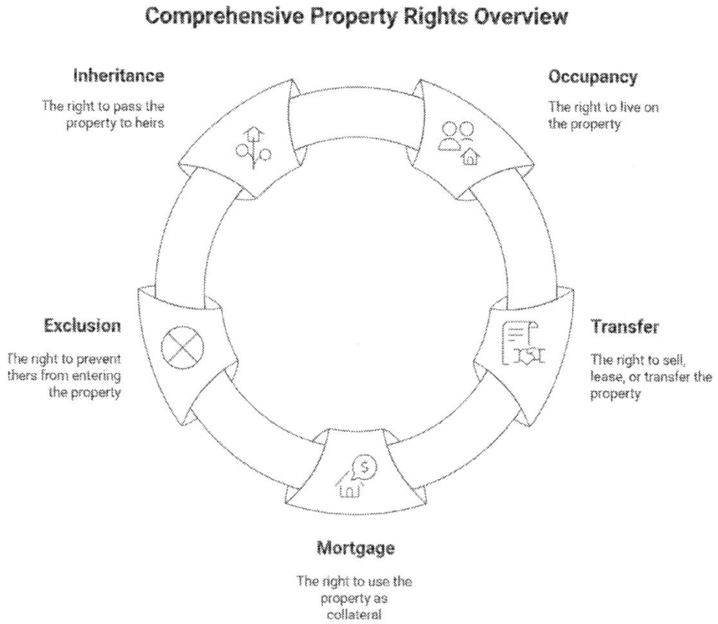

- The right to occupy and use the property
- The right to sell, lease, or transfer the property
- The right to mortgage the property
- The right to exclude others from your property
- The right to pass the property on to heirs

However, these rights are not absolute. Local, state, and federal laws—including zoning regulations, environmental restrictions, and public easements—can all limit how you use your property.

How Real Estate Is Acquired

The process of acquiring real estate in the U.S. follows a series of established legal steps, designed to protect both buyers and sellers:

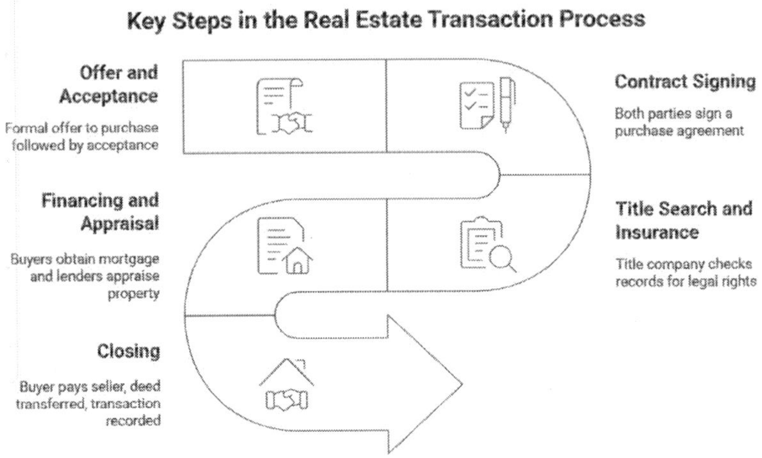

- **Offer and Acceptance**: The process begins with a formal offer to purchase, followed by acceptance by the seller.
- **Contract Signing**: Both parties sign a purchase agreement outlining the terms and conditions.
- **Title Search and Insurance**: A title company checks records to ensure the seller has the legal right to sell and that the property is free of liens or disputes.
- **Financing and Appraisal**: Most buyers obtain a mortgage. Lenders require an appraisal to confirm the property's value.
- **Closing**: At closing, the buyer pays the seller, the deed is transferred, and the transaction is recorded with the local government.

The Importance of a Clear Title

A **clear title** means the property is free from legal claims, disputes, or unpaid debts. Title insurance protects buyers from unforeseen issues, such as a previous owner's unpaid taxes or undetected heirs who might claim ownership.

Real-World Example: The Homestead Act

In the late 1800s, the **Homestead Act** opened vast tracts of land in the American West to settlers. Anyone willing to live on and improve the land could eventually own it outright. This law not only shaped migration and settlement patterns but also established the importance of land ownership in American society. While the Homestead Act is no longer in effect, its legacy endures, symbolizing how property rights are tied to opportunity and social mobility.

Responsibilities of Property Owners

With ownership come important obligations:

Property Taxes: Annual taxes fund local schools, roads, and services. Failure to pay can result in losing the property.

Maintenance and Safety: Owners must keep property safe and in compliance with local building codes.

Respecting Neighboring Rights: Actions on your property—like building a fence or cutting down trees—should not infringe on neighbors' rights or cause harm.

A Personal Story: Boundary Disputes

Consider the case of Maria, a new homeowner in a suburban neighborhood. She decided to build a fence to keep her dog safe, only to discover that her neighbor disputed the property line. After consulting a surveyor and reviewing property records, Maria found the original boundary markers. The dispute was resolved amicably, but the experience highlighted the importance of understanding your property's legal boundaries.

Diverse Perspectives: Global Property Ownership

While U.S. law generally favors individual ownership, in some countries, land is owned collectively or by the government. For example, in Switzerland, **cooperative housing** allows residents to own shares in a building rather than individual units. In China, all land is technically owned by the state, though individuals may lease use rights for extended periods. Understanding these differences can shed light on the unique features of American property law.

```
In most U.S. states, real estate transactions must be recorded with the county
or local government to be legally effective. This public record protects both
owners and buyers by providing a transparent history of ownership (the "chain
of title").
```

Owning real estate is a powerful right that comes with both opportunities and responsibilities. By understanding the legal steps, potential pitfalls, and broader context of property ownership, individuals can make informed decisions and safeguard their interests. As we turn to the next section, we'll explore what happens when you don't own property but still need a place to live—the world of renting, tenant rights, and landlord obligations.

6.2 Renting and Lease Agreements

When you choose to rent rather than own a home, you enter into a legal relationship defined by a **lease agreement**. This document isn't just a handshake or a casual promise—it's a binding contract that outlines the rights and responsibilities of both the **tenant** (the person renting) and the **landlord** (the property owner or manager). A lease typically specifies:

- The length of time you can stay (commonly 12 months, but sometimes month-to-month)
- The amount of rent and when it's due
- Security deposit requirements
- Rules about pets, guests, and property use
- Maintenance responsibilities
- Procedures for ending or renewing the lease

The law treats lease agreements seriously. Even if you don't sign a formal document—say, you move in after a verbal promise—local laws may still recognize an **implied lease**, affording you certain protections.

Key Rights and Responsibilities

Both tenants and landlords have specific legal rights and duties, which vary somewhat by state but share core principles:

Right to Habitable Housing: Tenants are entitled to a safe, clean, and livable environment. This means functional utilities, secure locks, and freedom from major hazards like mold or pest infestations.
Right to Privacy: Landlords cannot enter your home without notice (except in emergencies). Most states require at least 24 hours' notice before entry.
Timely Rent and Careful Use: Tenants must pay rent on time and avoid damaging the property beyond normal wear and tear.
Maintenance Obligations: Landlords must make necessary repairs, while tenants must keep the premises reasonably clean and notify landlords of issues.

The Security Deposit: More Than Just Money Upfront

A security deposit is money you pay at the start of your lease to cover potential damages or unpaid rent. State laws limit how much can be charged and require landlords to return the deposit (minus legitimate deductions) within a set period after you move out. Always document the condition of your home at move-in and move-out with photos or videos—this can be crucial if disputes arise.

A Real-World Example: Know Your Lease, Protect Your Rights

Consider the story of **Maria**, a recent college graduate who rented her first apartment in Chicago. She paid a $1,000 security deposit and moved in, only to discover a persistent leak in the kitchen. Despite repeated requests, her landlord delayed repairs for weeks. Maria learned from a local tenants' rights group that Illinois law required repairs within a reasonable time and allowed tenants to withhold rent if issues weren't fixed. Armed with this knowledge, she sent a written notice, and when the landlord still didn't act, she filed a complaint with the city's building department. The repairs were completed within days, and her security deposit was fully refunded when she moved out.

Maria's experience underscores the importance of understanding your lease and local laws. Knowing your rights can make the difference between a stressful ordeal and a fair resolution.

Lease Termination and Renewal: Ending the Relationship

When the time comes to move out, the lease will detail how to give notice—often 30 or 60 days in advance. Failing to follow these procedures can result in lost security deposits or even legal action. If you want to stay, many leases offer automatic renewal or a new lease negotiation.

The Eviction Process: Legal Protections for Tenants

Eviction is a legal procedure landlords must follow if a tenant violates the lease—such as not paying rent or causing damage. Tenants must receive proper notice and have the opportunity to correct the violation or contest the eviction in court. "Self-help" evictions—like changing the locks or shutting off utilities without a court order—are illegal in most states.

Global Perspective: Tenant Rights Around the World

The U.S. isn't alone in balancing landlord and tenant rights. In Germany, tenants enjoy strong protections, with limits on rent increases and strict eviction rules. Meanwhile, in Japan, rental agreements often include hefty upfront costs, but tenants benefit from legal clarity and efficient dispute resolution systems. Comparing these systems highlights the universal challenge of creating fair, safe housing for everyone.

Key Fact: In most U.S. states, landlords cannot evict tenants without going through the court system—and tenants have the right to a hearing before being removed from their home.

Renting brings legal responsibilities and rights for both tenants and landlords. Understanding your lease agreement, documenting your living space, and knowing your local laws are essential steps to protect yourself. As we continue, we'll examine what happens when property disputes arise—whether between neighbors, roommates, or even strangers—shedding light on how U.S. law resolves conflicts over property boundaries and shared spaces.

6.3 Buying and Selling Personal Property

Most Americans engage in the **buying and selling of personal property** more often than they realize—from purchasing a used bicycle at a garage sale to selling a smartphone online. Unlike real estate, which involves land and buildings, **personal property** refers to movable items: furniture, electronics, clothing, vehicles, and more. The legal foundation for these day-to-day exchanges is both simple and surprisingly robust, ensuring that buyers and sellers alike have clear rights and responsibilities.

At its core, a **sale** is a contract: one person agrees to transfer ownership of an item to another, usually in exchange for money. Under U.S. law, even casual, verbal agreements can be legally binding, though written records are always safer, especially for higher-value items. The **Uniform Commercial Code (UCC)**, adopted in some form by every state, governs most personal property sales and sets out important protections—for instance, ensuring that goods are as described, and clarifying what happens if a problem arises after the sale.

Key Principles in Buying and Selling

When it comes to personal property, several principles guide each transaction:

- **Ownership**: The seller must have the legal right to sell the item—selling stolen or misrepresented goods can result in criminal charges.
- **Condition and Disclosure**: Sellers should honestly represent the condition of the item. Many states require sellers to disclose any known defects, especially for vehicles or expensive goods.
- **Transfer of Title**: For certain items (like cars, boats, or firearms), the transfer of **title** (legal ownership) must be documented with a bill of sale and registered with the appropriate government agency.
- **Implied Warranties**: Unless a sale is explicitly "as is," the law often assumes the item works as described and is fit for its ordinary use. If it doesn't, buyers may have legal recourse.

- **Return Policies and Remedies**: While stores often offer return policies, private sales usually do not—unless agreed upon in advance.

Real-World Example: A Car Sale Gone Wrong

Consider the story of Marcus, a college student in Michigan who bought a used car through an online marketplace. The seller assured Marcus the car was in "excellent condition," but after two weeks, the engine failed completely. Because the seller had provided written statements about the car's condition, Marcus was able to take the matter to **small claims court**. The judge, applying the state's version of the UCC, found in Marcus's favor—demonstrating how even small transactions are protected by a legal safety net.

Historical Perspective: The Rise of Consumer Protection

Historically, consumers were left largely on their own if a purchase went bad. In the early 20th century, as mail-order catalogs and later, department stores, made cross-country sales common, states began to recognize the need for consistent rules. The **Uniform Sales Act** (later replaced by the UCC) and federal regulations like the **Magnuson-Moss Warranty Act** emerged to ensure that buyers had recourse if they were sold defective or misrepresented goods. These laws reflect the U.S. commitment to fair dealing and honest trade—principles echoed in many legal systems worldwide.

For example, in Germany, consumer protection laws require a two-year warranty on most goods, while in Japan, certain products carry lifetime guarantees. These global perspectives show that, despite differences, the right to fair treatment as a buyer or seller is a shared value.

Tips for Safe Transactions

To protect yourself in personal property transactions:

- Always get a written bill of sale, especially for high-value items.
- Check the item's history (for example, use **VIN checks** for vehicles).
- Meet in a safe, public place when exchanging goods.
- If selling, make sure you own the item outright and disclose any known problems.

When Things Go Wrong: Legal Remedies

If a dispute arises, possible remedies include:

Negotiating directly with the other party.

Filing a claim in **small claims court** for lower-value disputes (typically up to $10,000, depending on the state).

Contacting consumer protection agencies for help with fraudulent or deceptive sales.

```
In most U.S. states, selling stolen property—even unknowingly—can result in
both civil liability and criminal charges. Always verify ownership before
buying or selling valuable personal items.
```

The laws governing personal property sales in the U.S. are designed to protect fairness and transparency, balancing the interests of buyers and sellers. Whether you're purchasing a used appliance or selling your old car, understanding these principles empowers you to act confidently and responsibly. As we move forward, the next section explores the unique legal landscape of **intellectual property**, showing how ideas and creations are protected—both in the United States and around the world.

6.4 Resolving Property Disputes

Property disputes are among the most frequent legal challenges individuals encounter in the United States. Whether you own your home, rent an apartment, or share a fence line with a neighbor, disagreements can arise over boundaries, ownership, maintenance, or usage rights. Some of the most common sources of property disputes include:

- **Boundary disagreements**: Unclear property lines or encroachments, such as a neighbor's fence or tree extending onto your land.
- **Landlord-tenant conflicts**: Issues surrounding lease terms, eviction notices, security deposits, or repairs.
- **Easement and access issues**: Disputes over shared driveways, utility rights-of-way, or access to shared resources.
- **Co-ownership misunderstandings**: Arguments between family members or business partners who jointly own property.
- **Nuisance claims**: Activities or conditions on one property that negatively impact another, such as excessive noise, pollution, or blocked sunlight.

Understanding the roots of these disputes is the first step toward resolution. Let's explore the methods available for addressing them.

Steps to Resolving Property Disputes

Resolving property disputes often begins with communication, but sometimes requires formal legal steps. Here is a typical progression:

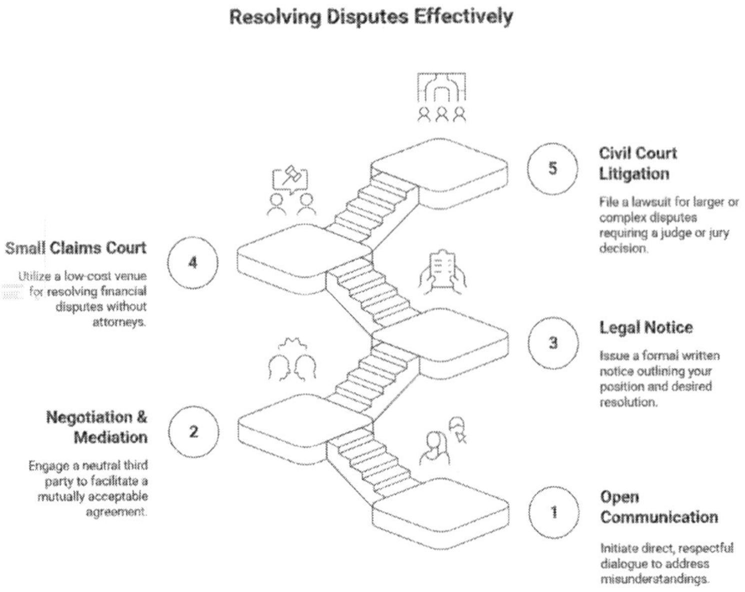

- **Open Communication**: The first effort should always be direct, respectful dialogue. Many disputes are the result of misunderstandings or lack of information.
- **Negotiation and Mediation**: If talking doesn't resolve the issue, mediation—a process where a neutral third party helps both sides reach an agreement—can often lead to a mutually acceptable solution. Mediation is often quicker and less expensive than going to court.
- **Legal Notice**: When informal solutions fail, formal written notice (such as a demand letter) may be necessary, laying out your position and what you seek as a resolution.
- **Small Claims Court**: For financial disputes involving smaller sums (the limit varies by state, usually between $5,000 and $10,000), small claims courts offer an accessible, low-cost venue for resolution without the need for attorneys.
- **Civil Court Litigation**: Larger or more complex disputes, such as those involving property titles or significant damages, may require filing a lawsuit in civil court. Here, a judge or jury will hear evidence and make a binding decision.

Real-World Example: The Case of the Overgrown Tree

Consider the story of Helen and Marcus, neighbors in a quiet California suburb. A massive oak tree on Marcus's property began to lean precariously over Helen's garage.

After several storms, large branches started to break off, damaging Helen's roof. Helen approached Marcus, but he insisted the tree was healthy and refused to trim it. Helen sought mediation, but Marcus did not participate. Left with no options, Helen filed a claim in small claims court for the cost of the roof repairs and trimming the tree. The court ruled in Helen's favor, ordering Marcus to cover the damages and maintain the tree. This case highlights the importance of knowing your rights and the stepwise escalation available in the U.S. legal system.

Legal Rights and Responsibilities

When resolving property disputes, it is essential to understand your legal rights and obligations:

- **Property owners** have the right to use their land, but not at the expense of their neighbors.
- **Tenants** have rights to safe, habitable living conditions and protection from unlawful eviction.
- **Landlords** must maintain the property and return security deposits in accordance with state law.
- **Courts** may order specific remedies, such as monetary damages, injunctions (orders to stop a particular activity), or even the removal of problem structures.

Global Perspective: Dispute Resolution Abroad

In many countries, property disputes are resolved through community mediation or local councils. For example, in some rural Indian villages, "panchayats" (village councils) mediate disagreements, balancing tradition and fairness. By contrast, the U.S. system emphasizes individual legal rights and court-based remedies, but alternative dispute resolution methods—like mediation—are increasingly encouraged.

Evidence in Property Disputes

Gathering evidence is critical. Courts rely on:

Deeds and surveys to determine property lines.
Photographs and repair receipts for damage claims.
Lease agreements and correspondence in landlord-tenant disputes.

The **burden of proof** typically lies with the party bringing the claim, who must provide credible evidence to support their case.

```
In most property disputes, local laws and homeowner association rules play a
crucial role. Always check these before escalating a disagreement.
```

Resolving property disputes can be challenging, but understanding your rights and the available legal pathways empowers you to protect your interests while maintaining civility. Disputes—whether over a tree, a fence, or a lease—are best settled with clear communication and, if needed, the structured help of the legal system. As we move forward, we'll turn our attention to the realm of intellectual property, where the "property" in question is not land or buildings, but the unique creations of the mind—ideas, inventions, and artistic works that shape our modern world.

6.5 Zoning, HOA, and Community Rules

When most people think about property rights, they imagine the freedom to use, modify, or sell their homes as they wish. However, these rights exist within a framework of **zoning laws**—local government regulations that dictate how land and buildings can be used in different areas. Zoning is a powerful tool used by cities and counties across the United States to shape the growth, safety, and character of neighborhoods.

Zoning categories typically include:

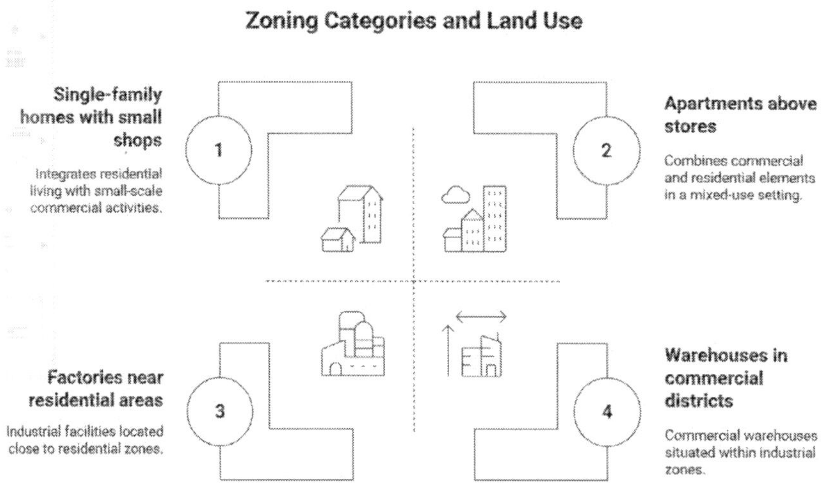

- **Residential** (single-family homes, apartments)
- **Commercial** (shops, offices)
- **Industrial** (factories, warehouses)
- **Mixed-use** (a blend, such as apartments above stores)

These laws may further specify restrictions on:

- Building height and size
- Lot coverage and setbacks (how far buildings must be from property lines)
- Types of permissible activities (for example, a home business or short-term rentals)

Historical Anecdote: New York City's Zoning Revolution

In 1916, **New York City** enacted the nation's first comprehensive zoning ordinance. The city's ever-growing skyscrapers were casting long shadows and crowding out light and air on the streets below. The new law addressed these issues by requiring setbacks for tall buildings—literally shaping the city's iconic skyline. Today, nearly every U.S. city uses some form of zoning to balance growth, safety, and livability.

Homeowners Associations (HOAs): Rules Within Rules

In addition to government regulations, many Americans live in communities governed by **Homeowners Associations (HOAs)**. An HOA is a private organization created by a real estate developer to manage and maintain a neighborhood, condo, or subdivision. When you buy a home within an HOA, you automatically become a member and agree to abide by its rules—known as **covenants, conditions, and restrictions (CC&Rs)**.

Typical HOA rules may include:

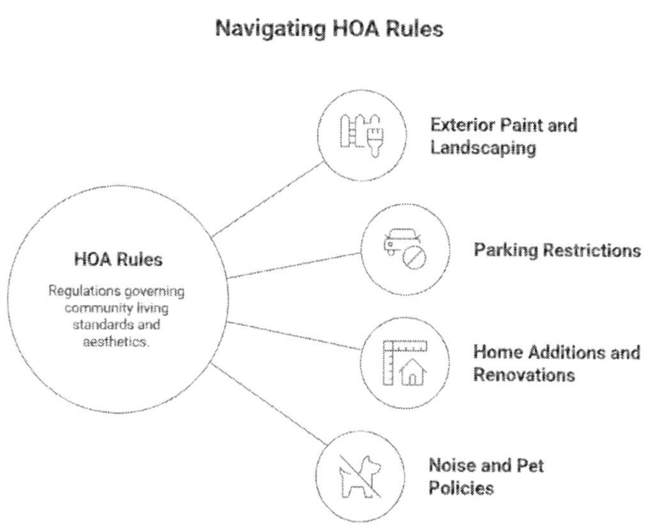

- Limits on exterior paint colors and landscaping
- Restrictions on parking (e.g., no boats or RVs in driveways)
- Guidelines for home additions or renovations
- Noise ordinances and pet policies

While some homeowners appreciate HOAs for maintaining property values and community standards, others find their rules overly restrictive. It's important to read and understand the CC&Rs before purchasing a home in such a community.

Real-World Example: The Satellite Dish Dispute

In the 1990s, as satellite television became popular, some HOAs tried to ban satellite dishes, arguing they were unsightly. Homeowners pushed back, citing their right to access television services. The federal government stepped in with the **Over-the-Air Reception Devices (OTARD) Rule**, which prevents HOAs and local governments from unreasonably restricting the use of satellite dishes. This example highlights the tension—and balance—between individual property rights and community standards.

Community Rules: Beyond the HOA

For those not living under an HOA, there may still be **community rules** created by local government or neighborhood groups. These can include:

- Noise ordinances (quiet hours)
- Trash and recycling regulations

- Rules regarding street parking or snow removal

Some cities even have historic preservation districts with special rules to protect the look and feel of old neighborhoods, requiring special approval for changes to certain homes.

Navigating Overlapping Authority

It's not uncommon for property owners to find themselves navigating the overlapping authority of zoning laws, HOA rules, and local ordinances. For example, even if your HOA approves a home addition, you may still need a city building permit. Conversely, the city may allow certain activities—like short-term rentals—that your HOA forbids.

Key steps for compliance:

- Review your city or county's zoning map and ordinances.
- Read your HOA's CC&Rs and bylaws carefully.
- Check for any additional community or local rules.

If you're ever unsure, consult your local planning department or a real estate attorney. Ignorance of the rules is rarely a valid defense if a violation occurs.

```
- Zoning violations can lead to fines, forced changes to your property, or
even lawsuits by neighbors or local government.
- HOA disputes often escalate to mediation or litigation; always keep written
records of all HOA correspondence.
```

Reflection and Looking Ahead

Understanding the layers of zoning, HOA, and community rules is essential for anyone owning or renting property in the U.S. These rules reflect a constant balancing act between private rights, collective interests, and public welfare. As we move forward, we'll examine how to protect your property rights and navigate disputes—ensuring you can enjoy your home while staying on the right side of the law. Next, we'll explore the practicalities and legalities of buying, selling, and leasing property, demystifying transactions that shape the places we call home.

6.6 Global Perspectives on Property Ownership

Property ownership is a deeply personal milestone—one that signifies stability, autonomy, and investment in the future. Yet, the rules governing what it means to own, rent, or transfer property vary widely across the globe. By examining these differences, we gain valuable perspective on the unique features of the U.S. legal system and its approach to property rights.

Systems of Property Ownership

Globally, property ownership systems generally fall into a few broad categories:

- **Private Ownership:** Individuals or entities have the legal right to own, use, and transfer property. This is the dominant model in the U.S., Canada, much of Europe, and Australia.
- **State Ownership:** The government retains legal ownership of land, granting use or lease rights to individuals. This model is seen in countries like China and, historically, in the former Soviet Union.
- **Communal or Customary Ownership:** Land is collectively managed by a community or tribe, common in parts of Africa and among Indigenous peoples worldwide.

Each system reflects unique cultural, historical, and political priorities. The U.S., with its roots in English common law, has long emphasized private property as a pillar of personal freedom and economic opportunity.

A Tale of Two Homes: U.S. vs. China

Consider the contrasting experiences of homeowners in the United States and China:

United States: When you buy a house, you typically receive a **deed**—a legal document proving your ownership of the property and the land on which it sits. This right is, in theory, indefinite, subject only to legal restrictions (like zoning laws) or government acquisition through eminent domain (with compensation).
China: All land is owned by the state. Urban homebuyers purchase long-term leases usually for 70 years for the right to use the land and build upon it
When these leases expire, the government decides whether to renew or reclaim the land. The concept of perpetual private ownership, as understood in the U.S., does not apply.

This divergence illustrates the profound impact of legal tradition on people's day-to-day lives—affecting everything from wealth accumulation to personal security.

Indigenous Land Rights: A Historical Perspective

In the United States, the history of property rights is inseparable from the experience of Native American nations. For centuries, tribal lands were held communally, governed by tradition rather than written law. European settlers, however, brought with them a different legal framework, rooted in individual ownership and formal deeds. Over time, U.S. policies—such as the **Dawes Act of 1887**—sought to assimilate Indigenous peoples by dividing communal lands into individual plots, often resulting in significant loss of tribal land.

Today, many Native American nations are reclaiming the right to self-govern property, blending traditional practices with modern legal tools. This ongoing dialogue reminds us that property law is not static; it evolves in response to cultural, political, and social change.

Renting: Rights and Responsibilities Worldwide

Just as ownership varies, so do the rights of renters. In some countries, tenant protections are robust—consider Germany, where long-term leases and strict eviction procedures are common, offering renters stability and peace of mind. In others, landlords wield more power, and tenants may have limited recourse if disputes arise.

In the U.S., tenant rights are defined by a patchwork of federal, state, and local laws. For example, the **Fair Housing Act** prohibits discrimination in renting, while state laws may regulate security deposits, eviction procedures, and habitability standards.

Lessons for U.S. Residents

Understanding the U.S. commitment to private property helps explain legal rights and responsibilities when buying, selling, or renting a home.

Comparing global systems highlights the importance of legal documentation, due process, and clear regulations in protecting property interests.

Exploring global perspectives reveals that property rights are shaped not just by laws, but by deep-seated values and histories. The U.S. system's emphasis on private ownership brings both opportunities and responsibilities, with legal protections grounded in centuries-old principles. As we move forward, we'll turn our attention to the practical steps involved in property transactions—demystifying the process of buying, selling, and leasing to empower you in one of life's most consequential decisions.

7 Family Law—Relationships, Children, and Change

7.1 Marriage and Civil Partnerships

Marriage in the United States is both a deeply personal commitment and a legally significant contract. When two individuals decide to marry, they are not only celebrating their relationship but also entering into a binding legal agreement recognized by the state. This contract brings with it a host of rights, responsibilities, and protections.

At its core, **marriage** establishes a legal partnership that affects property ownership, inheritance, medical decision-making, taxation, and parental rights. The requirements for marriage—such as age, consent, and licensing—vary somewhat by state, but all share the fundamental expectation that marriage is a voluntary union between two people.

Civil Partnerships and Domestic Partnerships

While marriage has long held a central place in U.S. society, alternative forms of legal partnership have emerged, especially for those who may not wish to—or, in the past, could not—marry. **Civil partnerships** and **domestic partnerships** provide many of the legal benefits of marriage without the title. These arrangements were especially important before the nationwide legalization of same-sex marriage in 2015, offering legal recognition and protection for same-sex couples.

States differ in how they recognize these partnerships:

Some offer civil unions or domestic partnerships with nearly all the benefits of marriage.
Others restrict such arrangements or have phased them out following marriage equality.

Marriage Equality: A Turning Point

One of the most significant legal developments in recent U.S. history was the Supreme Court's decision in **Obergefell v. Hodges (2015)**. This landmark case guaranteed the right to marry for same-sex couples across the nation, affirming that marriage is a fundamental right protected by the Constitution.

Personal Story:

Consider the story of Jim Obergefell and John Arthur, the couple at the heart of the Supreme Court case. When John became terminally ill, the couple wanted their marriage—legally performed in Maryland—to be recognized in their home state of Ohio for purposes such as inheritance and death certificates. Their fight for recognition became a rallying point for marriage equality and ultimately changed the legal landscape for millions of Americans.

Key Legal Effects of Marriage and Civil Partnerships

Being married or in a recognized partnership affects daily life in a multitude of ways:

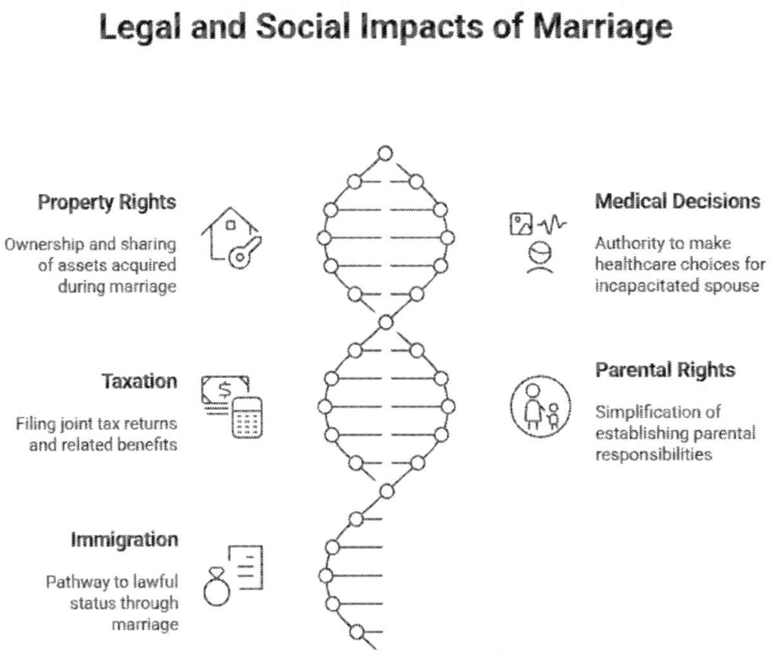

- **Property Rights:** Spouses often share ownership of property acquired during the marriage.
- **Medical Decisions:** Married partners typically have the right to make medical decisions if one partner becomes incapacitated.
- **Taxation:** Married couples can file joint tax returns, which can affect tax liabilities and benefits.
- **Parental Rights:** Marriage can simplify the process of establishing parental rights and responsibilities.

- **Immigration:** Marriage to a U.S. citizen can provide a pathway to lawful immigration status.

Entering and Dissolving Marriage or Partnerships

The process of entering a marriage or civil partnership typically involves:

- Obtaining a marriage or partnership license.
- Meeting state-specific requirements (such as minimum age and waiting periods).
- Completing a ceremony or registration process, often witnessed and officiated.

Ending these relationships can be more complex, involving issues like division of property, child custody, and spousal support. This is handled through divorce (for marriages) or dissolution (for partnerships), with courts aiming for fairness and the best interests of any children involved.

Global and Cultural Perspectives

While marriage and civil partnerships are common worldwide, the rules and cultural importance vary greatly. For example, in many European countries, civil partnerships were initially introduced to provide legal recognition for same-sex couples before marriage equality laws were passed. Meanwhile, some cultures maintain arranged marriages or communal marital traditions, illustrating the diversity in how societies structure family life.

```
Marriage provides over 1,000 federal legal benefits and protections in the
U.S., including Social Security survivor benefits and spousal privilege in
court.
```

Understanding the legal aspects of marriage and civil partnerships is crucial, as these relationships shape many facets of everyday life—from financial decisions to family structure. As we move forward, the next section will explore the legal frameworks surrounding children, parental rights, and the evolving nature of family in the U.S., further illuminating how the law intersects with our most personal relationships.

7.2 Divorce and Separation

When relationships undergo profound change, the law provides structured pathways to navigate the complexities of ending a marriage. **Divorce** and **legal separation** are two primary legal routes through which couples can redefine their commitments and responsibilities, each with distinct implications for property, finances, and children.

The Legal Framework for Divorce

In the United States, divorce is governed mainly at the state level, resulting in differing procedures and requirements from one jurisdiction to another. However, some core principles are widely shared:

- **No-Fault Divorce**: Most states now allow couples to dissolve their marriage without assigning blame, often citing "irreconcilable differences" or "irretrievable breakdown."
- **Fault-Based Divorce**: Some states still permit divorces on grounds such as adultery, abandonment, or cruelty, though these are less common.
- **Residency Requirements**: Typically, one or both spouses must reside in the state for a certain period before filing for divorce.

Consider the journey of **Linda and Carlos**, a married couple living in California. After years of growing apart, they opted for a no-fault divorce, citing irreconcilable differences. Their experience was shaped by California's community property laws, which required them to split marital assets equally. Their story reflects a broader shift toward less adversarial, more equitable divorce processes—a trend mirrored in many U.S. states.

Legal Separation: An Alternative Path

Unlike divorce, **legal separation** does not end a marriage but allows spouses to live apart while formalizing certain legal and financial arrangements. This option may be chosen for religious reasons, to retain health insurance benefits, or as a trial period before deciding on divorce. Legal separation agreements typically address:

- Child custody and visitation
- Spousal and child support
- Division of property and debts

Key Steps in the Divorce Process

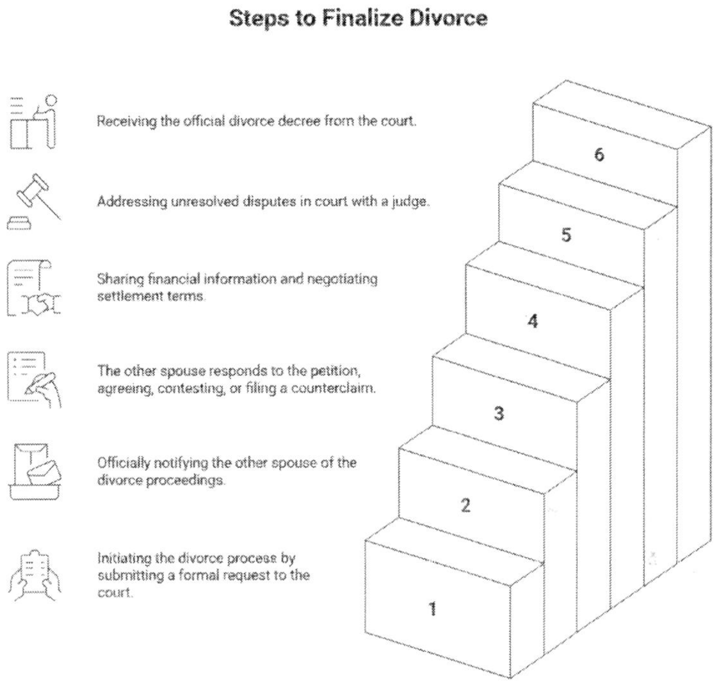

- **Filing a Petition**: One spouse files a divorce petition with the appropriate court, stating the grounds for divorce.
- **Serving Papers**: The other spouse is formally notified.
- **Response**: The respondent may agree, contest, or file a counterclaim.
- **Disclosure and Negotiation**: Both parties share financial information and negotiate settlement terms.
- **Court Hearings**: If disputes remain, a judge may hold hearings on property, custody, and support.
- **Final Decree**: The court issues a divorce decree, making the divorce official and enforceable.

Child Custody and Support

Divorce and separation often involve crucial decisions about children. U.S. courts act in the **best interests of the child**, considering factors like stability, parental involvement, and the child's needs. Arrangements can include:

- **Joint legal custody**: Both parents share decision-making rights.
- **Physical custody**: Where the child lives.
- **Child support**: Calculated based on parents' incomes and the child's expenses.

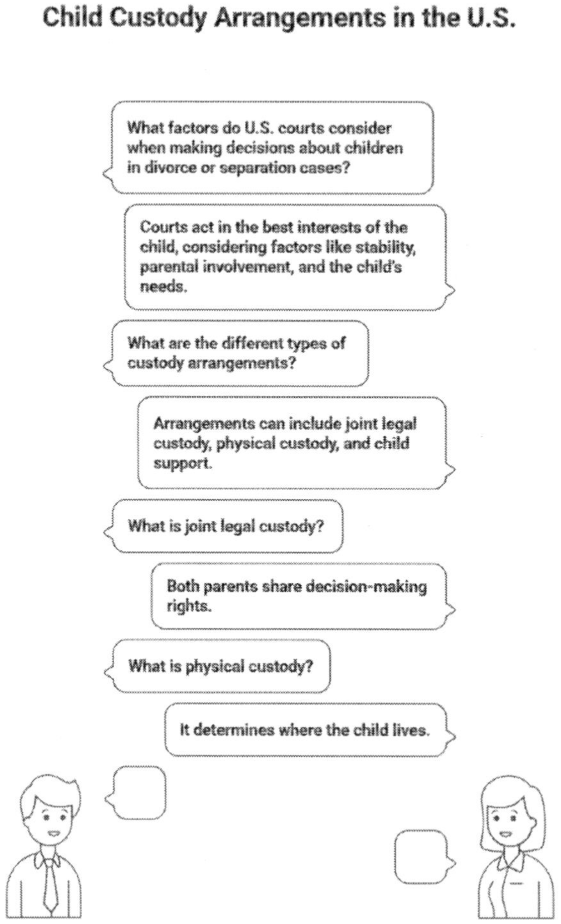

Real-World Example: The Evolution of No-Fault Divorce

In 1969, California became the first U.S. state to adopt no-fault divorce, a move that dramatically changed the landscape of family law. This reform was designed to reduce the stigma, acrimony, and perjury often involved in proving fault, setting a precedent that many other states soon followed. Today, no-fault divorce is widely recognized as a means of promoting fairness and reducing emotional harm.

Consequences and Considerations

Divorce and separation can have significant legal, financial, and emotional consequences:

Asset and debt division may affect long-term financial security.
Spousal and child support obligations are legally enforceable.
Custody arrangements can impact daily life and relationships with children.

```
A divorce decree is a legally binding court order. Failing to follow its
terms—such as paying child support or adhering to custody arrangements—can
result in serious legal consequences, including fines or jail time.
```

Divorce and separation are not just legal procedures; they are deeply personal journeys shaped by law, culture, and individual circumstance. By understanding their rights and obligations, individuals can navigate these transitions with greater clarity and protection. Next, we will turn our attention to the vital topic of **adoption and guardianship**, exploring how the law supports new family bonds and safeguards the well-being of children within evolving family structures.

7.3 Child Custody and Support

When families undergo significant transitions—such as separation, divorce, or the end of a domestic partnership—the question of **child custody** becomes paramount. The law is designed to prioritize the best interests of the child, aiming to provide stability, safety, and emotional well-being, even when parental relationships change.

Child custody encompasses two distinct but related concepts:

- **Legal custody**: The right to make major decisions about the child's upbringing, including education, healthcare, and religious instruction.
- **Physical custody**: Where and with whom the child lives on a daily basis.

Custody can be shared (**joint custody**) or granted to one parent (**sole custody**). Courts generally prefer arrangements that allow both parents to maintain relationships with their children unless circumstances—such as abuse or neglect—necessitate otherwise.

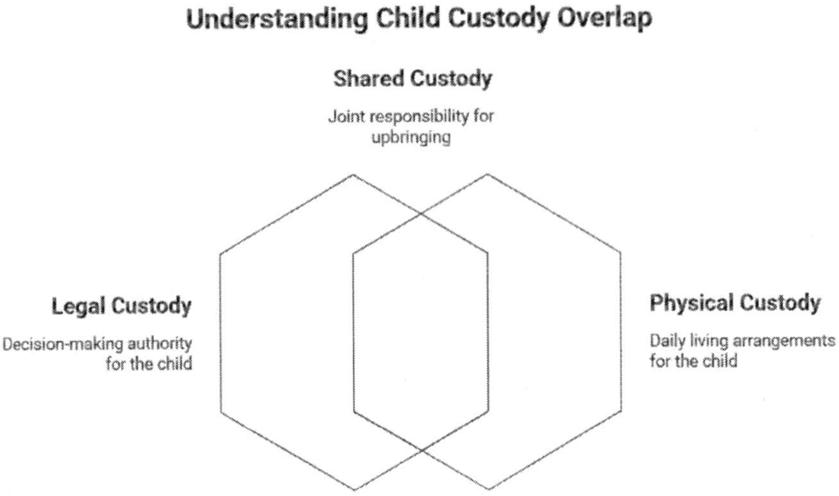

The Custody Process: From Dispute to Decision

The path to resolving custody can vary, but typically follows this sequence:

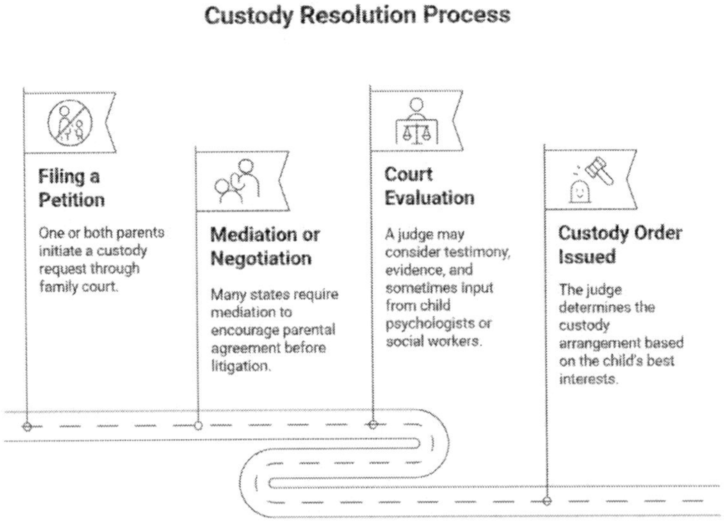

- **Filing a Petition**: One or both parents initiate a custody request through family court.
- **Mediation or Negotiation**: Many states require mediation to encourage parental agreement before litigation.
- **Court Evaluation**: A judge may consider testimony, evidence, and sometimes input from child psychologists or social workers.

- **Custody Order Issued**: The judge determines the custody arrangement based on the child's best interests.

Judges weigh factors such as:

- The child's age, health, and emotional ties to each parent.
- Each parent's ability to provide care and a stable environment.
- The child's own wishes, depending on their age and maturity.

Real-World Example

Consider the case of **Maria and James**, a divorced couple in Texas. Despite their personal differences, they agreed to joint legal custody, allowing both to participate in decisions about their daughter's schooling and medical care. However, due to James's frequent work travel, Maria was awarded primary physical custody, while James received generous visitation rights. This arrangement balanced parental involvement with the child's need for routine and stability.

Child Support: Ensuring Financial Security

Beyond custody, the law requires both parents to contribute financially to their child's upbringing. **Child support** is the monetary payment typically made by the non-custodial parent to assist with costs such as housing, food, education, and healthcare.

Key points about child support:

- Calculated using state-specific guidelines, often based on parental income and the child's needs.
- Payments are enforceable by law; failure to pay can result in wage garnishment, fines, or even jail time.
- Support orders can be modified if circumstances change (e.g., job loss or increased medical expenses).

Historical Anecdote

In the 1970s, the U.S. government recognized the growing problem of unpaid child support. This led to the creation of the **Office of Child Support Enforcement** in 1975, which provides tools for locating non-paying parents and enforcing support orders. The system has since helped millions of children receive the resources they need.

Cultural Perspective: Approaches Around the World

While the U.S. emphasizes judicial intervention, some countries, such as Sweden, prioritize mediation and government-funded support, aiming to reduce conflict and ensure children's well-being without protracted legal battles. This contrast highlights the importance of cultural values in shaping family law.

```
Very important: Child custody and support laws vary by state, but the best
interests of the child are always the central guiding principle in U.S.
courts.
```

Reflection and Transition

Child custody and support are complex, emotionally charged areas of law that shape the lives of countless families. By understanding the legal principles and processes, individuals can better navigate these transitions and advocate for the well-being of their children. As we turn next to adoption and guardianship, we'll explore how the law continues to evolve to protect children and support new family bonds, ensuring every child has the opportunity to thrive.

7.4 Domestic Violence and Protection Orders

Domestic violence is a serious and pervasive issue that affects individuals and families across the United States, cutting across social, economic, and cultural boundaries. Legally, **domestic violence** refers to patterns of abusive behavior—physical, emotional, psychological, or economic—used by one person to control or harm another within a household or intimate relationship. These behaviors can include physical assault, threats, stalking, intimidation, isolation, and financial control.

The law recognizes that domestic violence not only harms the immediate victim but can have lasting effects on children, extended family, and the broader community. As such, each state has enacted statutes aimed at protecting victims and holding perpetrators accountable. Federal laws, such as the **Violence Against Women Act (VAWA)**, provide additional protections, funding, and support for victims, regardless of gender.

The Role of Protection Orders

When someone is in immediate danger or fears for their safety due to domestic violence, the law provides a powerful tool: the **protection order** (sometimes called a restraining order). A protection order is a court-issued directive that restricts the alleged abuser from contacting or approaching the victim.

Types of Protection Orders

- **Emergency or Temporary Orders**: Issued quickly, often the same day as the request, to provide immediate safety. These typically last until a formal court hearing.
- **Permanent or Long-Term Orders**: After a court hearing where both parties can present their case, a judge may issue a longer-lasting order, sometimes for several years.

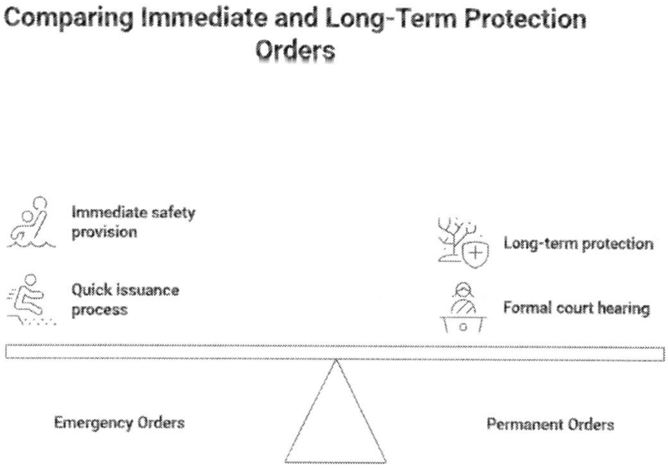

What Protection Orders Can Do

Protection orders may:

- Prohibit the abuser from making any contact with the victim (in person, by phone, by email, social media, etc.).
- Require the abuser to leave a shared home.
- Grant temporary custody of children to the victim.
- Order the abuser to surrender firearms.
- Set other specific conditions to ensure the victim's safety.

The Process of Obtaining a Protection Order

- **Filing a Petition**: The victim (or a representative, such as a parent or guardian) goes to court and files a petition outlining the abuse.
- **Judge's Review**: A judge reviews the petition and, if immediate danger is evident, may grant a temporary order.
- **Court Hearing**: Both parties have an opportunity to present evidence and testimony before the judge.

- **Final Order**: The judge decides whether to issue a longer-term protection order and what conditions it should include.

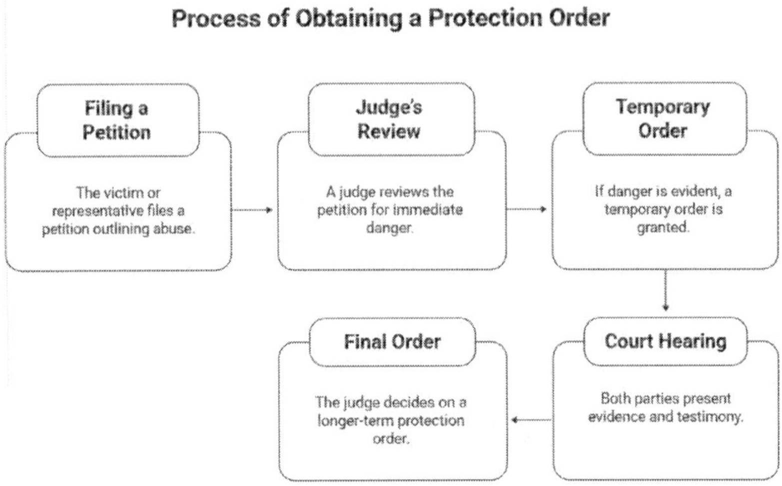

Real-World Example: A Path to Safety

Consider the case of **Maria**, a mother of two living in Texas. After enduring months of escalating threats and physical harm from her partner, Maria contacted a local domestic violence shelter. With their assistance, she filed for a protection order. The court granted her an emergency order the same day, requiring her partner to move out immediately. Later, at a hearing, evidence of repeated abuse led to a two-year order, giving Maria time to rebuild her life and seek further support.

Legal Obligations and Consequences

Violating a protection order is a crime. Consequences may include arrest, fines, and jail time. The law takes these violations seriously to deter further abuse and protect victims. Notably, protection orders are enforceable across state lines due to the **Full Faith and Credit Clause** of the U.S. Constitution, ensuring victims remain protected even if they move.

Cross-Cultural Perspectives

Globally, countries like Spain and Australia have adopted similar legal frameworks, emphasizing immediate intervention and victim protection. However, cultural stigmas and limited resources can impede access to justice in some regions, underlining the importance of ongoing legal reform and public education.

```
Protection orders can be issued without the alleged abuser present ("ex
parte") to ensure immediate safety, but a full hearing must follow promptly
for due process.
```

In summary, domestic violence laws and protection orders represent the legal system's commitment to safeguarding vulnerable individuals and families. As we move forward to explore adoption and guardianship, we'll see how the law continues to adapt, focusing on the best interests of those most in need of protection and stability.

7.5 Adoption and Guardianship

Adoption is the legal process by which an adult assumes the parenting of a child who is not biologically their own, granting the child all the rights and privileges of a biological child. The U.S. legal system has developed a thorough framework to ensure that adoption prioritizes the **best interests of the child**, protecting both the rights of biological parents and the needs of adoptive families.

Adoption can take several forms:

- **Agency Adoption:** Arranged through public or private agencies, often involving children in foster care.
- **Independent Adoption:** Arranged directly between birth and adoptive parents, sometimes facilitated by attorneys.
- **International Adoption:** Where U.S. citizens adopt children from other countries, subject to both U.S. and foreign legal requirements.
- **Stepparent or Relative Adoption:** When a stepparent or close relative legally adopts a child.

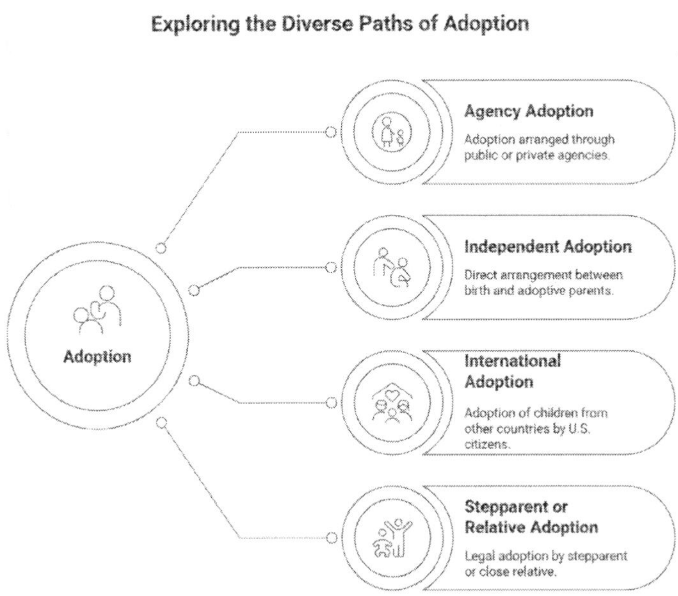

The adoption process typically involves the following steps:

- **Application and Background Checks:** Prospective parents apply and undergo background checks and home studies.
- **Termination of Parental Rights:** Biological parents' rights must be legally ended before adoption can proceed.
- **Court Approval:** A judge reviews the case, ensuring all legal requirements are met and the child's welfare is prioritized.
- **Finalization:** Once approved, the adoption is permanent, and the adoptive parent(s) assume full legal responsibility.

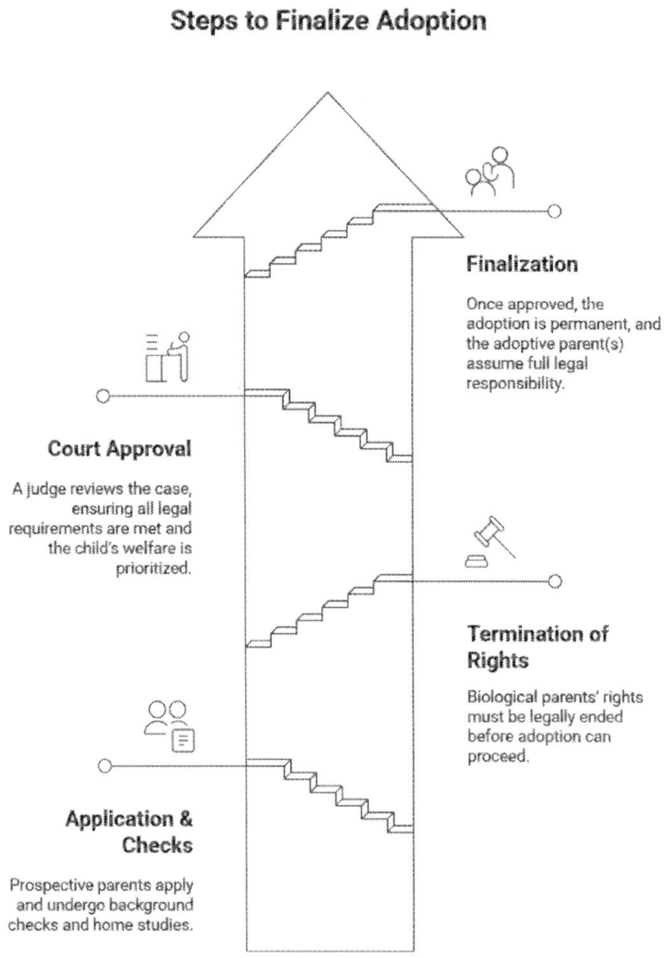

Real-World Example: The Dave Thomas Foundation

Dave Thomas, founder of Wendy's and himself adopted, became a major advocate for adoption reform. His foundation works to simplify adoption from foster care and promote permanent homes for waiting children. This real-world commitment has inspired many Americans to consider adoption and influenced legislation in several states.

Guardianship: Providing Care When Parents Cannot

Guardianship is a legal arrangement where someone other than a child's parent is granted responsibility for the child's care, often due to parental incapacity, illness, or absence. Unlike adoption, guardianship does not sever the legal relationship between parent and child; instead, it temporarily transfers decision-making authority.

Types of guardianship include:

- **Guardianship of the Person:** The guardian makes decisions about the child's daily life, education, and healthcare.
- **Guardianship of the Estate:** The guardian manages the child's financial affairs if the child owns property or assets.

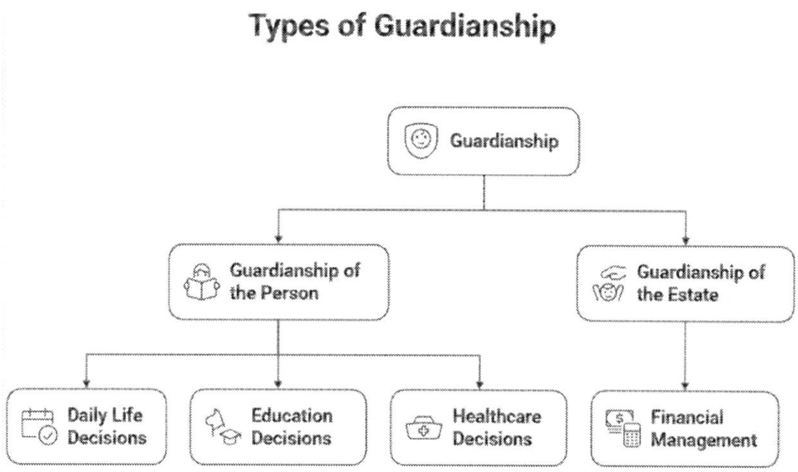

Guardians are appointed by a court, which will always consider:

- The **best interest of the child**
- The suitability of the proposed guardian
- The wishes of the child (especially if the child is older)

Historical Anecdote: Orphan Trains

In the late 19th and early 20th centuries, the Orphan Train Movement relocated over 200,000 orphaned or abandoned children from crowded Eastern cities to foster homes in the Midwest. This early form of guardianship and adoption illustrates the evolving attitudes and legal protections around child welfare in the U.S. Today, legal processes are far more rigorous and protective.

Key Considerations and Legal Protections

- The law requires that both adoption and guardianship proceedings are transparent, protecting all parties' rights.
- In both arrangements, courts may appoint attorneys or guardians ad litem to represent the child's interests.
- Adoption is generally permanent, while guardianship may be temporary or terminated if parents regain capacity.

```
In the U.S., adoption records are often sealed to protect the privacy of both
birth and adoptive families. However, laws regarding access to these records
vary by state and continue to evolve.
```

Adoption and guardianship embody the law's dedication to protecting vulnerable children and supporting new family structures. Understanding these processes helps individuals navigate significant life changes and ensures children's welfare remains at the forefront. As we continue, we'll turn our attention to another critical aspect of family law—how the legal system addresses domestic violence and safeguards those at risk, further highlighting the law's evolving role in promoting safety and justice within families.

7.6 Cultural Variations in Family Law

Family law in the United States is deeply influenced by a tapestry of cultural traditions and social norms. While American family law strives for consistency and fairness, it must also adapt to the diverse backgrounds of its residents. As families in the U.S. originate from all corners of the globe, the legal system is frequently called upon to navigate complex intersections of law and culture—balancing respect for tradition with the imperatives of justice and equality.

Marriage and Cultural Practices

The formation of a family often begins with marriage, but perceptions of marriage—and the legal obligations it entails—vary widely across cultures. In some communities, arranged marriages are customary, while in others, personal choice and romantic love are prioritized. U.S. family law does not explicitly prohibit arranged marriages, provided both parties are consenting adults. However, it strictly forbids **forced marriage**, aligning with the nation's commitment to individual rights and autonomy.

Example: In 2013, a case in Texas highlighted these tensions when a young woman of South Asian descent sought legal protection from a forced marriage. The court intervened, citing the fundamental right to personal liberty under U.S. law, while also mandating cultural sensitivity training for the family.

Parenting, Custody, and Cultural Identity

Child custody disputes can be particularly fraught when parents hail from different cultural backgrounds. American courts primarily use the **"best interest of the child"** standard, but they may also consider the importance of a child's cultural heritage. This approach recognizes that cultural identity can play a vital role in a child's development and well-being.

Real-World Example: In the landmark case of **Palmore v. Sidoti (1984)**, the U.S. Supreme Court ruled that custody decisions based on racial or cultural biases violate the Constitution. The case involved a white mother who lost custody of her child after remarrying a Black man. The Court's decision reaffirmed that legal judgments must be free from prejudice, emphasizing the need to respect diverse family structures.

International Families and Cross-Border Challenges

With increasing global mobility, U.S. family law courts frequently address issues involving international marriages, divorces, and child abduction. Treaties such as the **Hague Convention on the Civil Aspects of International Child Abduction** provide a framework for returning abducted children to their home countries. However, these cases can be complicated when cultural expectations about parental roles and children's rights differ sharply from American norms.

Anecdote: Consider the story of Maria, a Mexican-American mother whose ex-husband returned to Mexico with their son after a contentious custody battle. Through the Hague Convention, U.S. authorities worked with Mexican officials to facilitate the child's return, highlighting both the strengths and limitations of international legal cooperation.

The Role of Religion and Custom

Religious beliefs and customs often shape family structures and expectations. While the U.S. legal system upholds freedom of religion, it does not enforce religious laws—such as Islamic sharia, Jewish halakha, or Catholic canon law—in place of civil statutes. Instead, parties are free to follow religious practices so long as they do not conflict with American law or infringe on individual rights.

As we have seen, the U.S. legal system must continually adapt to meet the needs of a multicultural society, balancing cultural respect with the rule of law. Understanding these cultural variations is crucial—not just for legal professionals, but for anyone navigating family relationships in America. In the next section, we'll explore how family law evolves to address emerging issues, from changing definitions of family to the legal recognition of same-sex partnerships, underscoring the law's ongoing responsiveness to societal change.

7.7 When to Seek Legal Advice

Navigating family law can be deeply personal, often emotional, and sometimes confusing. As relationships, parenting, and family structures change, so do the legal issues that may arise. Although many family matters can be resolved amicably, there are crucial moments when seeking professional legal advice becomes not just helpful, but essential.

Recognizing Critical Moments

Family law covers a broad spectrum—marriage, divorce, child custody, adoption, guardianship, domestic violence, and more. While some situations allow for informal discussion or mediation, others require a clear understanding of your rights, responsibilities, and the potential consequences of your decisions.

Some key moments when legal advice is highly recommended include:

- **Divorce or Legal Separation:** Ending a marriage involves property division, possible spousal support, and decisions regarding children. Each state has unique laws that can significantly affect outcomes.
- **Child Custody and Support Disputes:** The well-being of children is paramount. Courts consider various factors, and a lawyer can help ensure that your interests—and those of your children—are fairly represented.
- **Adoption or Guardianship:** The legal process for adopting a child or becoming a guardian is complex, involving background checks, court appearances, and strict compliance with state and federal laws.
- **Allegations of Domestic Violence:** Immediate legal intervention can provide protection and clarify rights and options for all parties involved.
- **Prenuptial or Postnuptial Agreements:** These legal contracts can have lasting impacts on your financial and family future.

Real-World Example: A Tale of Custody and Change

Consider the experience of Maria, a recent immigrant to the United States. When her marriage ended, she was unsure of her legal standing regarding her children. Initially, she and her ex-husband tried to agree informally, but as tensions rose, disagreements about visitation and child support became frequent. Seeking the advice of a family law attorney not only clarified her rights but also helped her navigate the complex intersection of family and immigration law, ultimately securing a stable arrangement for her children.

Historical Perspective: Evolving Legal Definitions

In 2015, the U.S. Supreme Court's decision in **Obergefell v. Hodges** guaranteed the right to same-sex marriage nationwide. This watershed moment required many families to seek legal guidance to update wills, custody arrangements, and health care directives—demonstrating how shifts in the law can create a sudden need for expert advice, regardless of how amicable personal relationships may be.

The Value of Timely Legal Counsel

Delaying or avoiding legal advice can have lasting repercussions. Family law decisions often carry long-term financial, emotional, and legal consequences. Attorneys can:

- Interpret the law as it applies to your unique situation
- Help you understand potential outcomes
- Draft or review legal documents to ensure accuracy and fairness
- Represent you in court or during negotiations

Steps to Take When Seeking Legal Advice

1. **Assess the Situation:** Identify the issue and gather relevant documents (marriage certificates, court orders, financial records).
2. **Research**: Look for attorneys with expertise in the relevant area of family law.
3. **Consultation**: Schedule an initial meeting to discuss your options and potential strategies.
4. **Decision**: Decide whether to retain counsel for ongoing representation or limited consultation.

In most states, failing to respond to a family court summons can result in a default judgment, meaning the court may decide against you even if you are absent. Always seek legal advice if you receive court paperwork.

block Legal aid organizations and pro bono attorneys exist in every state to assist those who cannot afford private representation, especially in cases involving family safety and children.

In most states, failing to respond to a family court summons can result in a default judgment, meaning the court may decide against you even if you are absent. Always seek legal advice if you receive court paperwork.
block Legal aid organizations and pro bono attorneys exist in every state to assist those who cannot afford private representation, especially in cases involving family safety and children.

8 Employment and Labor Laws

8.1 Starting a New Job

Starting a new job is both exciting and daunting, often marking a significant milestone in one's life. Beyond learning the ropes of a new workplace, it's vital to understand your legal rights and responsibilities from the moment you accept an offer. The U.S. legal system, influenced by decades of reforms and historical developments, provides important protections for workers—while also setting expectations for professional conduct.

Before You Begin: Offer Letters, Contracts, and At-Will Employment

Most job offers in the United States are made "at-will," meaning either the employer or employee can end the employment relationship at any time, for almost any reason, with or without notice. However, there are exceptions:

- **Written Employment Contracts**: Some jobs, especially in specialized fields, use formal contracts specifying job duties, salary, and reasons for termination.
- **Union Agreements**: If your job is covered by a collective bargaining agreement, your rights and termination procedures may differ from at-will norms.

Offer Letters typically outline your position, salary, start date, and sometimes company policies. While not usually legally binding, they can serve as evidence of agreed-upon terms.

Key Steps When Accepting a Job

- **Review Documents Carefully**: Read all employment materials—offer letters, company handbooks, and contracts—before signing.
- **Ask Questions**: If anything is unclear, seek clarification from human resources or, for complex issues, consult an attorney.
- **Understand Workplace Policies**: Familiarize yourself with rules regarding time off, dress code, and workplace conduct.

Essential Legal Protections for New Employees

Federal and state laws provide safeguards for all workers, regardless of citizenship or background. Notably:

- **Equal Employment Opportunity**: Laws such as the Civil Rights Act and the Americans with Disabilities Act prohibit discrimination based on race, gender, religion, national origin, age, or disability.
- **Minimum Wage and Overtime**: The Fair Labor Standards Act (FLSA) guarantees a minimum wage and overtime pay for many employees.
- **Workplace Safety**: The Occupational Safety and Health Administration (OSHA) sets and enforces standards to ensure safe working conditions.

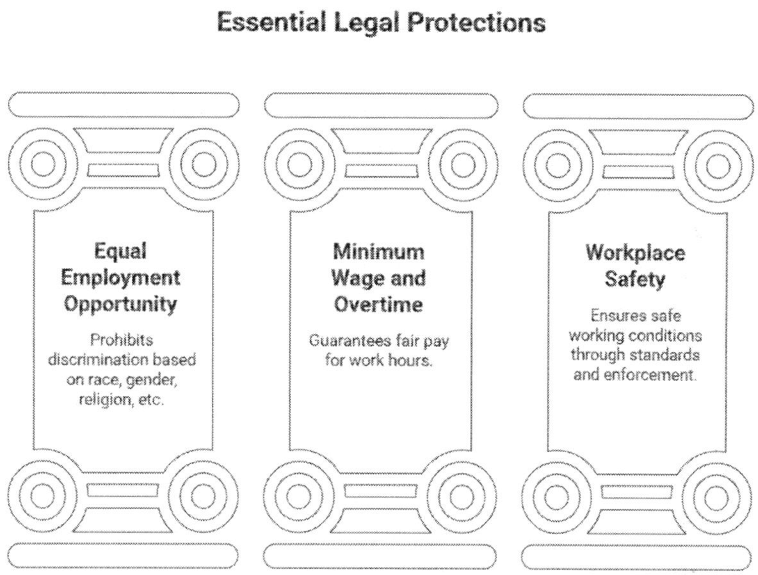

Real-World Example:

In 1964, when the Civil Rights Act was passed, it transformed the American workplace. For instance, Katherine Johnson, a mathematician at NASA, overcame both gender and racial barriers, ultimately contributing to the Apollo moon missions. Her story highlights how legal protections can unlock opportunities, benefiting not only individuals but society as a whole.

Know Your Obligations

Just as employees have rights, they have responsibilities:

- **Honesty and Integrity**: Providing accurate information on your application and in your work is essential.

- **Respect for Company Property and Policies**: Misuse of company resources or violation of workplace rules can be grounds for termination.
- **Confidentiality**: Many jobs require you to protect sensitive information, sometimes formalized through a non-disclosure agreement (NDA).

Starting Work: Your First Days

The initial period in a new job often involves paperwork and orientation. Expect to:

- Complete forms such as the I-9 (employment eligibility) and W-4 (tax withholding).
- Attend orientation or training sessions.
- Meet supervisors and coworkers, building relationships that can foster a positive work experience.

Global Comparison: At-Will vs. Contract Employment

While at-will employment is common in the United States, other countries like France or Japan often require employers to provide a legitimate reason for termination, and extensive notice periods or severance pay are the norm. Understanding these differences can be crucial for international workers or those contemplating work abroad.

```
Some of the most important protections for new employees include the right to
a safe workplace, freedom from discrimination, and guaranteed minimum wage.
```

Beginning a new job means more than mastering new skills—it's about knowing your place within the legal framework of employment. By understanding your rights and responsibilities, you set the stage for a successful and secure work experience. In the next section, we'll explore what happens when workplace issues or disputes arise, and how the law provides avenues for resolution, ensuring fairness and justice for all parties involved.

8.2 Workplace Rights and Protections

Navigating the modern workplace involves more than just showing up and doing your job—it's also about knowing your rights and protections under the law. In the United States, a robust framework of employment and labor laws has evolved over time to ensure that workers are treated fairly, provided safe environments, and protected against discrimination and exploitation. Whether you're an hourly wage earner, a salaried professional, or an independent contractor, these rights are designed to safeguard your dignity and well-being at work.

At the heart of these protections are several foundational statutes, including:

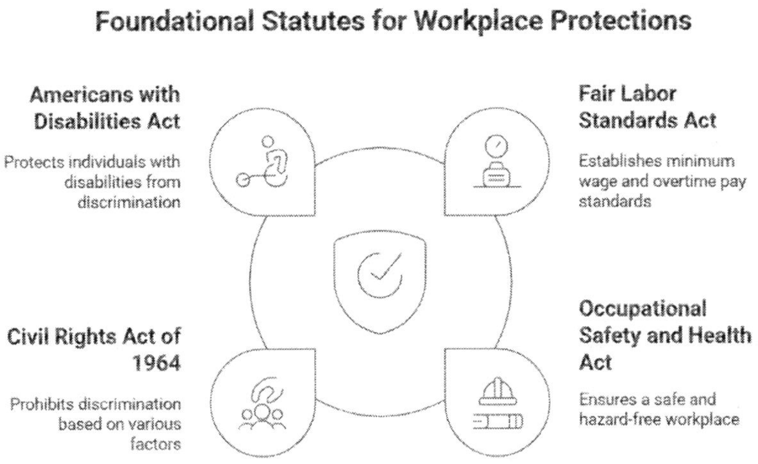

- **The Fair Labor Standards Act (FLSA):** Establishes minimum wage, overtime pay, and youth employment standards.
- **The Occupational Safety and Health Act (OSHA):** Requires employers to provide a workplace free from serious hazards.
- **The Civil Rights Act of 1964 (Title VII):** Prohibits discrimination based on race, color, religion, sex, or national origin.
- **The Americans with Disabilities Act (ADA):** Protects individuals with disabilities against discrimination in the workplace.

Key Protections Every Worker Should Know

Let's break down the major rights and protections employees have in the United States:

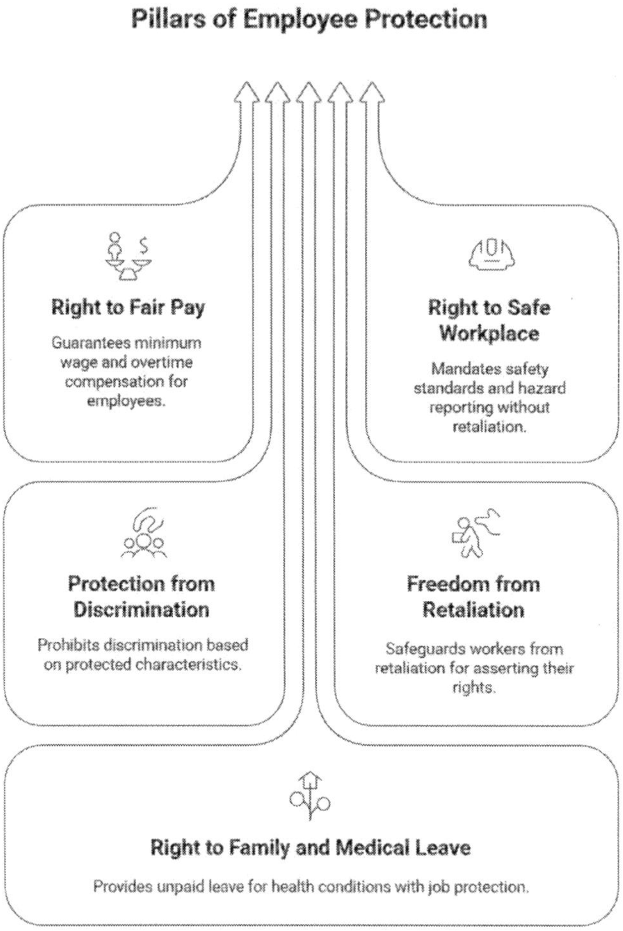

- **Right to Fair Pay:** Federal law sets a minimum wage, with many states and cities opting for higher rates. Overtime pay—typically "time and a half"—is required for hours worked over 40 in a week, unless you are exempt.
- **Right to a Safe Workplace:** Employers must maintain safety standards and can be held accountable for hazards. Workers have the right to report unsafe conditions without fear of retaliation.
- **Protection from Discrimination:** It is unlawful for employers to discriminate in hiring, promotion, or termination based on protected

characteristics. This extends to harassment and the creation of a hostile work environment.

- **Freedom from Retaliation:** Workers who assert their rights—such as reporting a safety violation or filing a discrimination claim—are protected from employer retaliation.
- **Right to Family and Medical Leave:** The Family and Medical Leave Act (FMLA) allows certain employees up to 12 weeks of unpaid leave for serious health conditions or to care for family, with job protection.

When Rights Are Violated: Real World Stories

Consider the story of **Rosa**, a hotel housekeeper in Los Angeles. After consistently being paid below minimum wage and denied overtime, she and her coworkers learned about their rights through a local worker center. With legal assistance, they filed a complaint with the Department of Labor. Their employer was ultimately required to compensate them for back wages—a powerful reminder that legal protections are meaningful only when workers know and assert their rights.

Another example comes from the early 20th century, when factory fires—like the infamous **Triangle Shirtwaist Factory fire of 1911**—exposed the dangerous conditions many workers faced. The tragedy, which claimed the lives of 146 garment workers, spurred sweeping reforms in workplace safety laws and the eventual creation of OSHA.

Global Perspectives: Comparing Workplace Rights

While U.S. laws offer vital protections, countries like Sweden and Germany have even broader safety nets, including guaranteed paid parental leave and strong collective bargaining rights. Conversely, some developing nations may lack robust enforcement, leaving workers vulnerable. Understanding these differences helps put American labor laws in a global context.

```
Did you know?
In the U.S., most employees are considered "at-will," meaning they can be
fired for any reason—or no reason—provided it isn't illegal (such as
discrimination or retaliation).
```

Workplace rights and protections are more than just legal concepts—they are essential tools for fairness and dignity in everyday life. By understanding these rights, workers can protect themselves and contribute to more just workplaces. In the next section, we'll delve into how disputes are resolved when things go wrong, guiding you through the processes of filing complaints, mediation, and legal recourse.

8.3 Discrimination and Harassment

Workplace discrimination is not just unfair; it's illegal. **Discrimination** occurs when employers treat individuals or groups unfavorably because of characteristics such as race, color, religion, sex, national origin, age, disability, or genetic information. These protections are enshrined in landmark federal laws, most notably the **Civil Rights Act of 1964**, the **Americans with Disabilities Act (ADA)**, and the **Age Discrimination in Employment Act (ADEA)**. State and local laws often expand these protections even further.

Common forms of discrimination include:

- **Hiring and Firing**: Refusing to hire or promoting someone due to their gender or ethnicity.
- **Compensation and Benefits**: Paying employees less or denying benefits because of age or disability.
- **Job Assignments**: Assigning undesirable tasks based on religious beliefs.
- **Retaliation**: Punishing employees for reporting discrimination.

Discrimination can be overt, such as using explicit slurs, or subtle, like consistently overlooking someone for advancement. Both forms are equally unlawful.

Recognizing Harassment

Harassment is a specific form of discrimination that creates a hostile or offensive work environment. It may involve unwelcome jokes, physical contact, threats, or intimidation, often related to one's protected status. Harassment can come from supervisors, coworkers, or even clients.

A well-known example is **sexual harassment**, which became a prominent issue in the 1990s after the high-profile hearings involving Supreme Court nominee Clarence Thomas and law professor Anita Hill. This event shined a national spotlight on how pervasive—and damaging—sexual harassment could be, leading to increased awareness and strengthened workplace policies.

Harassment isn't limited to sexual conduct. For instance, repeated jokes about someone's age or nationality, or displaying offensive symbols, can rise to the level of illegal workplace harassment.

Legal Protections and Responsibilities

Employers are required by law to maintain workplaces free from discrimination and harassment. They must:

- Develop clear anti-discrimination policies.
- Provide training to employees.
- Investigate complaints promptly and thoroughly.
- Take corrective action when necessary.

Employees also have responsibilities:

- Report discrimination or harassment if they witness or experience it.
- Cooperate with investigations.
- Refrain from retaliating against complainants.

A Real-World Case: The Story of Maria

Consider Maria, a first-generation immigrant working in a small manufacturing company. Despite her strong performance, she was repeatedly passed over for promotion in favor of less qualified male colleagues. After being subjected to derogatory remarks about her accent and background, Maria reported the behavior to her supervisor. The company failed to act, and Maria filed a complaint with the **Equal Employment Opportunity Commission (EEOC)**. Ultimately, the company was held accountable, leading to changes in its policies and compensation for Maria. Her courage not only protected her rights but also improved the workplace for others.

Global Perspectives

While U.S. laws are robust, other countries approach these issues differently. For example, the United Kingdom's **Equality Act 2010** offers broad protection against discrimination, while in Japan, laws prevent gender discrimination but social expectations often lag behind formal statutes. Recognizing these differences highlights the importance of cultural context in workplace rights.

```
Remember: Filing a discrimination complaint is protected by law. Employers
cannot legally retaliate against you for asserting your rights.
```

In summary, understanding your rights and responsibilities regarding discrimination and harassment is essential for navigating U.S. workplaces. These laws are not just rules—they're foundations for dignity and fairness on the job. Next, we'll explore how to take action when things go wrong, from filing formal complaints to seeking mediation or legal recourse, empowering you to stand up for yourself and others.

8.4 Unions and Collective Bargaining

Unions have played a defining role in shaping America's labor landscape. At their core, **unions** are organizations formed by workers who band together to advance their collective interests—chiefly fair wages, safe working conditions, and reasonable hours. When employees unite, their collective voice can be far more powerful than any single individual's, especially when negotiating with large employers.

Historically, the rise of unions in the U.S. coincided with the Industrial Revolution. Factories, mills, and mines were notorious for long hours and perilous conditions. Early union activists faced severe pushback, sometimes risking their jobs and safety. The 1886 **Haymarket Affair** in Chicago, where a peaceful rally for an eight-hour workday turned tragic after a bombing and subsequent riot, is a vivid example of the high stakes union members faced. Despite setbacks, unionization gradually gained legal protection, most notably through the **National Labor Relations Act (NLRA) of 1935**. This law cemented workers' right to organize and bargain collectively.

How Collective Bargaining Works

Collective bargaining is the process through which unions and employers negotiate the terms of employment. These discussions typically cover:

- Wages and salary structures
- Benefits (health insurance, retirement plans, paid leave)
- Working conditions and safety standards
- Grievance procedures and dispute resolution

The process usually unfolds as follows:

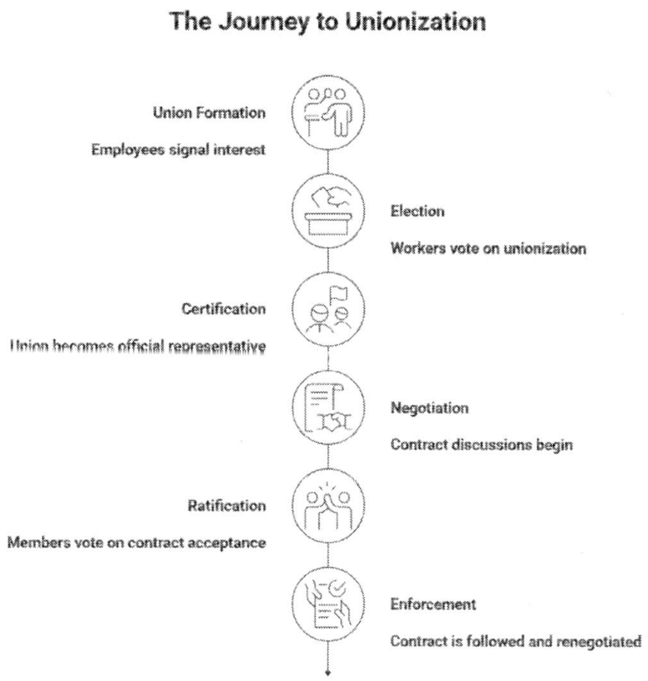

- **Union Formation:** Employees signal interest in forming a union, often by signing authorization cards.
- **Election:** If enough interest exists, workers vote on whether to unionize.
- **Certification:** Upon a successful vote, the union is certified as the official representative.
- **Negotiation:** Union leaders and employer representatives meet to negotiate a contract (collective bargaining agreement).
- **Ratification:** Members vote on whether to accept the proposed contract.
- **Enforcement:** Both sides abide by the contract, with future negotiations as needed.

For example, in 2021, warehouse workers at an Alabama facility sought to unionize, capturing national attention. Although the unionization vote was ultimately unsuccessful, the campaign highlighted contemporary debates about labor rights, employer influence, and the relevance of unions in the 21st century.

Legal Protections and Limitations

U.S. law provides significant protections for union activity. The **NLRA** makes it illegal for employers to retaliate against employees for organizing or participating in union activities. At the same time, not all workers are covered—public employees, agricultural workers, and independent contractors often fall outside federal protections, though some states extend additional rights.

Right-to-work laws in certain states give employees the freedom to choose whether to join or financially support a union, even in unionized workplaces. Proponents argue these laws uphold individual freedom, while critics say they weaken unions by reducing their resources.

A Global Perspective

While unions are a cornerstone of American labor law, their structure and influence vary worldwide. In Sweden, for instance, union membership remains high, and collective bargaining covers most workers—even those not in unions—due to national agreements. In contrast, some countries have stricter limitations on union activity or government-controlled unions.

Unions empower workers to negotiate collectively for better wages and conditions.

Collective bargaining is a structured process protected by U.S. law, though coverage and strength vary by state and sector.

```
Remember: Under the National Labor Relations Act, most private-sector
employees have the right to organize, join unions, and bargain collectively.
Retaliation by employers for union activity is illegal.
```

Unions and collective bargaining remain vital tools for securing workplace fairness and employee rights. As you consider your own employment situation, understanding these mechanisms can help you recognize both your rights and your options. Next, we'll examine what to do when workplace issues arise—how to file a complaint, seek mediation, or pursue legal remedies—ensuring you're fully equipped to protect your interests and those of your colleagues.

8.5 Termination and Unemployment

For many Americans, the end of a job—whether voluntary or involuntary—can be a time of uncertainty and confusion. U.S. employment law is built upon the principle of **at-will employment**, meaning that, unless bound by a contract or collective bargaining agreement, either the employer or the employee can end the working relationship at any time, for any lawful reason, or for no reason at all.

However, this does not mean that all reasons for termination are legal. Federal and state laws protect employees from being fired for certain reasons, including:

- **Discrimination** based on race, religion, sex, national origin, age, disability, or other protected categories.
- **Retaliation** for reporting illegal activity (whistleblowing) or for participating in a workplace investigation.
- **Taking protected leave** under laws like the Family and Medical Leave Act (FMLA).

A famous case that brought attention to wrongful termination was **Patterson v. McLean Credit Union (1989)**. In this case, an employee was terminated after complaining of racial harassment, prompting a Supreme Court decision that reinforced protections against discrimination in the workplace.

Unemployment Benefits: Who Qualifies and How They Work

Losing a job unexpectedly can create immediate financial stress. The **Unemployment Insurance (UI)** program, operated jointly by federal and state governments, helps eligible workers by providing temporary financial assistance while they search for new employment.

Qualification Criteria

While requirements vary by state, most UI programs require that you:

Have lost your job through no fault of your own (for example, due to layoffs).
Meet minimum earnings or work history thresholds during a "base period."
Be actively seeking employment and able to work.

Application Process

- **File a claim** with your state's unemployment office, usually online or by phone.
- **Provide information** about your recent employment history and the circumstances of your job loss.
- **Await determination**—the agency will review your claim and notify you of your eligibility, the amount of benefit, and the duration.

As a real-world example, consider the surge in unemployment filings during the 2020 COVID-19 pandemic. Millions of Americans lost their jobs due to business closures and economic downturn, prompting federal and state governments to expand UI programs and introduce pandemic-specific relief measures. This period underscored the critical safety net provided by unemployment insurance, as well as the complexity and delays many faced in accessing benefits.

Rights and Next Steps After Termination

If you believe you were terminated unlawfully, you have options:

- **File a complaint** with the Equal Employment Opportunity Commission (EEOC) or your state labor agency.
- **Consult an attorney** specializing in employment law for guidance.
- **Seek mediation** or arbitration, especially if required by your employment contract.

Severance and Final Pay

Employers are not required by federal law to provide **severance pay**, but some offer it voluntarily or under company policy. State laws vary on when final pay (including unused vacation or sick leave) must be provided after termination.

Global Perspectives: Comparing Systems

In many countries, such as Germany and Japan, firing an employee often requires cause and a formal process, offering greater job security than at-will employment. Understanding these differences can provide valuable context for U.S. workers and employers navigating domestic and international workplaces.

```
Remember: In the U.S., most employment is at-will, but you cannot be fired for
discriminatory or retaliatory reasons. If terminated, apply for unemployment
benefits as soon as possible.
```

In summary, understanding your rights and obligations surrounding termination and unemployment is essential for navigating the end of a job. With knowledge of legal protections, benefit programs, and available recourse, you can better manage transitions and safeguard your well-being. Next, we'll explore the intricacies of workplace safety and health regulations, further empowering you to thrive in every stage of your employment journey.

8.6 Global Labor Standards and Practices

As we examine the landscape of employment and labor laws, it's essential to recognize that the rights and responsibilities we encounter in the United States are part of a broader, interconnected global conversation. Labor standards and practices, while rooted in national traditions and economies, increasingly reflect international norms and expectations. Understanding these global influences not only broadens our perspective but also helps us appreciate the protections and challenges faced by workers worldwide—and how those dynamics shape U.S. law and everyday life.

International Frameworks for Fair Work

At the heart of global labor standards is the **International Labour Organization (ILO)**, a specialized agency of the United Nations. Since its founding in 1919, the ILO has established core conventions that advocate for:

- The elimination of forced labor
- The abolition of child labor
- The promotion of non-discrimination in employment
- The right to collective bargaining and freedom of association

These principles serve as benchmarks. While not legally binding in the U.S., they influence domestic policy and labor movements, and many American laws echo these ideals.

The U.S. Approach in a Global Context

While the United States has a robust system of labor protections, it has not ratified all ILO conventions. Instead, U.S. labor law—such as the **Fair Labor Standards Act (FLSA)** and **Occupational Safety and Health Act (OSHA)**—reflects a unique blend of federalism, market priorities, and advocacy. This approach emphasizes:

- Minimum wage and overtime protections

- Workplace safety
- Prohibitions against discrimination
- The right to organize and form unions

However, the U.S. model also exhibits distinctive features, such as the "at-will employment" doctrine, allowing employers or employees to terminate employment for nearly any reason, as long as it's not illegal or discriminatory. This differs from many European countries, where employment protections are often more stringent, requiring just cause for dismissal.

Real-World Example: The Garment Industry

A powerful illustration of global labor standards in action (and the consequences of their absence) is the 2013 **Rana Plaza disaster** in Bangladesh. The collapse of a factory building killed over 1,100 garment workers, many producing clothes for international brands. The tragedy sparked worldwide outrage and led to the creation of the **Accord on Fire and Building Safety**, a legally binding agreement signed by dozens of global apparel companies.

This event demonstrates how international pressure and consumer awareness can drive improved labor standards abroad—and how American consumers and companies are connected to global labor practices. It also highlights the importance of supply chain accountability, influencing U.S. companies to adopt codes of conduct that align with global standards.

Comparative Perspectives: Paid Leave

Consider the issue of paid parental leave. The U.S. stands apart from most developed nations by not mandating paid family leave at the federal level. In contrast, countries like Sweden and Canada offer extensive paid leave benefits, reflecting broader societal commitments to work-life balance. This difference informs ongoing debates in the U.S. about the future of family and medical leave policies.

```
The United States is one of only a handful of countries worldwide that does
not guarantee paid maternity leave at the federal level.
ILO conventions influence many U.S. labor laws, but the U.S. has not ratified
all core ILO labor standards.
```

Looking Ahead

Global labor standards and practices remind us that workplace rights and responsibilities are never static—they evolve in response to social movements, economic realities, and international influence. By understanding the global context, workers and employers in the U.S. can better navigate their roles, advocate for fairness, and contribute to a more just world of work.

As we continue, we'll delve into the specifics of workplace safety and health regulations, examining how these protections safeguard your well-being and ensure fair treatment on the job. By connecting global trends to your everyday experience, you gain the tools to thrive—no matter where your career journey takes you.

8.7 Balancing Work and Life

In the United States, the pursuit of a healthy **work-life balance** is more than a personal aspiration—it is, in many respects, supported and protected by law. While the phrase "work-life balance" evokes images of flexible schedules and family time, its legal underpinnings are rooted in a complex web of federal and state regulations designed to safeguard employees' time, health, and dignity.

Federal Protections: The Backbone of Balance

Key federal laws set the minimum standards for workplace fairness and time off:

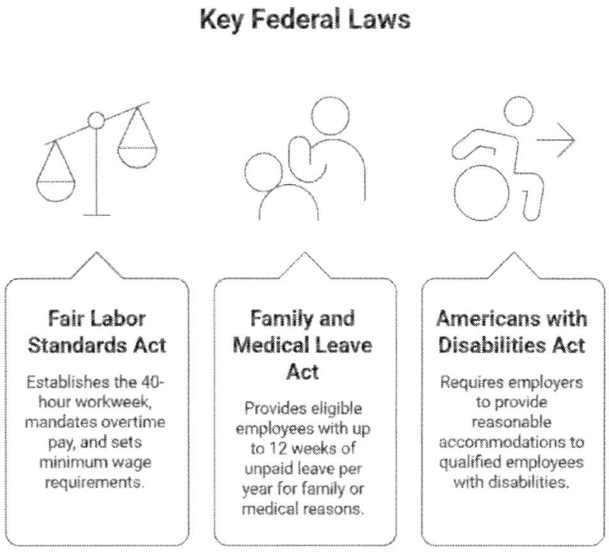

- **Fair Labor Standards Act (FLSA):** Establishes the 40-hour workweek, mandates overtime pay, and sets minimum wage requirements.

- **Family and Medical Leave Act (FMLA):** Provides eligible employees with up to 12 weeks of unpaid leave per year for family or medical reasons, including the birth or adoption of a child or the serious illness of the employee or a close family member.
- **Americans with Disabilities Act (ADA):** Requires employers to provide reasonable accommodations, which can include flexible schedules or remote work, to qualified employees with disabilities.

These laws are foundational, but it's important to know that states and municipalities can—and often do—extend additional protections.

The Realities of Enforcement and Access

Despite these legal frameworks, not every worker's experience is equal. Coverage under the FMLA, for instance, is limited to businesses with 50 or more employees, leaving out millions of workers at smaller companies. Moreover, FMLA leave is unpaid, which can make taking time off financially challenging for many families.

Consider the story of **Maria Santiago**, a nurse in Texas. When Maria's mother fell seriously ill, Maria requested FMLA leave to care for her. Her employer, a hospital with more than 50 staff, was legally required to grant her the time off. However, because the leave was unpaid, Maria faced significant financial strain, highlighting a gap between legal rights and practical realities.

Global Perspectives and Evolving Standards

The U.S. approach to work-life balance contrasts sharply with other nations. For example:

Sweden offers generous paid parental leave—up to 480 days per child, which can be shared between parents.
Japan has recently taken steps to address "karoshi," or death from overwork, by instituting caps on overtime hours and encouraging more flexible work arrangements.

These global examples have sparked conversations in the U.S. about the adequacy of existing protections and the importance of both legislative and cultural change.

Employer Practices: Beyond Legal Minimums

Forward-thinking employers often go beyond legal requirements to attract and retain talent:

- Flexible work hours
- Remote work opportunities
- Paid parental leave
- Wellness programs

The tech industry, for example, has led the way in normalizing remote work, a trend accelerated by the COVID-19 pandemic. Some companies, like **Salesforce**, now offer "flex team agreements," allowing employees to set schedules that best suit their personal lives—demonstrating how workplace norms can shift in response to both legal and cultural change.

```
Did you know?

The FMLA does not require paid leave, meaning many workers must choose between
their health (or their family's health) and their financial stability.
```

Knowing Your Rights—and Your Options

Understanding your legal rights is the first step to advocating for a better work-life balance. If you feel your rights are being violated, you can:

- Review your employee handbook and company policies.
- Consult with your HR department.
- Contact the Department of Labor or a local employment attorney for guidance.

Work-life balance is not just a personal preference—it's a legal issue with real implications for your well-being and family life. By knowing what the law provides (and where it falls short), you can make more informed decisions about your job, your time, and your future. Next, we will explore **workplace discrimination**: understanding your rights and remedies if you experience unfair treatment on the job.

9 Business and Consumer Law

9.1 Starting and Registering a Business

Starting a business in the United States is both an exciting opportunity and a significant legal responsibility. At its core, forming a business means creating a separate legal entity—distinct from your personal identity—that can own property, enter contracts, and be held accountable in court. The process involves a series of legal steps and decisions, each with lasting implications.

Types of Business Structures

Choosing the right **business structure** is a foundational step, as it determines your liability, tax obligations, and ability to raise capital. The main options in the U.S. include:

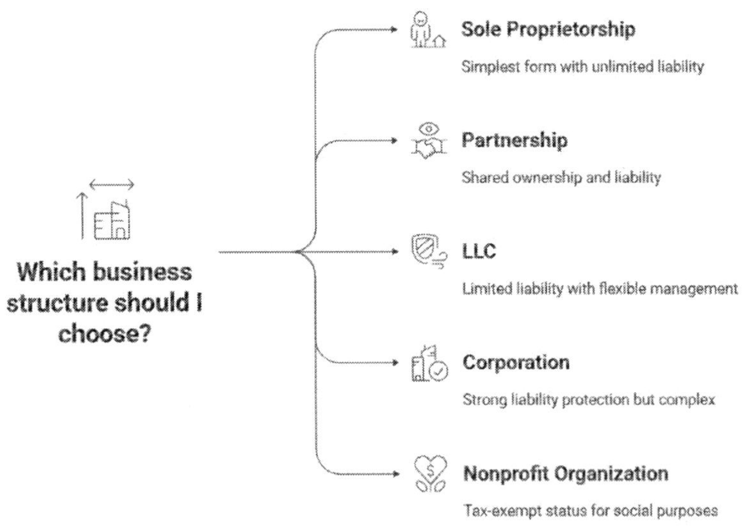

- **Sole Proprietorship:** Owned and operated by one individual; simplest form but with unlimited personal liability.
- **Partnership:** Two or more people share ownership; liability and profits are shared as well.
- **Limited Liability Company (LLC):** Combines limited liability protection with flexible management and pass-through taxation.

- **Corporation:** A separate legal entity owned by shareholders; offers strong liability protection but involves more regulations and tax complexity.
- **Nonprofit Organization:** Operates for charitable, educational, or social purposes; can receive tax-exempt status.

Each structure has unique legal requirements and advantages, so consulting with a legal or tax professional is often wise before making a decision.

The Registration Process: Step by Step

Once you've selected a business structure, it's time to make your business official. While requirements vary by state, the general steps are as follows:

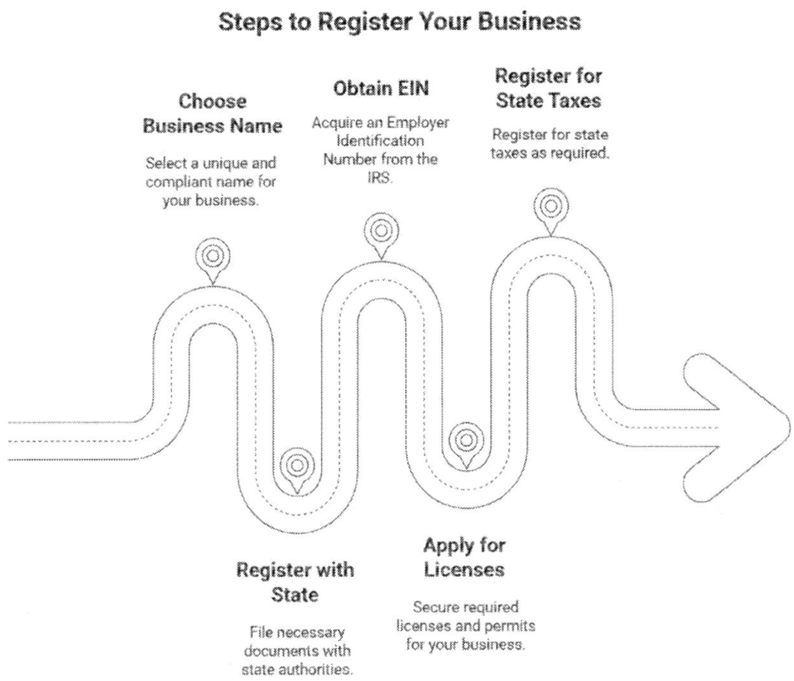

- **Choose a Business Name:** Your business name must be unique and comply with state regulations. Conduct a name search through your state's business registry.
- **Register with State Authorities:** Most businesses must register with the Secretary of State or a similar office. This usually involves filing **Articles of Incorporation** (for corporations) or **Articles of Organization** (for LLCs).

- **Obtain an EIN:** The **Employer Identification Number** (EIN) is issued by the IRS and is necessary for tax purposes, hiring employees, and opening bank accounts.
- **Apply for Licenses and Permits:** Depending on your business type and location, you may need federal, state, or local licenses and permits.
- **Register for State Taxes:** If applicable, register for state sales tax, unemployment insurance, and other required taxes.

Real-World Example: A Coffee Shop's Journey

Consider the experience of Maria and Jay, two friends who dreamed of opening a neighborhood coffee shop in Atlanta, Georgia. They started as a partnership but soon realized the risk to their personal assets if something went wrong—such as a customer injury or a contract dispute. On advice from a local small business association, they formed an LLC, providing them both flexibility and protection. After registering with Georgia's Secretary of State and obtaining the necessary permits, they were ready to open—legally and securely.

Navigating Federal, State, and Local Rules

It's important to recognize that the U.S. legal system is layered. Federal laws set the broad framework, but state and local governments have their own regulations that must be followed. For example, while the IRS issues EINs nationwide, business licenses and zoning permits are governed by city or county offices.

A Global Comparison

In many countries, starting a business is a centralized, national process. In the U.S., the decentralized approach means entrepreneurs must be diligent about compliance at multiple levels—a unique feature that shapes the American business landscape.

```
Very Important: Operating an unregistered business can result in significant
fines, legal liability, and even forced closure. Always check your state and
local requirements before launching operations.
```

Registering your business is the gateway to legal legitimacy and protection in the U.S. By understanding the process, choosing the right structure, and complying with all regulations, you set your venture on a path to success. In the next section, we'll explore the crucial topic of **contracts and consumer protection**, ensuring your business dealings are both fair and legally sound.

9.2 Contracts in Everyday Transactions

A **contract** is much more than a formality signed in boardrooms or law offices. Every day, individuals and businesses enter into agreements—some as simple as buying a cup of coffee, others as complex as purchasing a home. At its heart, a contract is a legally binding promise between two or more parties, setting out what each expects from the other. Whether you realize it or not, contracts shape countless routine interactions in the U.S. legal system.

What Makes a Contract Legally Binding?

To be enforceable in court, a contract must generally contain certain elements:

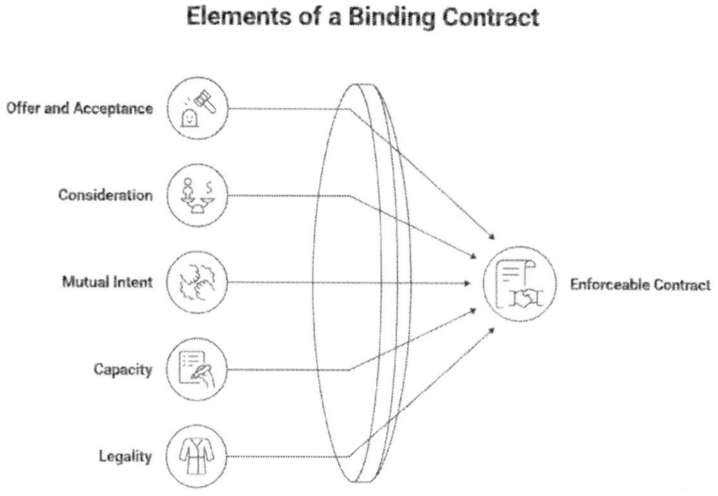

- **Offer and Acceptance**: One party proposes the terms, and the other accepts them.
- **Consideration**: Something of value (money, services, goods) changes hands.
- **Mutual Intent**: Both parties intend to enter into a legal agreement.
- **Capacity**: Parties must have the legal ability to contract (e.g., not minors or mentally incapacitated).
- **Legality**: The contract's subject must be lawful.

If any of these are missing, the agreement may not be recognized by courts.

Everyday Examples of Contracts

Contracts are not just for big business deals. Consider these familiar scenarios:

Cell Phone Plans: Signing up for mobile service involves a contract outlining monthly fees, data limits, and termination penalties.

Apartment Rentals: A lease agreement spells out each party's rights and responsibilities, from rent payments to maintenance duties.

Online Purchases: Clicking "I agree" to terms and conditions while shopping online usually creates a legally binding contract.

Real-World Example: The Unseen Contract

Imagine Maria, who buys a coffee at her neighborhood café. She gives $3 at the counter, and in return, the barista hands her a hot latte. Though nothing is written, an **implied contract** exists: Maria offers payment, the café accepts, and both expect the agreed-upon exchange. If the coffee is undrinkable due to contamination, Maria may have legal grounds for a complaint, based on the café's implied promise of a safe product.

When Contracts Go Wrong

Sometimes, parties disagree over what was promised or delivered. These disputes can lead to lawsuits, where courts examine the contract's terms and the parties' actions. Courts may:

- **Enforce the contract as written**.
- **Order compensation** for losses (damages).
- **Cancel the contract** if it's invalid or was made under duress or deception.

Historical Anecdote: Contracts and Consumer Rights

In the early 20th century, the landmark case of **Henningsen v. Bloomfield Motors** (1960) changed how U.S. law protects consumers. After buying a new car, Mrs. Henningsen was injured due to a defect. The manufacturer claimed a small-print warranty limited its liability, but the court sided with Mrs. Henningsen, ruling that unfair, one-sided contract terms could not strip consumers of basic rights. This case helped shape modern consumer protection laws and made it clear that not all contracts are enforced if they violate fairness or public policy.

Key Takeaways for Everyday Life

- **Read before you sign**: Whether it's a lease or a gym membership, always review contract terms.

- **Keep records**: Save copies of important agreements and receipts.
- **Know your rights**: Unfair or illegal contract terms can sometimes be challenged in court.

As we have seen, contracts are everywhere—silent guardians of trust and commerce. By understanding how they work, you protect yourself and your business from misunderstandings and legal pitfalls. Next, we'll examine the broad landscape of consumer protection laws, providing further tools to ensure your daily transactions are both fair and secure.

9.3 Consumer Rights and Protections

Every time you buy a cup of coffee, sign up for a phone plan, or shop online, you are engaging in transactions protected by a body of law known as **consumer protection law**. In the United States, these laws exist to create a fair marketplace, guard against deceptive business practices, and ensure that consumers have access to accurate information about the goods and services they purchase.

Consumer rights have evolved significantly since the early 20th century. One watershed moment came in 1962, when President John F. Kennedy delivered a special message to Congress outlining the **Consumer Bill of Rights**. These four cornerstone rights—**the right to safety, the right to be informed, the right to choose, and the right to be heard**—became the foundation for modern American consumer law.

Key Consumer Protections in Everyday Life

When you participate in the marketplace, your rights are safeguarded by a patchwork of federal, state, and local laws. Some of the most important protections include:

- **Truth in Advertising**: Businesses may not make false claims about their products. The Federal Trade Commission (FTC) enforces rules that require advertisements to be truthful, not misleading, and, when appropriate, backed by scientific evidence.
- **Product Safety**: The Consumer Product Safety Commission (CPSC) ensures that common household items—from toys to electronics—meet safety standards. Dangerous products can be recalled.
- **Fair Credit and Lending Practices**: The Truth in Lending Act (TILA) and Fair Credit Reporting Act (FCRA) guarantee that credit terms are transparent and that your credit information is handled fairly.

- **Privacy Protections**: Laws such as the Children's Online Privacy Protection Act (COPPA) and the Gramm-Leach-Bliley Act (GLBA) provide safeguards for your personal data in commercial transactions.

Real-World Example: The Case of the Recalled Toy

Consider the story of Linda, a mother in Michigan who bought a popular toy for her three-year-old son. Within days, she noticed small parts breaking off—posing a choking hazard. Linda reported the incident to both the retailer and the CPSC. Within weeks, the toy was recalled nationwide, preventing potential injuries to thousands of children. This example highlights the vital role of vigilant consumers and responsive agencies in maintaining public safety.

The Complaint Process: How to Stand Up for Your Rights

If you believe your rights have been violated—perhaps by a defective product or a misleading advertisement—you have several avenues for recourse:

- **Contact the Seller or Service Provider**: Most disputes can be resolved directly.
- **File a Complaint with a Government Agency**: The FTC, state attorneys general, and local consumer protection offices accept complaints and investigate patterns of wrongdoing.
- **Seek Legal Action**: In cases of significant harm, you may pursue a lawsuit or join a class-action case.
- **Alternative Dispute Resolution**: Mediation and arbitration can offer quicker, less expensive solutions than court.

Global Perspectives and Memorable Facts

Consumer protection is a global concern. For example, the **European Union's General Data Protection Regulation (GDPR)** sets some of the world's strictest rules for data privacy, influencing companies worldwide—even those based in the United States. Meanwhile, in Japan, the **Consumer Contract Act** provides strong safeguards against unfair terms in consumer agreements.

```
Did you know?

The Federal Trade Commission was established in 1914 to combat unfair or
deceptive business practices—making it one of the oldest consumer protection
agencies in the world.
```

Understanding your rights as a consumer is critical to navigating modern life with confidence and security. From buying groceries to signing a rental agreement, these protections ensure that fairness is more than just an ideal—it is a legal requirement. As we move forward, let's explore how these consumer laws intersect with the world of contracts, and what happens when disagreements arise over promises made and kept in the marketplace.

9.4 Credit, Debt, and Collections

Every day, millions of Americans rely on **credit**—the ability to borrow money, purchase goods now, and pay later. Whether it's using a credit card at the grocery store or financing a car, credit is a powerful tool, but it comes with strict legal frameworks. The **Fair Credit Reporting Act (FCRA)** and the **Truth in Lending Act (TILA)** ensure that both lenders and consumers play by clear rules.

For example, the FCRA gives you the right to:

- Access your credit report annually for free
- Dispute incorrect information
- Know if information in your file has been used against you

Meanwhile, TILA requires lenders to:

- Clearly disclose interest rates and fees
- Provide a standardized way to compare credit offers

A memorable story comes from the late 1970s, when a group of consumers in California discovered unauthorized charges on their credit cards. Their complaints led to the passage of the **Fair Credit Billing Act**, empowering consumers to challenge billing errors and withhold payment during investigations.

Managing Debt: Responsibilities and Consequences

Debt is a double-edged sword. Used wisely, it enables opportunity. Mismanaged, it can lead to financial strain and legal headaches. When you borrow, you enter a **binding contract**—a legal promise to repay.

Key points to remember:

- Missing payments can lead to late fees, interest hikes, and negative credit marks.
- After a certain period of nonpayment (often 30–90 days), lenders may declare your account "in default."
- Defaulting can trigger collection actions or lawsuits.

Personal story: Consider Maria, a recent college graduate. She took out several credit cards to furnish her first apartment. When unexpected medical bills piled up, she struggled to keep up with payments. Soon, collection calls began, and her credit score dropped, making it difficult to secure a car loan or rent a new apartment.

Collections: Legal Protections and Practices

When debts go unpaid, creditors may turn to **collections**—a process strictly regulated by law. The **Fair Debt Collection Practices Act (FDCPA)** is the backbone of consumer protections in this area.

Collectors must:

- Identify themselves and provide information about the debt
- Refrain from harassment or making false statements
- Honor written requests to cease communication

If a collector violates your rights, you can report them to the **Consumer Financial Protection Bureau (CFPB)** or take legal action.

Timeline of the Collections Process

- Debt becomes overdue (typically after 30–90 days).
- Creditor attempts to collect directly.
- Account may be sold to or assigned to a collection agency.
- Debt collector contacts you; you have the right to dispute the debt.

- If unresolved, collectors may file a lawsuit. If they win, they can seek court orders to garnish wages or seize assets within legal limits.

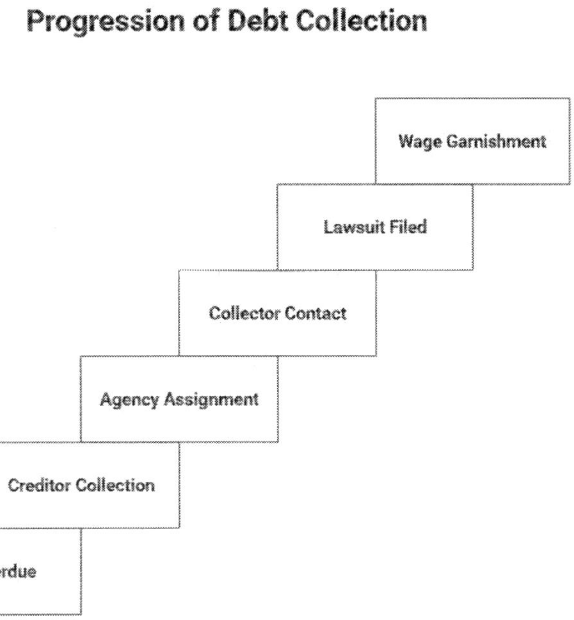

Global Perspective: Debt and Collections Abroad

While the U.S. has robust protections for debtors, approaches vary worldwide. For instance:

In the UK, the **Financial Conduct Authority** enforces strict rules on how collectors interact with debtors.

In Sweden, the **Kronofogden** (enforcement authority) manages collections transparently, focusing on rehabilitation over punishment.

Understanding credit, debt, and collections is essential for navigating modern life and safeguarding your financial future. By knowing both your rights and responsibilities, you can avoid costly mistakes and handle disputes confidently. Next, we'll delve into what happens when financial promises break down—exploring small claims court, mediation, and your options when you and a business can't agree.

9.5 Fraud, Scams, and Identity Theft

Fraud, in its many forms, is a persistent threat in both business and daily life. Whether it's a deceptive sales tactic, a sophisticated online scam, or a case of identity theft, understanding how these crimes work—and how the law responds—is essential for safeguarding yourself and your community. Let's explore the landscape of fraud, scams, and identity theft, and learn how the U.S. legal system protects both consumers and businesses from these ever-evolving risks.

What Constitutes Fraud?

At its core, **fraud** is an intentional act of deception for personal or financial gain. The law distinguishes between civil fraud (addressed in lawsuits for damages) and criminal fraud (prosecuted by the state). Common elements include:

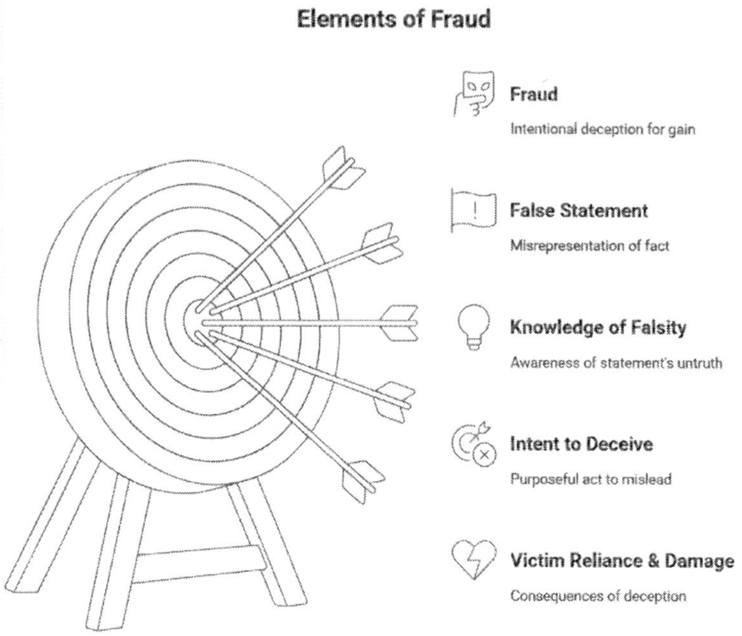

- A false statement or misrepresentation of fact.
- Knowledge that the statement is false.
- Intent to deceive the victim.
- Justifiable reliance by the victim on the false statement.
- Damage or injury suffered by the victim as a result.

Fraud can occur in countless contexts—online marketplaces, real estate transactions, investment pitches, or even everyday retail purchases.

Scams: Old Tricks, New Technology

While scams have existed for centuries, modern technology has given rise to new forms of deception. Consider the infamous **Nigerian prince email scam**—a simple yet effective ruse in which fraudsters promise vast sums of money in exchange for personal banking details. Such scams exploit trust and often target the most vulnerable.

A more recent example is the rise of **phishing**, where criminals impersonate legitimate businesses or government agencies through email, phone calls, or text messages. Their goal: coax individuals into revealing private data like passwords, Social Security numbers, or credit card details.

Identity Theft: When Your Life Becomes Someone Else's

Perhaps the most personal form of fraud is **identity theft**. In these cases, a criminal obtains key pieces of someone's personal information—such as their Social Security number, date of birth, or bank account numbers—and uses them to commit fraud or theft. The consequences can be devastating: ruined credit, drained bank accounts, and years spent unraveling the damage.

Case Study:

In 2017, a major credit reporting agency, **Equifax**, suffered a data breach exposing the personal information of over 147 million Americans. Thieves gained access to names, Social Security numbers, birth dates, addresses, and even some driver's license numbers. This breach highlighted just how vulnerable personal data can be, and the far-reaching impact when it falls into the wrong hands.

Legal Protections and Your Rights

The U.S. legal system provides several layers of protection against fraud and identity theft:

- **Federal Laws:** The Federal Trade Commission (FTC) enforces consumer protection laws and investigates fraudulent practices. The **Identity Theft and Assumption Deterrence Act** makes identity theft a federal crime.
- **State Laws:** All 50 states have laws addressing various forms of fraud, including consumer fraud, insurance fraud, and credit card fraud.
- **Reporting Mechanisms:** Victims can file complaints with the FTC, local law enforcement, and credit bureaus to begin resolving issues and restoring their identities.

Steps to Take if You're a Victim

1. Notify your bank and credit card companies immediately.
2. File a report with the FTC and your local police.
3. Place a fraud alert or freeze on your credit reports.
4. Keep detailed records of all communications and actions taken.

Staying Safe: Prevention Tips

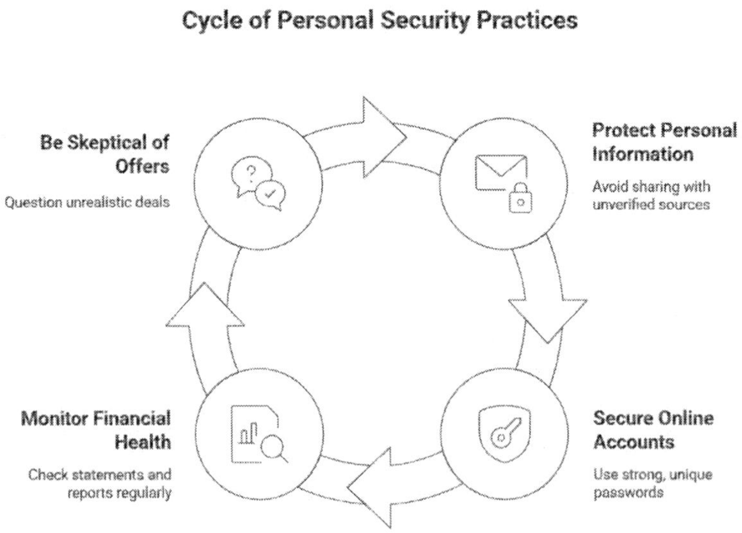

- Never share personal information with unverified sources.
- Use strong, unique passwords for online accounts.
- Monitor your financial statements and credit reports regularly.
- Be skeptical of offers that sound too good to be true.

Identity theft is one of the fastest-growing crimes in the U.S.; over 1 million reports are filed annually with the FTC.

If you suspect fraud, act quickly timely reporting can limit your financial loss and help law enforcement stop further crimes.

Fraud, scams, and identity theft are not just stories from the headlines—they can impact anyone. By understanding the legal landscape and taking preventive steps, you can protect yourself and your loved ones. As we move forward, we'll examine the rights and responsibilities of both consumers and businesses in more detail, focusing on how to resolve disputes and enforce legal protections in everyday transactions.

9.6 E-Commerce and Online Transactions

In the past two decades, the way Americans buy and sell goods has transformed dramatically. **E-commerce**—the buying and selling of products and services over the internet—has opened global markets to local consumers and entrepreneurs alike. From ordering groceries online to running a small business through a website, digital transactions have become an integral part of daily life. With this evolution comes a unique set of legal frameworks and challenges that both consumers and business owners must understand to protect their interests.

Key Legal Protections in Online Transactions

Online shopping offers convenience, but it also introduces risks such as fraud, identity theft, and disputes over quality or delivery. To address these issues, U.S. laws and regulations have adapted:

- The Electronic Signatures in Global and National Commerce Act (E-SIGN Act): Passed in 2000, this law gives electronic signatures the same legal standing as handwritten ones, making contracts and agreements signed online binding.
- Federal Trade Commission (FTC) Regulations: The FTC enforces rules against deceptive advertising, requiring that online businesses clearly disclose prices, terms of sale, refund policies, and privacy practices.
- The Fair Credit Billing Act (FCBA): Offers consumers protection against unauthorized charges on their credit cards, including those made online.
- Children's Online Privacy Protection Act (COPPA): Regulates the collection of personal information from children under 13 by websites and online services.

What Consumers Should Know

- Always verify the legitimacy of the website before entering personal or financial information.
- Review return, refund, and shipping policies before completing a purchase.

- Use secure payment methods—credit cards often provide better fraud protection compared to debit cards or wire transfers.

What Businesses Must Remember

- Clearly communicate terms and conditions to avoid misunderstandings or legal disputes.
- Follow data protection laws and safeguard customer information against breaches.
- Make sure all advertising is truthful and not misleading, as false claims are subject to FTC enforcement.

Real-World Example: The Case of the Disappearing Seller

Consider the story of **Maria**, who ordered a custom piece of furniture from a small online retailer. She paid in advance, but the piece never arrived, and the website disappeared. Maria reported the fraud to her credit card company, which reversed the charge under the FCBA's protection. The incident highlights the importance of consumer vigilance and the value of legal safeguards in e-commerce.

Global Perspectives: E-Commerce Law Around the World

Other countries have enacted similar protections. For instance:

- The European Union's General Data Protection Regulation (GDPR) sets strict rules for handling customer data, affecting even U.S. businesses that serve European consumers.
- In China, the E-Commerce Law requires platforms to verify the identity of sellers and resolve consumer complaints promptly.

These global trends point to a universal need for balance: fostering innovation in online commerce while safeguarding the rights of buyers and sellers.

law gives electronic signatures and contracts the same legal validity as paper and ink agreements—always read online terms carefully before agreeing.

The Future of Online Transactions

As technology evolves, so too do the legal challenges. Cryptocurrency transactions, virtual goods, and app-based marketplaces are expanding the boundaries of traditional commerce law. Staying informed about legal responsibilities and protections is essential for both consumers and businesses in this ever-changing digital landscape.

In summary, understanding the legal aspects of e-commerce empowers individuals to shop and conduct business online with confidence. Next, we'll explore how these protections extend to resolving disputes between consumers and businesses, including mediation, arbitration, and small claims court procedures.

9.7 International Perspectives on Consumer Protection

Consumer protection is not unique to the United States; it is a foundational element of modern economies worldwide. While the U.S. system has its own distinctive features—such as the prominent role of the Federal Trade Commission (FTC) and the patchwork of federal and state laws—many countries have developed robust legal frameworks to safeguard consumers from unfair practices. By examining international models, we can better appreciate the strengths and limitations of the U.S. approach and see how global cooperation shapes the everyday experiences of buyers and sellers.

International Models and Approaches

Different countries have tailored their consumer protection laws to reflect their cultural values, economic structures, and legal traditions. Here are a few notable approaches:

Consumer Protection Laws by Region

Characteristic	European Union	Japan	Brazil
Regulations	Comprehensive regulations	Clear labeling, strict recalls	Broad rights for consumers
Key Laws	GDPR, product safety directives	Consumer Affairs Agency enforcement	Consumer Defense Code (CDC)
Consumer Focus	Strong rights, returns	Education, clear information	Burden of proof on businesses

- **European Union (EU):** The EU has some of the world's most comprehensive consumer protection regulations. The General Data Protection Regulation (GDPR) and directives on product safety, unfair commercial practices, and digital content give EU consumers strong rights, such as the right to return most online purchases within 14 days—no questions asked.
- **Japan**: Japan's Consumer Affairs Agency enforces laws that require clear labeling, prohibit deceptive advertising, and establish strict recall processes for

unsafe products. Consumer education is also a priority, with regular campaigns to inform citizens of their rights.

- **Brazil**: Brazil's Consumer Defense Code (CDC), enacted in 1990, is considered pioneering in Latin America. It grants consumers broad rights and places the burden of proof on businesses in many disputes, making it easier for consumers to seek redress.

Real-World Example: The Horsemeat Scandal

In 2013, European supermarkets were rocked by the **horsemeat scandal**, in which beef products were found to contain undeclared horsemeat. This incident highlighted the importance of transparent supply chains and cross-border cooperation. EU agencies and national regulators worked together to trace the problem, enforce recalls, and strengthen labeling laws—demonstrating how international collaboration can address consumer risks that extend beyond national borders.

U.S. vs. Global Protections: A Comparative View

While the U.S. emphasizes enforcement through agencies like the FTC and through civil lawsuits brought by individuals, many other countries favor administrative mechanisms, such as ombudsmen or government-led complaint resolution services. Some key contrasts include:

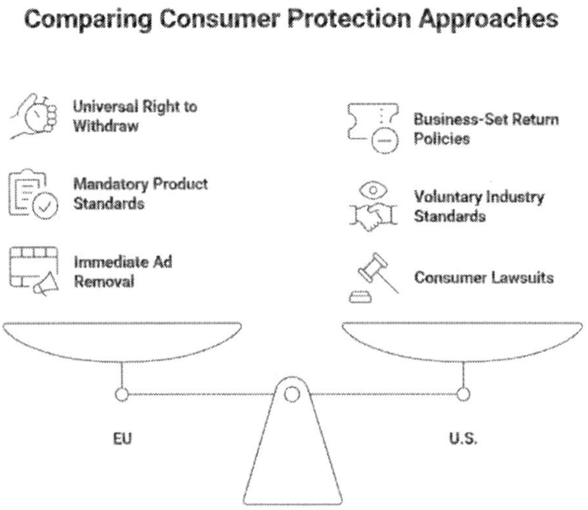

- **Right to Withdraw:** In the EU, consumers have a universal right to cancel most distance sales within 14 days, whereas in the U.S., return policies are often set by individual businesses, with only limited federal requirements.

- **Product Safety:** The U.S. Consumer Product Safety Commission (CPSC) operates alongside voluntary industry standards, while countries like Australia have "mandatory standards" for many goods, making compliance a legal requirement.
- **Advertising**: Misleading advertising is prohibited worldwide, but enforcement varies. The U.S. often relies on consumer lawsuits, while the United Kingdom's Advertising Standards Authority (ASA) can order immediate removal of deceptive ads.

Lessons from Abroad

Global consumer protection efforts underscore the benefits of harmonization—where common standards allow for safer, more predictable marketplaces. For travelers, immigrants, or those shopping internationally, knowing your rights in each jurisdiction is essential. For instance, a U.S. tourist buying electronics in Germany enjoys strong return rights under EU law, while a German visitor in New York must rely on store policies.

10 Immigration and Citizenship

10.1 Immigration Statuses and Visas

The United States is often described as a nation of immigrants, a characterization reflected in its complex and layered immigration system. Whether someone is arriving for a new job, reuniting with family, seeking refuge, or pursuing educational opportunities, their **immigration status** determines their legal rights, responsibilities, and pathways to permanent residency or citizenship.

At its core, U.S. immigration law recognizes several primary statuses:

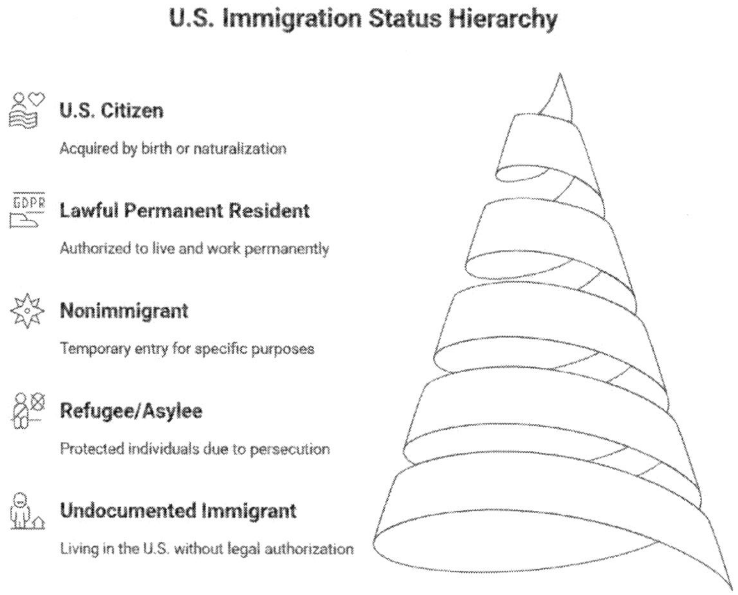

- **U.S. Citizen**: Acquired by birth within the United States or through naturalization.
- **Lawful Permanent Resident (LPR)**: Often called a "green card" holder, authorized to live and work permanently in the U.S.
- **Nonimmigrant (Visa Holder)**: Permitted to enter the U.S. temporarily for specific purposes such as tourism, study, or work.
- **Refugee or Asylee**: Protected individuals unable to return to their home countries due to persecution.
- **Undocumented Immigrant**: Living in the U.S. without legal authorization.

Each status confers different rights and imposes varying obligations, as well as eligibility for public benefits, paths to citizenship, and vulnerability to deportation.

Common Types of U.S. Visas

Visas are official endorsements permitting foreign nationals to enter, stay, or work in the U.S. Depending on the purpose and duration of stay, visas fall into two broad categories:

Nonimmigrant Visas

These are temporary visas for individuals who plan to stay in the U.S. for a specific period. Common examples include:

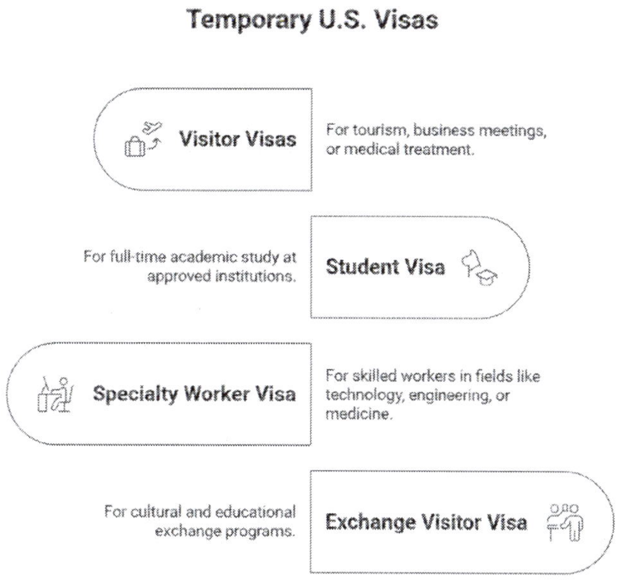

- **B-1/B-2 (Visitor Visas)**: For tourism, business meetings, or medical treatment.
- **F-1 (Student Visa)**: For full-time academic study at approved institutions.
- **H-1B (Specialty Occupation Worker Visa)**: For skilled workers in fields like technology, engineering, or medicine.
- **J-1 (Exchange Visitor Visa)**: For cultural and educational exchange programs.

Immigrant Visas

These are for people seeking to live permanently in the U.S. Most immigrant visas are issued based on:

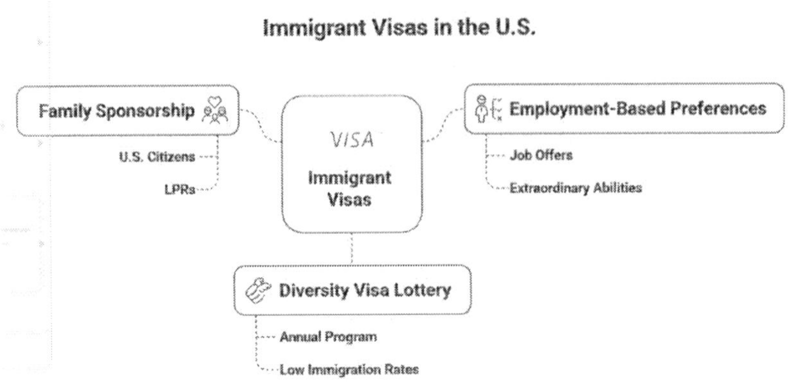

- **Family Sponsorship**: Close relatives of U.S. citizens or LPRs may qualify.
- **Employment-Based Preferences**: For individuals with specific job offers or extraordinary abilities.
- **Diversity Visa Lottery**: An annual program for residents of countries with low rates of immigration to the U.S.

Timeline: The Path from Arrival to Permanent Residency

- **Entry with a Visa**: Whether arriving as a student, worker, or visitor, the individual must comply with the terms of their visa.
- **Status Adjustment**: Some may seek to adjust their status to permanent resident (e.g., marrying a U.S. citizen or receiving a job offer).
- **Green Card Application**: Applicants submit paperwork, undergo background checks, and attend an interview.
- **Permanent Residency Granted**: If approved, the individual becomes an LPR, with a path to citizenship through naturalization after several years.

Real-World Example: The Student's Journey

Consider the story of Priya, who arrived in the U.S. on an F-1 student visa to pursue a master's degree in engineering. After graduation, she secured a job with a tech company willing to sponsor her H-1B work visa. Several years into her career, she applied for a green card through her employer. Priya's journey, while typical for many skilled immigrants, underscores the layered and sometimes lengthy process of navigating U.S. immigration law.

Historical Perspective: The Evolution of Immigration Law

In 1965, the U.S. fundamentally changed its approach to immigration by abolishing national origins quotas and prioritizing family reunification and skilled workers. This shift, embodied in the **Immigration and Nationality Act of 1965**, opened new pathways for millions and continues to shape the diverse fabric of American society.

```
Remember: Overstaying a visa—even by a single day—can have serious long-term consequences, including bars on re-entry to the U.S. and disqualification from future visas.
```

Reflection and Transition

Understanding immigration statuses and visa options is essential not only for newcomers but also for all residents who interact with a diverse community. The stories behind these legal categories reflect both the promise and the challenges of U.S. immigration. In the next section, we'll explore the process of becoming a naturalized citizen, examining the rights and responsibilities that come with this important step in the American legal journey.

10.2 The Path to Citizenship

For millions, the journey to American citizenship is a defining chapter in their lives, marked by determination, hope, and the pursuit of new opportunities. The **naturalization process**—the legal pathway by which a foreign national becomes a U.S. citizen—is both rigorous and rewarding, reflecting the nation's commitment to upholding its values while welcoming new members into the fabric of society.

Eligibility Requirements: Who Can Apply?

Before beginning the process, applicants must meet specific requirements established by U.S. law:

- **Lawful Permanent Residency:** Most applicants must have a valid green card (permanent resident status) for at least five years, or three years if married to a U.S. citizen.
- **Physical Presence:** Applicants must have lived in the U.S. for at least half of the required residency period.
- **Good Moral Character:** Evidence of upstanding behavior, including no serious criminal record.

- **English Proficiency:** Ability to read, write, and speak basic English.
- **Civics Knowledge:** Understanding of U.S. history and government.
- **Attachment to Constitutional Principles:** Willingness to support and defend the U.S. Constitution.

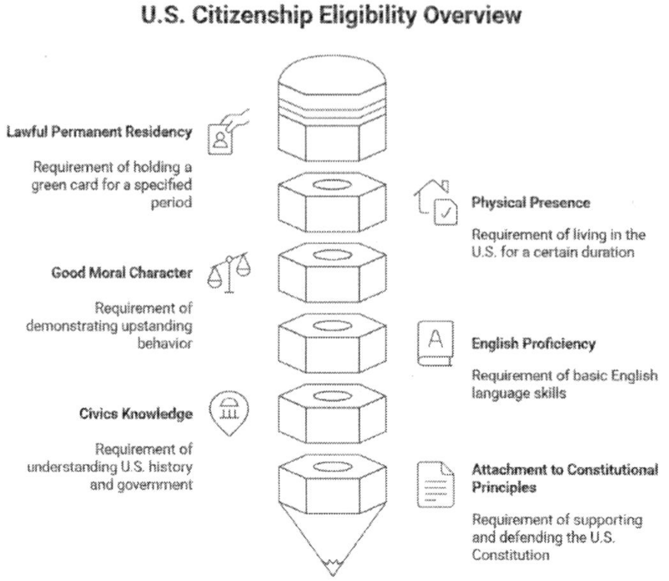

These requirements ensure that new citizens are integrated into American society and understand the rights and responsibilities of citizenship.

The Steps of Naturalization

The path to citizenship unfolds through a series of steps:

- **Application (Form N-400):** The process begins with the submission of Form N-400 to U.S. Citizenship and Immigration Services (USCIS), along with supporting documents and fees.
- **Biometrics Appointment:** Applicants attend a local USCIS office to provide fingerprints, photographs, and a signature for background checks.
- **Interview and Exam:** A USCIS officer conducts an in-person interview, which includes questions about the applicant's background, English proficiency, and a civics test covering U.S. history and government.
- **Decision:** USCIS reviews the case and issues a decision. If approved, the applicant is scheduled for a naturalization ceremony.
- **Oath of Allegiance:** The final step is taking the Oath of Allegiance, at which point the individual becomes a U.S. citizen.

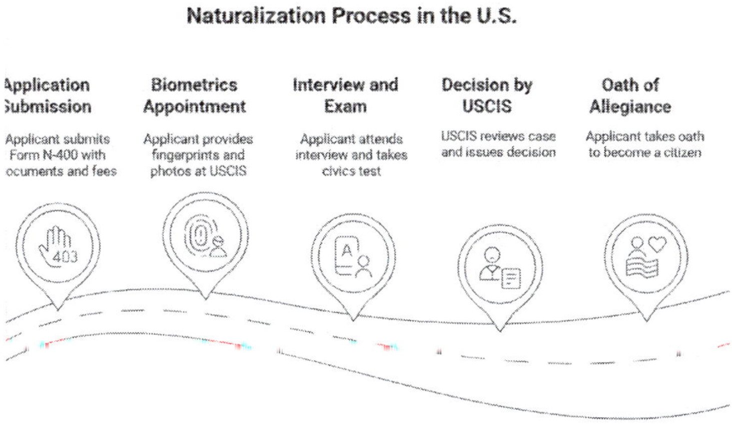

Real-World Stories: From Newcomer to Citizen

Consider the story of **Li Wei**, who emigrated from China as a student. After years of studying, working, and volunteering in her adopted community, Li met all the requirements and successfully completed the naturalization process. She describes her swearing-in ceremony as one of the proudest moments of her life—a culmination of perseverance and a symbol of her new identity as an American.

Similarly, **Jose Martinez**, originally from El Salvador, spent nearly two decades in the U.S. as a lawful permanent resident. After naturalizing, he was able to petition for his parents to join him, illustrating how citizenship can have ripple effects, strengthening families and communities alike.

Key Points to Remember

- The naturalization process is designed to ensure that new citizens are prepared for the rights and duties of citizenship.
- Each step, from application to oath, reflects a commitment to American values and legal principles.
- Real-life stories highlight the deeply personal and transformative nature of becoming a U.S. citizen.

```
The U.S. Constitution grants naturalized citizens the same rights and
protections as those born in the United States, with only a few exceptions
such as eligibility for the presidency.')
startswith('Naturalization applicants must pass both an English language test
and a civics exam.
```

The path to citizenship is more than a legal process—it is a testament to the enduring promise of the United States as a nation of opportunity. In the next section, we'll examine the rights and responsibilities that come with citizenship, exploring how new Americans contribute to and shape their communities under the law.

10.3 Rights of Non-Citizens

One of the most remarkable features of the U.S. legal system is its commitment to fundamental rights for everyone within its borders—not just citizens. The U.S. Constitution, particularly the **Bill of Rights**, extends many protections to **non-citizens** (sometimes called "aliens" in legal terms), regardless of immigration status. This principle is grounded in the idea that certain rights are inherent to all people, not just to those holding citizenship.

Key constitutional rights that apply to non-citizens include:

- **Due Process:** Under the Fifth and Fourteenth Amendments, everyone—citizen or not—has the right to fair legal procedures before being deprived of life, liberty, or property.
- **Equal Protection:** The Fourteenth Amendment requires states to provide equal protection under the law to all people within their jurisdiction.
- **Freedom of Speech, Religion, and Assembly:** The First Amendment protects these freedoms for non-citizens, allowing them to express opinions, practice religion, and gather peacefully.
- **Protection Against Unreasonable Searches and Seizures:** The Fourth Amendment gives all persons the right to be free from unwarranted government intrusion.

Legal Rights in Practice

For non-citizens, these constitutional protections have real-world implications:

- **Criminal Proceedings:** Non-citizens accused of crimes have the right to a fair trial, legal representation, and protection against self-incrimination.
- **Deportation and Removal Proceedings:** Even those facing removal from the U.S. are entitled to a hearing before an immigration judge and the right to present their case.
- **Access to the Courts:** Non-citizens can file lawsuits and seek protection in U.S. courts.

Real-World Example: Plyler v. Doe (1982)

In **Plyler v. Doe**, the U.S. Supreme Court struck down a Texas law that denied public education funding for undocumented immigrant children. The Court ruled that denying these children access to public schools violated the Equal Protection Clause. This decision affirmed that basic rights and opportunities—such as education—cannot be denied based on immigration status.

Limitations on Non-Citizen Rights

While non-citizens enjoy many constitutional protections, there are important distinctions.

- **Voting:** Only U.S. citizens can vote in federal and most state elections.
- **Jury Service:** Generally, only citizens are eligible to serve on juries.
- **Government Jobs and Benefits:** Certain jobs and public benefits are reserved for citizens or lawful permanent residents.
- **Travel and Re-Entry:** Non-citizens may face restrictions on travel outside the U.S. and re-entry, depending on their legal status.

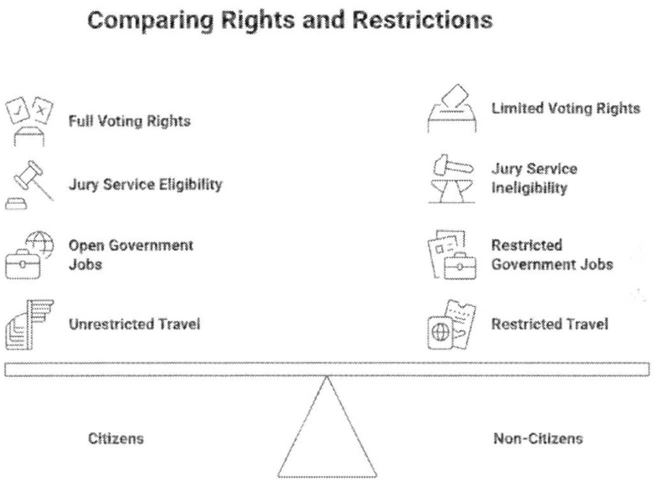

Personal Story: A Dreamer's Experience

Consider the story of Ana, a young woman brought to the U.S. as a child without legal status. Despite her status, Ana graduated from a public high school and attended a public university—rights protected by court decisions like **Plyler v. Doe**. However, Ana faced uncertainty about her ability to work legally or travel abroad. Her story highlights both the protections and the limitations non-citizens encounter under U.S. law.

```
Very Important: Non-citizens in the U.S. have constitutional rights such as
due process and equal protection—but some rights, like voting in federal
elections, are reserved for citizens only.
```

Reflection and Transition

Understanding the rights of non-citizens is crucial for fostering fairness and inclusion in American society. While the legal system upholds many fundamental protections for all, it also draws clear lines around certain privileges of citizenship. As we move forward, the next section will explore the responsibilities that come with citizenship, emphasizing how every member of the community can contribute to the legal and civic fabric of the nation.

10.4 Deportation and Removal Proceedings

For many immigrants, the word **deportation** conjures images of sudden upheaval, families separated, and futures put on hold. But the legal process behind deportation, officially called **removal proceedings**, is governed by clear rules and steps within the U.S. legal system. Understanding how these proceedings work—and what rights individuals have throughout—is crucial for anyone navigating immigration or supporting those who do.

The Legal Framework

Removal proceedings are initiated by the U.S. government when it believes a non-citizen (including lawful permanent residents, or "green card" holders, in some cases) has violated immigration law. Common grounds include:

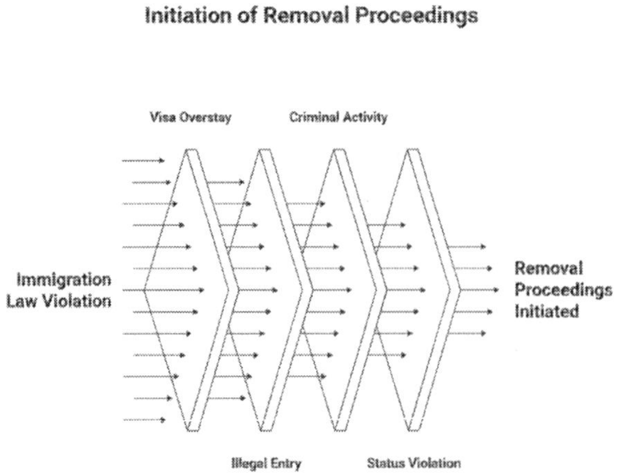

- Overstaying a visa
- Entering the U.S. without proper documentation
- Committing certain crimes
- Violating terms of lawful status

The process is overseen by the **Executive Office for Immigration Review** (EOIR), a branch of the Department of Justice, and cases are heard before immigration judges, not in traditional criminal courts.

The Step-by-Step Process

- **Notice to Appear (NTA):** The process begins when an individual receives a formal document called a **Notice to Appear**. This outlines the government's charges and the reasons removal is sought.
- **Master Calendar Hearing:** The first court appearance, where the judge explains rights, reviews charges, and schedules further hearings.
- **Individual Hearing:** The main event, where the individual can present evidence, call witnesses, and argue their case—often with the assistance of a lawyer, if they can obtain or afford one.
- **Judge's Decision:** The immigration judge decides whether removal is warranted or if the individual qualifies for relief (such as asylum, cancellation of removal, or adjustment of status).
- **Appeals:** Both the government and the individual have the right to appeal the judge's decision to the **Board of Immigration Appeals (BIA)**, and in some cases, to federal courts.

Rights and Representation

Unlike criminal defendants, those in removal proceedings are not guaranteed government-appointed attorneys. However, they do have the right to:

- Hire an attorney at their own expense
- Receive interpretation services in court
- Present evidence and witnesses
- Appeal unfavorable decisions

These protections, while limited, are essential for due process and ensuring fair treatment.

Real-World Story: The Case of Juana

Consider the experience of **Juana**, a mother from Guatemala who fled violence and entered the U.S. without documentation. After years living quietly and working in California, she was stopped for a minor traffic violation. The resulting background check revealed her undocumented status. Juana was given a Notice to Appear and entered removal proceedings. With the help of a local legal aid organization, she applied for asylum, presenting evidence of the dangers she faced back home. Though her case was ultimately successful, it vividly illustrates both the risks and the protections available in the U.S. system.

Historical Perspective

The U.S. approach to deportation has evolved over time. For example, during the **Great Depression**, thousands of Mexican Americans—many of them U.S. citizens—were forcibly removed in a wave of mass deportations. This history underscores the importance of legal safeguards, transparency, and advocacy in today's system.

```
In removal proceedings, individuals are not entitled to a free government
attorney, unlike in criminal cases. However, legal representation can
significantly improve the chances of a favorable outcome.

Appealing an immigration judge's decision must be done quickly—usually within
30 days—making timely action and legal advice critical.
```

Deportation and removal proceedings are complex and often deeply personal, affecting families and communities across the country. Understanding the process—and the rights of those involved—empowers individuals to make informed decisions and seek help when needed. As we move forward, the next section will focus on the responsibilities that come with citizenship, highlighting how each person's actions contribute to the strength and resilience of the nation's legal and civic fabric.

10.5 Documenting Status and Avoiding Scams

Navigating the process of immigration in the United States is often complex, requiring a clear understanding of what documents are necessary to prove legal status. Whether you are applying for a visa, seeking permanent residency, or pursuing citizenship, maintaining accurate and up-to-date paperwork is essential. Not only does proper documentation grant access to benefits and protections, but it also acts as a safeguard during interactions with law enforcement or government agencies.

Essential Documents for Immigrants

- **Passport:** The foundational identity document for most non-citizens.

- **Visa or Entry Permit:** Shows permission to enter the U.S. for a specific purpose and duration.
- **I-94 Arrival/Departure Record:** Confirms legal entry and authorized stay period.
- **Permanent Resident Card ("Green Card"):** Proof of lawful permanent residency.
- **Employment Authorization Document (EAD):** Allows non-citizens to work legally.
- **Social Security Card:** Necessary for employment, banking, and access to some public services.

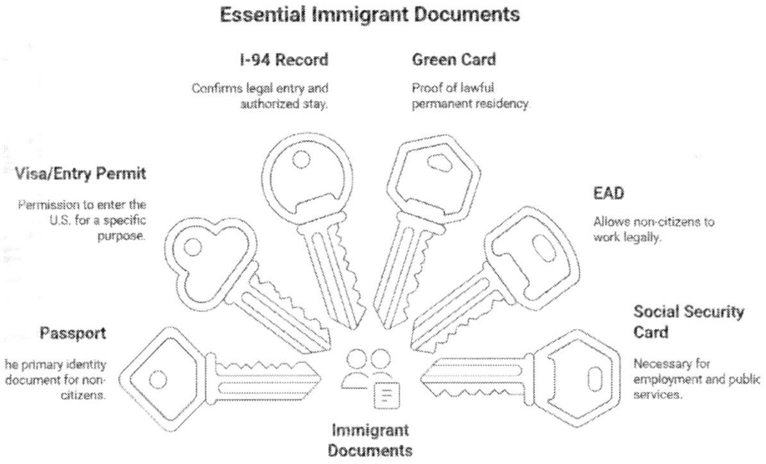

Keeping these documents safe and making certified copies for personal records is crucial. In the event of loss or theft, promptly reporting and applying for replacements can prevent legal complications.

Recognizing and Avoiding Immigration Scams

Unfortunately, the complexities of the immigration process can make individuals vulnerable to scams. Fraudsters often prey on those seeking legal status, promising quick solutions or guaranteed results in exchange for high fees or personal information. Understanding the most common tactics used by scammers can help protect yourself and loved ones.

Common Types of Immigration Scams

- **Fake Legal Representatives:** Unlicensed individuals or "notarios" who claim they can provide legal advice or expedite applications.

- **Phishing and Impersonation:** Emails, phone calls, or texts that appear to be from U.S. Citizenship and Immigration Services (USCIS) or other official agencies, requesting payments or personal information.
- **False Promises:** Offers of "guaranteed" visas, green cards, or citizenship—no legitimate representative can make such guarantees.

Real-World Example

Consider the story of Maria, a recent immigrant from Honduras. She was approached by a man in her community who claimed he could "fix" her papers for a fee. He provided her with documents that looked official, but after paying him, Maria never heard from him again. Worse, the documents were fraudulent, putting her at risk for deportation. Maria's experience is sadly common, highlighting the importance of seeking help only from qualified, licensed immigration attorneys or accredited representatives.

Protecting Yourself

- **Verify Credentials:** Always check that anyone offering immigration assistance is a licensed attorney or an accredited representative recognized by the Department of Justice.
- **Never Pay for Blank Forms:** USCIS forms are free and available online.
- **Beware of Pressure Tactics:** Legitimate representatives will not rush you or demand immediate payment.
- **Keep Records:** Document all interactions, payments, and correspondence.

Global Perspective

Immigration scams are not unique to the United States. In Canada, similar fraud rings have targeted newcomers, while the United Kingdom has seen a rise in fake "immigration advisors." Worldwide, the best defense is education and vigilance.

```
Never share personal documents or immigration details with unlicensed
individuals. Always verify the credentials of anyone offering immigration
assistance.
```

Documenting your status carefully and remaining vigilant against scams are foundational steps in protecting your rights and future in the United States. These practices don't just serve your individual interests—they uphold the integrity of the legal system and ensure fair access to justice for all. As we move forward, the next section will explore the rights and responsibilities that come with citizenship, emphasizing how your participation and conduct can strengthen the nation's legal and civic framework.

10.6 Stories from Immigrant Communities

Every journey toward U.S. citizenship is unique, shaped by personal circumstance, cultural identity, and the ever-evolving landscape of American law. The stories of immigrant communities across the nation reveal how the legal system intersects with daily life, testing resilience, shaping families, and redefining what it means to belong. These experiences not only illustrate the challenges and opportunities of immigration but also highlight the essential role law plays in fostering—or complicating—the American dream.

The Path to Belonging: One Family's Journey

In 1992, the **Nguyen family** left Vietnam, seeking refuge from political upheaval and hope for a better future. Arriving in California with limited English and uncertain prospects, their first encounter with the U.S. legal system was at the border, where they applied for **asylum**. Navigating complex paperwork and court hearings, they found guidance through a local non-profit specializing in immigration law.

Through the following years, the Nguyens experienced both setbacks and triumphs:

- **Initial Application**: Their asylum claim was scrutinized, with extensive documentation required to prove credible fear of persecution.
- **Legal Representation**: Pro bono legal aid helped them understand their rights, prepare for interviews, and respond to government requests.
- **Community Support**: The local Vietnamese-American community offered translation services and emotional support, underscoring the importance of cultural networks.
- **Path to Citizenship**: After being granted asylum, the family applied for permanent residency, followed by citizenship—a process spanning over a decade.

Their story underscores how U.S. immigration law, while complex, offers avenues for protection and integration. Yet, the process demands patience, legal awareness, and community engagement.

Legal Hurdles and Everyday Life

For many immigrants, legal status dictates everyday realities—from employment opportunities to interactions with law enforcement. Consider the experience of **Maria Rodriguez**, a DACA recipient from Mexico, who grew up in

Texas. Despite excelling in school and contributing to her community, Maria faced unique legal challenges:

Employment Authorization: Her ability to work legally hinged on maintaining her DACA status, requiring regular renewal and legal vigilance.
Travel Restrictions: Without permanent residency, traveling abroad—even for family emergencies—posed significant risks.
Civic Participation: Maria could not vote or serve on a jury, reflecting the limitations of her legal status.

Maria's narrative illustrates how laws shape the contours of daily life, determining not only what is possible but also what remains out of reach.

Bridging Legal Systems: Global Perspectives

Immigrant stories resonate worldwide. In **Canada**, for instance, refugees are met by government-sponsored resettlement programs that provide immediate legal assistance and integration support, reflecting a different approach from the largely decentralized U.S. model. Meanwhile, in **Germany**, the 2015 refugee influx prompted reforms in asylum law, spurring debate on the balance between national security and humanitarian responsibility.

These global perspectives enrich our understanding of how legal systems mediate the immigrant experience and reveal the shared challenges of forging new lives in unfamiliar lands.

Key Takeaways

DACA (Deferred Action for Childhood Arrivals) does not grant permanent legal status but allows certain undocumented immigrants who arrived as children to receive renewable work permits and protection from deportation.

Legal representation and community support are often critical in navigating the U.S. immigration system, highlighting the intersection of law and everyday life.

The stories above remind us that immigration law is not merely a set of rules—it is a living framework that shapes destinies. By understanding these lived experiences, we gain insight into the profound responsibilities and privileges that come with citizenship. As we turn to the next section, we will explore the full spectrum of rights and duties that define civic participation, deepening our appreciation for the legal bonds that unite us as a nation.

10.7 Comparative Immigration Systems

When considering the rights and duties that define civic participation, it is essential to place the U.S. immigration system within a broader global context. Immigration policies vary widely around the world, shaped by each nation's history, economy, and values. A comparative look not only highlights what is distinctive about the American approach but also offers insights into alternative models and their outcomes.

Models of Immigration: A Global Overview

Nations generally structure their immigration systems according to their social needs and philosophies. Broadly, these systems fall into several categories:

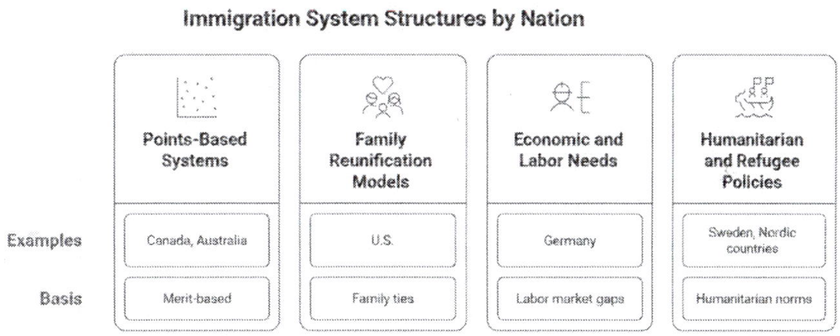

- **Points-Based Systems:** Countries like Canada and Australia use a merit-based approach, assigning points for factors such as education, language proficiency, work experience, and age.
- **Family Reunification Models:** The U.S. places significant emphasis on family ties, allowing citizens and lawful permanent residents to sponsor relatives for immigration.
- **Economic and Labor Needs:** Some nations, such as Germany, tailor their immigration flow to fill specific labor market gaps, offering temporary or permanent visas based on industry demands.
- **Humanitarian and Refugee Policies:** Sweden and other Nordic countries have historically provided generous pathways for asylum seekers and refugees, reflecting a commitment to international humanitarian norms.

Real-World Example: The U.S. and Canadian Systems

Consider the experience of Maria, a software engineer from Brazil. Seeking to immigrate, she investigates her options:

United States: Maria discovers that the U.S. primarily offers employment-based visas through employer sponsorship (like the H-1B program), with a complex lottery system and annual caps. Alternatively, she could pursue family-based immigration if she has relatives who are U.S. citizens or permanent residents.

Canada: In contrast, Canada's Express Entry system evaluates Maria's education, language skills, and work experience, assigning her a comprehensive score. If her score meets the annual cutoff, she could receive an invitation to apply for permanent residency without needing a job offer.

This comparison underscores how policy design affects individual opportunities and shapes the broader immigrant experience.

Historical Anecdote: Shifting American Priorities

The U.S. immigration system has evolved through several landmark changes. In 1965, the Immigration and Nationality Act replaced an ethnicity-based quota system with preferences for family reunification and skilled labor. This shift dramatically altered the demographic makeup of new arrivals, reflecting a broader commitment to equality and economic growth. Other countries have also adapted their laws in response to changing global realities—for example, Germany's recent reforms to attract skilled workers in response to demographic decline.

Key Differences and Shared Challenges

Despite differences, most developed nations face similar challenges:

- **Balancing Economic Needs and Social Integration:** How to attract talent while fostering community cohesion.
- **Responding to Humanitarian Crises:** Creating flexible pathways for refugees and asylum seekers.
- **Ensuring Security and Rule of Law:** Protecting borders without undermining civil liberties.

Nations frequently revisit their policies, learning from one another's successes and setbacks.

```
Remember: The U.S. immigration system is unique for its emphasis on family
reunification, but it is just one approach among many. Globally, immigration
```

```
laws reflect each country's priorities, and systems can change rapidly in
response to social or economic pressures.
```

In summary, understanding comparative immigration systems deepens our awareness of the U.S. legal framework and the global forces that shape it. By examining how other countries manage newcomers, we gain perspective on our own rights, responsibilities, and opportunities as members of a diverse and dynamic society. As we move to the next section, we will focus more closely on the practical steps and legal requirements for obtaining citizenship—a process that ties these comparative insights back to everyday life in the United States.

11 Crime, Punishment, and the Criminal Justice System

11.1 The Criminal Justice Process

When a crime is committed in the United States, the path from investigation to potential punishment follows a series of well-defined steps. Understanding this journey helps demystify what happens when individuals—or even entire communities—find themselves entangled in the criminal justice system.

1. Investigation and Arrest

The process begins with an **investigation**. Law enforcement officers gather evidence, interview witnesses, and, if there is enough **probable cause** (a reasonable belief that a crime has been committed), proceed to make an **arrest**. Probable cause is a crucial standard; without it, an arrest may violate constitutional rights.

> **Example:** In 2015, a widely publicized robbery in a New York City neighborhood was solved when detectives followed a trail of surveillance footage and eyewitness accounts, leading to the suspect's lawful arrest. The transparency and careful documentation of evidence were critical for ensuring a fair start to the process.

2. Booking and Initial Appearance

After arrest, the individual is **booked**—personal information is recorded, fingerprints and photos are taken, and the alleged crime is noted. Soon after, the accused appears before a judge in an **initial appearance**. Here, the judge reviews the charges and decides on bail, which is money or property pledged to ensure the accused's return for future court dates.

3. Charging and Arraignment

The **prosecutor** then reviews the evidence to determine what charges, if any, should be filed. In some cases, a **grand jury** reviews the evidence and votes on whether to indict (formally accuse) the defendant.

Arraignment is the defendant's first court appearance after charges are filed, where the charges are formally read, and the defendant enters a plea—typically "guilty," "not guilty," or "no contest."

4. Pretrial Motions and Discovery

Before trial, both sides exchange evidence in a process called **discovery**. Attorneys may file **pretrial motions** to exclude certain evidence, dismiss charges, or request a change of venue.

Historical Anecdote: The famous 1966 Miranda v. Arizona case established that suspects must be informed of their rights ("You have the right to remain silent...") before interrogation. This safeguard was born from the pretrial phase, ensuring that evidence gathered respects constitutional protections.

5. Trial

If the case goes to trial, both the prosecution and defense present their evidence and arguments. In most felony cases, a **jury** decides guilt or innocence. The **burden of proof** is on the prosecution, who must prove the defendant's guilt "beyond a reasonable doubt."

6. Sentencing

If found guilty, the defendant is sentenced—punishments may range from fines or community service to probation or incarceration, depending on the severity of the offense and sentencing guidelines.

7. Appeals

After sentencing, the defendant may appeal the verdict or sentence, arguing that legal errors affected the trial's outcome. Appeals courts review the case but do not retry facts.

```
Very Important:
A person is presumed innocent until proven guilty in a court of law. This
```

```
foundational principle protects individual rights and shapes every stage of
the criminal justice process.
```

The criminal justice process is designed to balance the interests of society and the rights of the accused, aiming for fairness and justice. Each stage—from arrest to appeal—offers safeguards intended to prevent abuses of power and wrongful convictions. As we move forward, we'll explore the consequences of criminal convictions and their impact on everyday life, highlighting why understanding this process is so vital for all residents.

11.2 Rights of the Accused

When someone is accused of a crime in the United States, the legal system is designed to protect their rights at every step. These protections are rooted in the U.S. Constitution, particularly in the **Bill of Rights**—the first ten amendments. The most crucial rights for the accused are found in the **Fourth**, **Fifth**, **Sixth**, and **Eighth Amendments**. These safeguards ensure justice and prevent abuses of power by the government.

Key rights of the accused include:

- **Protection against unreasonable searches and seizures** (Fourth Amendment): Law enforcement must have probable cause or a warrant to search you or your property.
- **Right to remain silent** (Fifth Amendment): You cannot be forced to testify against yourself—commonly known as "pleading the Fifth."
- **Right to due process** (Fifth and Fourteenth Amendments): Legal proceedings must be fair, and the government must respect all legal rights owed to a person.
- **Right to an attorney** (Sixth Amendment): If you cannot afford a lawyer, one will be appointed to you.
- **Right to a speedy and public trial by an impartial jury** (Sixth Amendment): This prevents indefinite detention and ensures your case is heard openly.
- **Protection against cruel and unusual punishment** (Eighth Amendment): Punishments must fit the crime and cannot be excessively harsh.

Miranda Rights: Words That Matter

One of the most recognizable examples of these protections in action is the **Miranda warning**. Originating from the 1966 U.S. Supreme Court case **Miranda v.**

Arizona, this requirement ensures that anyone taken into custody is informed of their rights before questioning begins. You've likely heard the familiar words in movies or television: "You have the right to remain silent. Anything you say can and will be used against you in a court of law..."

A real-world example: In 1963, Ernesto Miranda was arrested in Phoenix, Arizona, but was not informed of his rights before confessing to a crime. The Supreme Court later overturned his conviction, ruling that suspects must be informed of their rights to silence and legal counsel. This case reshaped police procedures nationwide.

The Importance of Legal Representation

The right to an attorney is more than a formality—it's a fundamental safeguard. Take the story of **Clarence Earl Gideon**, a Florida man accused of burglary in 1961. Too poor to hire a lawyer, Gideon was forced to defend himself and lost. From his prison cell, he petitioned the Supreme Court, which ruled in **Gideon v. Wainwright (1963)** that states must provide an attorney to anyone unable to afford one in criminal cases. This decision transformed the criminal justice system, ensuring legal support for millions of Americans.

The Legal Process: Step by Step

From arrest to trial, the accused has rights at every stage:

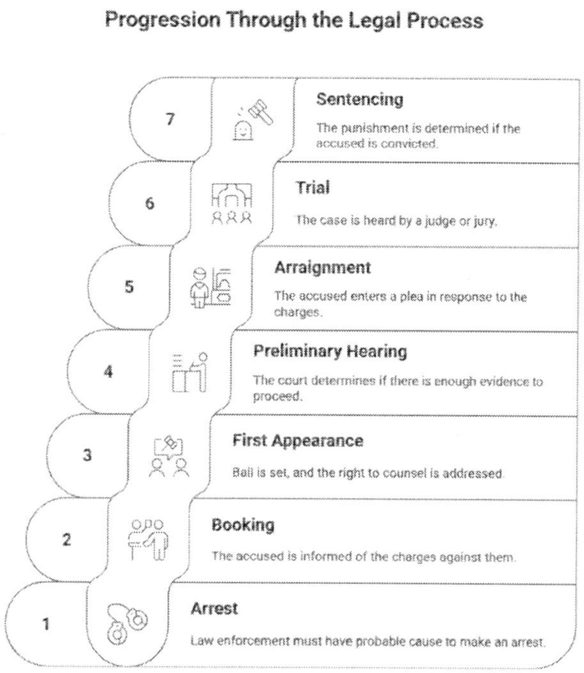

- **Arrest:** Law enforcement must have probable cause.
- **Booking:** The accused is informed of the charges.
- **First appearance:** Bail is set, and the right to counsel is addressed.
- **Preliminary hearing or grand jury:** The court determines if there is enough evidence to proceed.
- **Arraignment:** The accused enters a plea.
- **Trial:** The case is heard by a judge or jury.
- **Sentencing (if convicted):** The punishment is determined.

Global Perspectives: A Comparative View

While the U.S. system provides robust protections, other countries approach these rights differently. For example, in the United Kingdom, suspects have the right to remain silent but may face adverse inferences if they do not answer police questions. In Japan, suspects can be detained for up to 23 days before being charged, a stark contrast to the speedy trial rights in the U.S.

> Fact: The right to remain silent and the right to an attorney are not just formalities–they are critical protections that can be the difference between freedom and wrongful conviction.

The rights of the accused form the bedrock of the U.S. criminal justice system. By ensuring fairness and due process, these rights protect individuals from government overreach and uphold the principle of "innocent until proven guilty." As we move forward, we'll examine the consequences of criminal convictions—how they affect everything from employment to housing—emphasizing why understanding your rights is essential for navigating everyday life in America.

11.3 Types of Sentences and Punishments

After a criminal conviction—whether through a guilty plea or a trial verdict—the court must determine an appropriate punishment. The process of **sentencing** is guided by the severity of the crime, prior criminal history, state or federal guidelines, and sometimes, the specific circumstances of the offense. Sentences serve multiple purposes: punishing the offender, deterring future crime, rehabilitating the individual, and protecting society.

Common Types of Sentences

American courts have several sentencing options at their disposal. Each type reflects a different approach to justice and public safety.

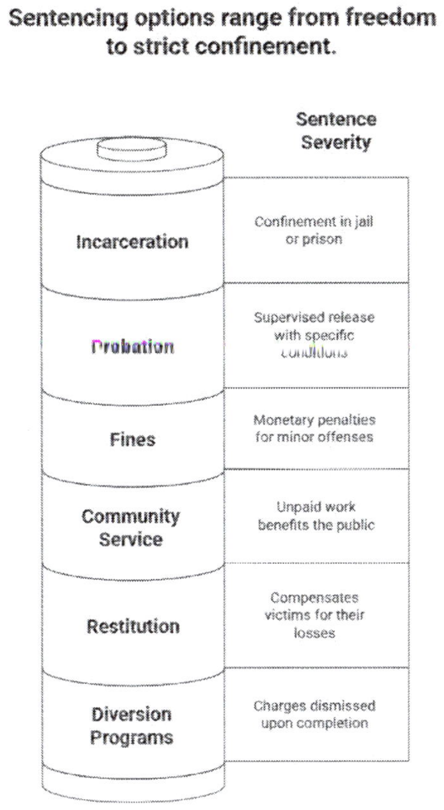

- **Incarceration:** The most severe and well-known penalty, incarceration involves confinement in jail (typically for less than a year) or prison (for longer sentences). For example, a felony conviction for armed robbery may result in a multi-year prison term.
- **Probation:** Rather than serve time behind bars, an individual may be placed under supervision in the community. They must comply with specific conditions, such as regular check-ins with a probation officer, drug testing, or attending counseling.
- **Fines:** Monetary penalties are often imposed for lesser offenses, such as traffic violations or misdemeanors like petty theft.
- **Community Service:** Courts sometimes require offenders to complete a certain number of unpaid work hours for public benefit, such as cleaning parks or assisting charitable organizations.
- **Restitution:** Offenders may be ordered to compensate victims directly for losses suffered, such as property damage or medical bills.

- **Diversion Programs:** For first-time or low-level offenders, some jurisdictions offer programs focused on treatment or education, allowing charges to be dismissed upon successful completion.

Sentencing Example: The Case of Shoplifting

Consider the story of Maria, a first-time offender caught shoplifting a $50 item. Instead of jail, the judge placed her on probation, required her to attend a theft-awareness class, and ordered restitution to the store. Maria's experience illustrates how sentencing can be tailored to the crime's context and the offender's background, focusing on accountability and rehabilitation rather than harsh punishment.

Severity of Punishments: Misdemeanors vs. Felonies

The law distinguishes **misdemeanors** (less serious crimes) from **felonies** (more severe crimes), with corresponding differences in punishment:

Misdemeanors: Typically carry a maximum sentence of one year in jail, lower fines, or both. Examples include disorderly conduct or minor assault.
Felonies: Can result in prison sentences exceeding one year, substantial fines, and long-term consequences such as loss of voting rights or difficulty securing employment.

Historical Perspective: The Three Strikes Law

In the 1990s, several states enacted "Three Strikes" laws, mandating severe sentences for repeat offenders. In California, for example, a third felony conviction—even for a nonviolent crime—could mean 25 years to life in prison. These laws were intended to deter habitual criminals but sparked debate over fairness and effectiveness, prompting reforms in later years.

Alternatives and Global Comparisons

Other countries often take different approaches to sentencing. For instance, Scandinavian nations emphasize rehabilitation over incarceration, with markedly lower prison populations and recidivism rates. The U.S. system, by comparison, has historically leaned toward longer sentences, especially for drug-related offenses.

Collateral Consequences

Beyond the immediate sentence, a criminal conviction can have lasting effects—known as **collateral consequences**—such as loss of professional licenses, housing difficulties, or ineligibility for federal benefits. These impacts underscore why understanding sentencing is vital for every resident.

```
Remember: Even a minor criminal conviction can affect your life for years to
come—impacting your job prospects, housing, and more. Always seek legal
counsel if you face criminal charges.
```

In summary, sentencing in the U.S. legal system reflects a balance of punishment, deterrence, and rehabilitation. Understanding the types and consequences of sentences helps individuals better navigate their rights and responsibilities. Next, we'll explore the appeals process and what options are available when a conviction or sentence seems unjust, continuing our journey through the complexities of the criminal justice system.

11.4 Juvenile Justice

The **juvenile justice system** is a specialized branch of the U.S. legal system designed to address crimes committed by persons under the age of 18. Unlike the adult system, which emphasizes punishment and deterrence, juvenile justice prioritizes **rehabilitation, education, and the welfare of young offenders**. This approach recognizes that children and teenagers are still developing, both emotionally and cognitively, and that early intervention can help redirect them toward productive, law-abiding futures.

Key Features of the Juvenile Justice System

- **Separate Courts and Facilities:** Juvenile cases are typically handled in family or juvenile courts, with proceedings closed to the public to protect minors' privacy. Detained juveniles are held in facilities distinct from adult jails or prisons.
- **Different Terminology:** Juvenile offenders are often called "respondents" or "delinquents" rather than "defendants" or "criminals." Sentences are referred to as "dispositions."
- **Emphasis on Rehabilitation:** Courts often order counseling, community service, education, or treatment programs instead of incarceration.
- **Limited Public Record:** Juvenile records are generally sealed or expunged once the individual reaches adulthood, allowing them to move forward without the stigma of a criminal record.

The Path of a Juvenile Case

A juvenile's journey through the justice system typically follows these steps:

- **Arrest or Detention:** Law enforcement may take a minor into custody if they are suspected of a crime. In many cases, the officer has discretion to release the youth to their parents or refer the case to juvenile court.

- **Intake:** A probation officer or prosecutor reviews the case to determine if formal charges are necessary or if the matter can be handled informally.
- **Adjudication Hearing:** If the case proceeds, a judge (not a jury) hears the evidence and decides if the minor is "delinquent"—the juvenile equivalent of being found guilty.
- **Disposition:** If adjudicated delinquent, the judge orders a disposition, which may include probation, community service, counseling, or placement in a juvenile facility.

When Juveniles Are Tried as Adults

In some cases, particularly where violent felonies are involved, juveniles may be transferred to adult court. Factors considered include:

- The nature and severity of the offense
- The minor's age and prior record
- The likelihood of rehabilitation within the juvenile system

Case Example: In 1999, the tragic Columbine High School shooting led to national debate over whether young offenders accused of serious crimes should be tried as adults. Many states subsequently passed laws lowering the age at which juveniles can be transferred to adult court, especially for violent offenses.

Real-World Impact: A Second Chance

Consider the story of "Jordan," a 16-year-old from California who was arrested for burglary. Instead of incarceration, he participated in a restorative justice program: meeting with the victims, apologizing, and completing community service. This approach, common in many juvenile systems, allowed him to repair harm and avoid a criminal record, highlighting the system's rehabilitative focus.

Global Perspectives

While the U.S. juvenile justice system is distinct, many countries share similar principles. For example, Sweden emphasizes mediation and family involvement, while Japan encourages community-based rehabilitation. This reflects a global understanding that young people deserve opportunities for growth and change.

```
Juvenile court records are generally sealed to protect a young person's future
opportunities, but serious offenses may still impact eligibility for some jobs
or college admissions.
```

In summary, the juvenile justice system embodies the belief that youth deserve a chance to learn from their mistakes and build better lives. As we continue, we'll examine the appeals process—another vital component in ensuring fairness and justice within both adult and juvenile systems—helping you understand what options exist when a decision seems unjust.

11.5 Victims' Rights and Support

The U.S. criminal justice system has historically focused on prosecuting offenders and ensuring due process for the accused. For much of American history, crime victims had little formal role in legal proceedings. However, as public awareness grew regarding the impacts of crime on individuals and communities, so too did the movement to recognize and protect **victims' rights**. The 1980s marked a turning point: advocacy groups and survivors themselves demanded greater consideration and institutional support.

One foundational milestone was the passage of the **Victims of Crime Act (VOCA) of 1984**. This federal law established a fund to support victim assistance programs, helping to provide much-needed resources such as counseling, shelters, and compensation for medical bills or lost wages. Today, all 50 states have some form of a **victims' bill of rights**, which typically guarantees certain protections and participation for those harmed by crime.

Key Rights Afforded to Crime Victims

While laws vary by state, most U.S. jurisdictions recognize several core rights for crime victims:

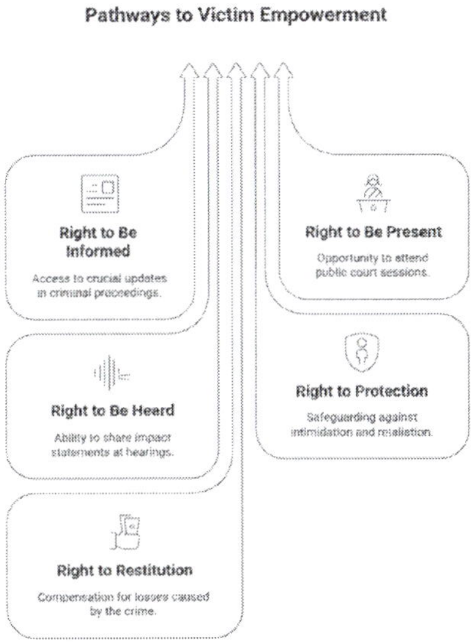

- **The right to be informed** about significant stages in the criminal process, including arrest, bail hearings, trial dates, and parole decisions.
- **The right to be present** at public court proceedings involving the accused.
- **The right to be heard**, often through a victim impact statement at sentencing or parole hearings.
- **The right to protection** from intimidation, harassment, or retaliation.
- **The right to restitution**, meaning the offender may be ordered to pay for losses directly resulting from the crime.

These rights are not just symbolic; they aim to restore a sense of voice and agency to those affected by crime.

Real-World Example: The Role of Victim Impact Statements

Consider the case of **Mary Johnson**, whose son was killed in a violent crime. At the sentencing hearing, Mary was able to deliver a powerful victim impact statement describing the emotional and financial toll her son's death had on her family. Her testimony didn't change the verdict, but it influenced the judge's sentencing decision and allowed her to express her grief and hopes for justice. Experiences like Mary's have led many states to formalize the right of victims to participate directly in the judicial process.

Support Services for Victims

Beyond legal rights, a network of support services exists to help victims recover and rebuild:

- **Crisis hotlines** offer immediate emotional support.
- **Victim advocacy organizations** provide guidance through complex legal processes.
- **Compensation programs** may reimburse out-of-pocket expenses related to the crime.
- **Shelters and counseling** services address the needs of victims of domestic violence, sexual assault, and other trauma.

Victims are often overwhelmed, confused, or fearful after a crime. These services help ensure that people receive not just justice, but also compassion and practical assistance.

Diverse Perspectives: Learning from Global Practices

Globally, the recognition of victims' rights varies. For example, **South Africa's Truth and Reconciliation Commission** in the 1990s placed victims' stories at the center of national healing, offering public acknowledgment and restitution as part of restorative justice. In contrast, some countries in Europe, such as Sweden, offer stronger government-funded support for victims, including automatic legal representation and long-term mental health care. These models have influenced American advocacy efforts, reminding us that justice is not only about punishment but also about healing and restoration.

```
Victim impact statements allow individuals harmed by a crime to address the
court directly—this right is now protected in all 50 states.
Victims of Crime Act (VOCA) funding has provided billions of dollars in aid
for crime victims since 1984.
```

As we reflect on the progress and ongoing challenges in supporting victims, it's clear that their voices are now a central part of the criminal justice process. Ensuring their rights and providing comprehensive support is essential for a just society. Next, we'll explore the ways legal evidence shapes the outcomes of criminal cases, and why understanding the rules of evidence is crucial for both the accused and the accuser.

11.6 Social Impact of Crime and Punishment

When a crime is committed, its effects rarely end with the accused and the victim. Instead, the impact spreads outward, touching families, neighborhoods, and sometimes entire communities. The **social impact of crime and punishment** is a complex web, influencing public trust, economic stability, and even the way people interact with one another in daily life.

Consider the aftermath of a burglary in a small town. Beyond the immediate loss for the victim, neighbors may feel anxious, leading to increased security measures, changes in routines, or even mistrust among residents. **Fear of crime** can discourage social gatherings, decrease property values, and erode the sense of community that binds people together.

The Cycle of Punishment and Its Broader Effects

Punishment, intended to deter and correct criminal behavior, carries its own set of consequences. The U.S. criminal justice system, particularly through incarceration, has a profound effect not only on offenders but also on their families and social networks.

- **Family disruption:** When a parent is incarcerated, children may face emotional trauma, financial instability, and diminished educational opportunities.
- **Economic fallout:** Formerly incarcerated individuals often struggle to find employment due to criminal records, perpetuating cycles of poverty.
- **Community disintegration:** High rates of incarceration within certain neighborhoods can weaken social ties, foster distrust in institutions, and reduce political participation.

A Closer Look: The Story of "Three Strikes" Laws

In the 1990s, many states adopted **"three strikes" laws**, mandating significantly harsher sentences for individuals convicted of a third felony. While these laws aimed to deter repeat offenders, their social impact was far-reaching. In California, for example, the law led to a dramatic increase in the prison population, disproportionately affecting communities of color. Families found themselves separated for decades, and communities with high rates of incarceration faced increased unemployment, strained public resources, and deepening poverty.

Restorative Justice: An Alternative Approach

Recognizing the limitations and unintended consequences of traditional punishment, some communities have turned to **restorative justice**. This approach emphasizes repairing harm, reconciliation, and community involvement rather than simply punishing offenders.

- **Victim-offender dialogues:** Direct meetings between victims and offenders can foster understanding, closure, and sometimes forgiveness.
- **Community service:** Offenders contribute positively to their neighborhoods, helping to restore trust and demonstrate accountability.
- **Reduced recidivism:** Studies show that restorative justice programs can reduce the likelihood of repeat offenses, benefitting both individuals and society at large.

Global Perspective: Norway's Emphasis on Rehabilitation

Globally, different countries approach crime and punishment in varied ways. Norway's criminal justice system, for example, prioritizes rehabilitation over retribution. Prisons focus on preparing inmates for reintegration into society, with education, job training, and counseling. As a result, Norway boasts one of the lowest recidivism rates in the world—a stark contrast to the U.S., where punishment often eclipses rehabilitation.

Public Perception and Policy Shifts

The social impact of crime and punishment shapes, and is shaped by, public opinion and political will. Events such as the **war on drugs** in the 1980s and 1990s led to tougher sentencing laws and a dramatic increase in incarceration rates, especially for nonviolent offenses. In recent years, growing awareness of these consequences has spurred calls for reform, including sentencing changes, expanded reentry programs, and efforts to address the root causes of crime.

Reflecting on these dynamics reminds us that the law is not just an abstract set of rules, but a living force with real world consequences for all. By understanding the broader social effects of crime and punishment, we prepare ourselves to advocate for a justice system that serves everyone fairly. Up next, we'll dive into the rules of legal evidence—how facts are established in court, and why this process is at the heart of both justice and fairness in the U.S. legal system.

11.7 Global Approaches to Justice

The U.S. criminal justice system is just one approach among many, shaped by the nation's unique history, values, and constitutional framework. To better understand how justice is served—and sometimes denied—it's enlightening to look beyond our borders. Different societies have crafted their own methods for addressing crime, punishment, and rehabilitation, each reflecting their cultural priorities and historical challenges.

Civil Law vs. Common Law Traditions

Globally, two dominant legal traditions prevail: **common law** and **civil law** systems.

In **common law** countries like the United States, United Kingdom, and Canada, court decisions (precedents) play a major role. Judges interpret laws, and these interpretations shape future rulings.

Civil law systems, found in nations such as France, Germany, and Japan, rely more heavily on comprehensive legal codes. Judges apply these written statutes and have less discretion to interpret law creatively.

Both systems strive for justice, but they differ in how rules are created, interpreted, and enforced.

Restorative Justice in New Zealand

One global example that challenges conventional punishment is New Zealand's use of **restorative justice**—particularly in its treatment of juvenile offenders and in partnership with the indigenous Māori community. Instead of focusing solely on punishment, restorative justice aims to repair harm by bringing together victims, offenders, and community members to discuss the impact of the crime and develop a plan for making amends.

This process may involve apologies, restitution, community service, or other acts of reparation.

Studies have shown that restorative justice in New Zealand often leads to lower recidivism rates and greater victim satisfaction.

This model is increasingly influential worldwide, prompting U.S. communities to experiment with similar practices, especially for non-violent offenses.

The Scandinavian Model: Rehabilitation Over Retribution

In contrast, Scandinavian countries like Norway and Sweden emphasize **rehabilitation** over retribution. Their prisons are designed to resemble small communities, with comfortable living conditions, educational programs, and psychological support. The underlying philosophy holds that treating offenders humanely and preparing them for reintegration into society reduces the likelihood of reoffending.

A famous example is **Halden Prison** in Norway, often described as the "world's most humane prison." Inmates have private rooms, access to nature, and are encouraged to maintain contact with families. Norway's recidivism rate is among the lowest globally—roughly half that of the U.S.—suggesting that fostering dignity and growth might serve public safety as well as, or better than, harsher punishments.

Perspectives from the United States

While the U.S. system is grounded in due process and constitutional rights, it has historically leaned toward punitive measures—mandatory minimum sentences, three-strikes laws, and lengthy incarcerations. However, recent years have seen a growing interest in integrating rehabilitative and restorative practices, inspired by global examples.

For instance, some U.S. states are piloting diversion programs that direct non-violent offenders to counseling or treatment instead of jail. Others are revisiting sentencing laws to reduce overcrowding and address systemic inequalities.

Global Lessons for Everyday Life

These international examples show that justice is not a one-size-fits-all concept. Each system reflects its society's values and priorities—whether it's the U.S. focus on due process, New Zealand's communal healing, or Norway's emphasis on rehabilitation. By understanding these global approaches, Americans can better appreciate both the strengths and limitations of their own system, and perhaps find inspiration for reform.

```
A fair trial is a core principle shared by most legal systems worldwide; in
the U.S., the right to due process is protected by the Constitution and
ensures everyone receives a fair hearing before punishment is imposed.
```

```
Restorative justice and rehabilitation are gaining traction globally,
influencing reforms in the U.S. criminal justice system, especially for
juveniles and non-violent offenders.
```

As we've seen, justice takes many forms across the globe, each offering valuable lessons for creating a fairer society. Next, we'll turn our attention to the rules of legal evidence—how facts are established in court, why these rules matter, and how they help ensure justice is more than just an ideal, but a reality for all.

12 Everyday Legal Safety and Taking Action

12.1 Preventing Legal Trouble

Staying on the right side of the law is not just about avoiding trouble—it's about developing habits and attitudes that foster responsible citizenship and personal well-being. Every day, people make choices that, knowingly or not, can have legal consequences. By understanding the most common pitfalls and adopting preventative strategies, you can safeguard yourself, your loved ones, and your community.

Common Scenarios Leading to Legal Issues

Legal trouble often arises from routine situations—sometimes, a simple oversight is all it takes. Consider these everyday examples:

- **Driving without a valid license or insurance**: Many states report thousands of citations each year for this infraction.
- **Unknowingly trespassing**: Walking through a shortcut in a neighbor's yard might seem harmless, but it can lead to a civil suit.
- **Signing contracts without reading the fine print**: This can result in unexpected debts or obligations.
- **Posting defamatory comments online**: In today's digital age, online statements can have serious, lasting legal repercussions.

One real-world example involves **Maria**, a recent college graduate, who agreed to sublet her apartment to a friend. She failed to check her lease agreement, which prohibited subletting without landlord approval. When the landlord discovered the arrangement, Maria faced eviction and lost her security deposit. This scenario underscores the importance of understanding and following contractual obligations.

Steps to Prevent Legal Trouble

Legal awareness is your best defense. Here are practical strategies to help you avoid common mistakes:

Educate Yourself

- Familiarize yourself with local, state, and federal laws relevant to your daily life.
- Take advantage of community legal clinics or online resources for up-to-date information.

Keep Records

- Maintain copies of important documents: contracts, receipts, correspondence, and legal notices.
- In disputes, documentation can be your strongest ally.

Pause Before You Act

- If you're unsure whether something is legal—such as starting a home business or modifying your property—pause and research or seek professional advice.

Communicate Clearly

- Be transparent and honest in your dealings, whether with neighbors, employers, or authorities.

Practice Responsible Digital Behavior

- Remember, what you post online is often permanent and can be used as evidence in legal proceedings.

Global Perspective: Learning from Other Systems

Other countries' legal systems provide instructive contrasts. In **Japan**, for instance, the concept of **giri** (social duty) strongly influences behavior—people often avoid legal disputes through mediation and mutual agreement, rather than litigation. Similarly, **Germany's** comprehensive system of public signage and clear rules helps minimize misunderstandings that could lead to legal violations, especially for newcomers.

When the Unexpected Happens

Even with the best intentions, misunderstandings or honest mistakes can occur. The key is to respond promptly and appropriately:

- Acknowledge the issue if you are at fault.
- Seek legal advice before making statements or signing agreements related to the incident.
- Cooperate respectfully with law enforcement or regulatory authorities.

```
In the U.S., ignorance of the law is not a valid defense—everyone is presumed
to know the law, even if they have never read it.
```

Preventing legal trouble is less about fear and more about proactive, informed living. By staying aware, organized, and thoughtful in your actions, you can navigate daily life with greater confidence and security. As we move forward, the next section will guide you through what to do if you find yourself facing a legal issue—empowering you with knowledge to protect your rights and interests when challenges arise.

12.2 Finding and Working with Legal Professionals

Legal challenges often come unexpectedly—a car accident, a landlord dispute, or receiving a court summons. In these moments, knowing when and how to seek professional help is crucial. While some everyday issues can be managed independently, others require the expertise of a trained **attorney** to navigate complex laws, protect your rights, and advocate on your behalf.

- **Criminal Charges:** If you're accused of a crime, an attorney ensures due process and may significantly affect the outcome.
- **Civil Disputes:** Property disagreements, contract issues, or personal injury claims often benefit from legal guidance.
- **Family Matters:** Divorce, custody, or immigration cases involve sensitive laws and high stakes.

How to Find the Right Legal Professional

The U.S. legal system offers a variety of resources to connect people with qualified attorneys. Whether you need a specialist in immigration, real estate, or criminal defense, the following steps can help:

- **Identify Your Legal Need:** Clarify the issue—criminal, civil, family, or business law—to search for attorneys with relevant experience.
- **Seek Referrals:** Ask friends, family, or coworkers for recommendations. Personal experiences often reveal trustworthy professionals.
- **Use Bar Association Directories:** State and local bar associations provide searchable databases by specialization and location.
- **Explore Legal Aid Organizations:** For those with limited means, nonprofits and legal clinics offer free or low-cost assistance.
- **Check Credentials:** Confirm the attorney's license and standing via your state bar's website.

Real-World Example: Navigating a Car Accident

When **Maria**, a recent immigrant, was involved in a minor car accident, she faced not only damage to her vehicle but also confusion about insurance claims and potential liability. Unsure of her rights and obligations, Maria reached out to a local legal aid clinic. The attorney helped her understand her responsibilities, draft her insurance claim, and negotiate with the other party, preventing unnecessary costs and stress.

What to Expect When Working with an Attorney

Once you've selected an attorney, the relationship is built on clear communication, mutual respect, and confidentiality. Here's what the process typically looks like:

- **Initial Consultation:** Many attorneys offer a first meeting—sometimes free—to discuss your situation and outline possible strategies.
- **Fee Agreements:** Understand costs upfront. Fees may be hourly, flat, or contingency-based (the attorney only gets paid if you win).
- **Attorney-Client Privilege:** Anything you share is confidential, encouraging honesty and openness.
- **Active Participation:** Stay engaged—ask questions, provide documents, and update your attorney about new developments.

Historical Anecdote: Gideon v. Wainwright

In 1963, **Clarence Earl Gideon** was charged with a felony in Florida but couldn't afford an attorney. He represented himself and was convicted. Later, the Supreme Court ruled in **Gideon v. Wainwright** that every criminal defendant has the right to legal counsel, regardless of ability to pay. This landmark decision ensures fair trials and underscores the importance of access to professional legal help.

```
Did you know?

In the U.S., every person accused of a serious crime has the constitutional
right to an attorney—even if they cannot afford one. This right is a
cornerstone of justice and due process.
```

Finding and working with legal professionals can make the difference between confusion and confidence when legal issues arise. By understanding when to seek help, how to choose the right attorney, and what to expect from the professional relationship, you empower yourself to navigate the legal system wisely. In the next section, we'll explore what steps to take if you're facing a legal dispute—so you can act strategically and protect your interests from the very start.

12.3 Resolving Disputes Without Court

For many, the idea of stepping into a courtroom conjures images of drama and high stakes. While courts are essential for justice, they are not always the best or only path to resolving disputes. In fact, most conflicts between individuals, neighbors, or businesses never reach a judge's bench. Instead, people often turn to **Alternative Dispute Resolution (ADR)**—a set of practical methods designed to settle disagreements efficiently, privately, and often at lower cost.

Common Approaches to Alternative Dispute Resolution

- **Negotiation**: The most informal approach, negotiation involves the parties directly communicating to reach a mutually agreeable solution. No outside parties are needed—just a willingness to talk and compromise.
- **Mediation**: Here, a neutral third party called a **mediator** helps both sides discuss the issue and explore solutions. Mediators do not decide the outcome but guide the conversation, helping the parties find common ground.
- **Arbitration**: More formal than mediation, arbitration involves a neutral third party (the **arbitrator**) who listens to both sides and makes a binding or non-binding decision, much like a judge, but usually in a private setting.

Pathways to Agreement

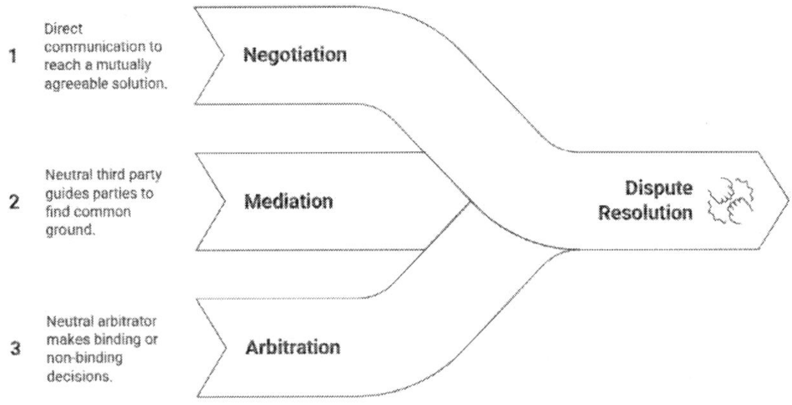

When Should You Consider ADR?

ADR can be highly effective for:

- Family disagreements, such as custody or property division
- Landlord-tenant disputes
- Consumer complaints against businesses

- Workplace issues, including wrongful termination or discrimination claims
- Small business contract disagreements

A Real-World Example: Mediation in the Neighborhood

Consider the story of Maria and James, neighbors in a bustling suburban community. When a tree on Maria's property grew so large its roots threatened James's driveway, tempers flared. Rather than filing a lawsuit, they agreed to mediation through a local community program. The mediator facilitated a respectful dialogue, helping them agree that Maria would trim the tree and share the cost of driveway repairs. They avoided court fees, preserved their neighborly relationship, and reached a solution neither could have managed alone.

The Process: What to Expect

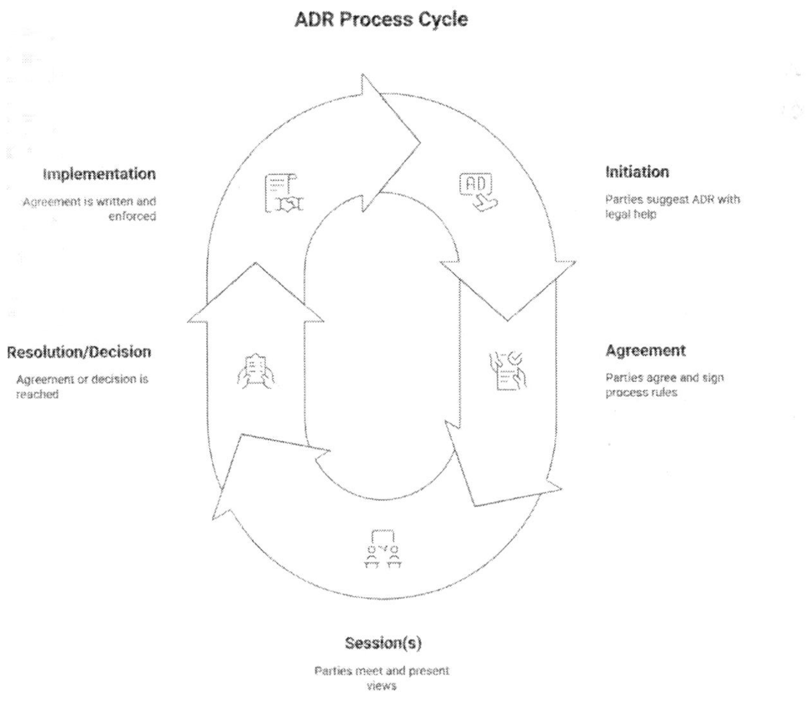

- **Initiation**: One or both parties suggest ADR, often with the help of a lawyer or community organization.
- **Agreement**: Both sides agree to participate and may sign a document outlining the process and ground rules.

- **Session(s)**: At a scheduled time, parties meet with the mediator or arbitrator. Each side presents their view.
- **Resolution or Decision**: In mediation, parties craft their own agreement. In arbitration, the arbitrator issues a decision.
- **Implementation**: If an agreement is reached, it is put in writing and, if necessary, made legally enforceable.

The Benefits and Limitations

Benefits:

- Lower cost and faster resolution than court
- Privacy and confidentiality
- Flexibility in crafting creative solutions
- Preservation of relationships

Limitations:

- ADR relies on the willingness of both parties to participate and compromise
- Not suitable for all cases, such as serious criminal matters or when urgent legal protection is needed

A Global Perspective

In Japan, **conciliation** centers have long provided a culturally accepted, non-adversarial way to resolve civil disputes. In South Africa, community-based mediators have played a vital role in post-apartheid reconciliation, showing that peaceful resolution is valued across cultures and legal systems.

```
Most civil disputes in the U.S. are resolved without going to court—through
negotiation, mediation, or arbitration. Choosing ADR can save time, money, and
stress, and often leads to more satisfying outcomes for everyone involved.
```

In summary, resolving disputes without court not only preserves resources but often leads to fairer, more durable solutions. By understanding and considering ADR, you empower yourself to act wisely when conflicts arise. In the next section, we'll examine what to do when legal action becomes unavoidable—so you can face the courtroom with confidence and preparation.

12.4 Taking Action in Your Community

When legal issues touch your neighborhood or community, knowing how to take effective action is vital. Every resident has a stake in shaping local laws and ensuring they are applied fairly. Whether advocating for safer streets, responding to unfair housing practices, or addressing environmental concerns, community engagement is a cornerstone of a healthy legal system.

Steps to Getting Involved

Taking action doesn't always mean going to court. Often, meaningful change begins with a few determined individuals who understand their rights and responsibilities—and know how to mobilize others. Here's how you can get started:

Identify the Issue

Begin by clarifying the legal or safety concern. Is it a new traffic pattern causing confusion? A landlord neglecting basic repairs? Document what you see, collect evidence, and talk with others affected.

Know the Law

Research local ordinances, state statutes, or federal regulations related to your concern. This knowledge empowers you to speak confidently and propose solutions rooted in law.

Build Coalitions

Connect with neighbors, local organizations, or advocacy groups who share your concerns. Collective voices carry more weight than individuals acting alone.

Engage with Authorities

Attend city council meetings, contact local representatives, or write formal complaints. Use public comment periods to express your views and present evidence.

Use Legal Tools

Sometimes, formal legal action—like filing a complaint with a housing authority or seeking a court order—may be necessary. If so, consider seeking guidance from local legal aid organizations.

Real-World Example: The Power of Grassroots Advocacy

In the early 2000s, residents of a small town in California noticed an increase in bicycle accidents at a dangerous intersection. Rather than waiting for a tragedy, they organized neighborhood meetings, gathered statistics on accidents, and launched a petition. By presenting their findings at city hall and working with local officials, they secured funding for new signage and a crosswalk. This example demonstrates how everyday people, armed with legal awareness and determination, can effect real change.

Historical Anecdote: Civil Rights and Community Action

During the Civil Rights Movement, ordinary citizens used their understanding of constitutional rights to challenge unjust laws. The Montgomery Bus Boycott (1955-1956) began when Rosa Parks refused to give up her seat. The boycott was organized not just as a protest, but as a carefully coordinated legal action—resulting in a Supreme Court decision that desegregated public transportation. This moment in history highlights the profound impact of community-led legal action.

Global Perspective: Participatory Governance

Other countries also recognize the value of civic participation. In Brazil, for example, participatory budgeting allows citizens to propose and vote on local government projects, giving legal weight to community voices. This approach strengthens democracy and legal accountability—a reminder that the U.S. system is part of a broader global movement toward community empowerment.

Key Takeaways for Taking Action

Stay informed: Understanding the law is your first line of defense and advocacy.

Collaborate: Individual voices are powerful, but coalitions amplify impact.

Engage constructively: Work with, not against, authorities where possible.

```
Did you know?

Community members can request access to many government records through the
Freedom of Information Act (FOIA), strengthening transparency and
accountability.
```

Reflection and Looking Ahead

Taking action in your community bridges the gap between legal knowledge and everyday impact. Whether advocating for better services or fighting injustice, your participation strengthens the legal fabric that protects everyone. As we move to the next section—navigating the courtroom—you'll learn how to build on this foundation, ensuring your rights are protected when legal action becomes necessary.

12.5 Digital Tools and Legal Resources

In today's world, access to legal information and assistance has been transformed by technology. Where once a simple legal query might have required a trip to a law library or a costly consultation, now a wealth of resources is available at your fingertips. Digital tools have made it easier than ever to stay legally safe, informed, and prepared for action—whether you're facing a traffic ticket, reviewing a lease, or preparing for court.

Online Legal Platforms

Several reputable websites and mobile apps provide **legal advice**, document templates, and research tools. These platforms often cater to individuals without legal backgrounds, using plain language and user-friendly interfaces. Some of the most notable include:

- **LegalZoom**: Offers affordable legal forms and the option to consult with attorneys for personal or business matters.
- **Nolo**: Provides extensive guides, articles, and do-it-yourself forms for common legal issues.
- **Rocket Lawyer**: Allows users to create and sign legal documents, and access on-demand attorney advice.
- **LawHelp.org**: Connects people with local legal aid and information tailored to specific states and regions.

For urgent matters, many state court systems now maintain official websites with up-to-date information on filing procedures, court calendars, and downloadable forms. These can be invaluable for those representing themselves—commonly called **pro se litigants**.

Accessing Public Records

Transparency is a cornerstone of the U.S. legal system. Many court records, criminal histories, property deeds, and business licenses are searchable online. Knowing how to access these records can empower you to:

Check the background of a potential tenant or employee
Verify the legal status of a property before making a purchase
Monitor the progress of a legal case

A remarkable example of this digital shift is the **Public Access to Court Electronic Records (PACER)** system, which provides electronic access to federal court records. While some records require a nominal fee, many are free or can be accessed through local libraries.

Legal Aid and Hotlines

For individuals facing urgent legal trouble or who cannot afford private counsel, digital tools have expanded access to help:

- **National Domestic Violence Hotline**: Offers confidential legal and safety resources online and by phone.
- **Immigration Advocates Network**: Maintains a searchable directory of nonprofit immigration legal services.
- **State Bar Association Websites**: Most states offer lawyer referral services and guidance on how to file complaints or seek low-cost legal assistance.

Real-World Example

Consider the story of Maria, a recent immigrant who received an eviction notice. Unsure of her rights, she turned to LawHelp.org, where she found detailed state-specific information about tenant protections. Using free templates and guides, Maria responded to her landlord and connected with a local legal aid organization, ultimately reaching a fair agreement without going to court. Digital access transformed a potentially devastating situation into an empowering one.

```
Very important: Not all online legal resources are created equal. Always
verify the credibility of digital legal tools and consult a licensed attorney
for serious or complex matters.
```

Global Glimpses

The U.S. is not alone in integrating technology into its legal system. Countries like Estonia have pioneered digital court filings, while India's eCourts initiative aims to reduce backlog and improve transparency. These examples show a growing international trend: technology as a tool for justice, not just convenience.

Digital tools are reshaping how everyday people interact with the law, breaking down barriers and building new pathways to justice. As you explore these resources, remember the importance of discerning fact from fiction online. Next, we'll step into the courtroom—demystifying what happens in legal proceedings, and equipping you with knowledge to navigate these pivotal moments with confidence.

12.6 Reflections from Diverse Voices

Legal safety is not just a matter of knowing statutes—it is a lived experience, shaped by community, culture, and personal history. As we explore how to protect ourselves and take action in everyday situations, it's vital to listen to diverse voices.

Their stories illuminate not only the challenges within the U.S. legal system, but also the resilience and resourcefulness people bring to their encounters with the law.

Lessons from Immigrant Communities

For many newcomers, understanding the U.S. legal system can be daunting. Take the story of **Marisol**, who arrived from El Salvador with her family. At a routine traffic stop, she was unsure whether she was required to show identification beyond her driver's license. Drawing on advice from her local immigrant support group, Marisol learned that she had the right to remain silent and to ask if she was free to leave. This awareness transformed a moment of fear into one of empowerment. Her experience highlights key points:

Knowing your rights during police interactions can prevent misunderstandings.
Community organizations often provide culturally relevant legal education.
Language barriers can complicate legal safety; having key phrases or a translator can be invaluable.

Marisol's story is echoed in communities around the world. In the United Kingdom, for instance, "stop and search" procedures similarly challenge immigrants and minorities, sparking public debates about fairness and accountability.

Youth and the Power of Legal Awareness

Younger generations are also shaping the meaning of legal safety. **Darius**, a high school senior from Chicago, became an advocate after witnessing friends detained for minor infractions. His school's "Know Your Rights" club now teaches students about:

- The difference between **arrest** and **detainment**.
- How to record police encounters safely and legally.
- Paths to seek legal assistance if rights are violated.

Darius's initiative was inspired by global movements, such as the "Street Law" program in South Africa, which uses peer education to foster legal confidence among youth in historically marginalized communities.

Bridging Gaps in Rural America

Legal safety concerns are not exclusive to cities or newcomers. In rural regions, where legal resources may be sparse, everyday challenges require creative solutions. **Sarah**, a farmer in Nebraska, faced a property dispute with a neighboring landowner.

With limited access to attorneys, she relied on her local library's legal self-help materials and online forums to prepare her case. For Sarah and many like her:

- Public libraries serve as vital legal information hubs.
- Online legal clinics can bridge geographic gaps.
- Knowing how to document evidence—such as taking photographs or keeping written records—can make a crucial difference.

The Ongoing Journey Toward Justice

These stories underscore the universal importance of legal safety, as well as the unique ways individuals and communities respond to legal challenges. Whether through grassroots education, peer support, or self-advocacy, ordinary people are shaping a more accessible and accountable legal system.

```
In the U.S., you always have the right to remain silent when questioned by law
enforcement-a right protected by the Fifth Amendment. Exercising this right
cannot be used against you in court.

Legal aid organizations provide free or low-cost assistance to millions of
people each year, ensuring access to justice regardless of financial means.
```

In summary, everyday legal safety is best achieved when individuals are informed, connected, and empowered. From city streets to rural farmlands, diverse voices remind us that legal knowledge is not just a shield—it's a bridge to mutual understanding and justice. As we turn to the next chapter, we'll step inside the courtroom, demystifying what happens during legal proceedings and equipping you with the tools to navigate these pivotal moments with confidence.

12.7 Looking Forward: The Evolving Role of Law

The law is not a static set of rules etched in stone but a living framework that evolves alongside society. As our communities, technologies, and values shift, so too does the way the law operates in our everyday lives. The role of law is to provide order and fairness, but it also responds to new challenges—sometimes slowly, sometimes with surprising speed.

One striking example is how U.S. laws have adapted to the digital age. From the way we shop and communicate online to concerns about privacy and cybercrime, lawmakers face the constant task of updating statutes to cover virtual interactions. **The Children's Online Privacy Protection Act (COPPA)**, enacted in 1998, is still being revised to keep pace with the ever-changing ways children use the internet. This ongoing process shows how legal systems strive to protect citizens, even as the landscape shifts underfoot.

The Expanding Reach of Everyday Law

Everyday legal safety is no longer just about following traffic regulations or understanding your rights during a police stop. The law increasingly touches on activities that didn't exist a generation ago:

- **Ride-sharing** regulations now dictate safety and insurance requirements for drivers using apps like Uber and Lyft.
- **Drone operation laws** guide where and how individuals can fly unmanned aircraft in neighborhoods.
- **Data privacy** rules govern how companies can collect, store, and share your personal information.

Each of these areas illustrates how the law's reach grows with innovation, aiming to ensure safety, fairness, and accountability in new domains.

Responding to Social Movements and Global Events

The law also evolves in response to social movements and global events. Consider the civil rights era of the 1960s, when widespread activism prompted landmark legislation like the **Civil Rights Act of 1964**. More recently, the COVID-19 pandemic led to emergency legal measures—mask mandates, business closures, and eviction moratoriums—that directly affected daily life. These shifts demonstrate the law's flexibility and its essential role in safeguarding both individual and collective well-being during times of change.

Global Perspective: Comparative Legal Adaptations

While the U.S. legal system is unique, the adaptive role of law is a global phenomenon. For instance, **Germany's strict data protection laws** influenced the European Union's General Data Protection Regulation (GDPR), which has become a global model for digital privacy. Meanwhile, countries like Japan have rapidly modernized traffic laws in response to advances in autonomous vehicles. These global examples underscore how legal systems worldwide strive to balance innovation, safety, and individual rights.

The Citizen's Role: Staying Engaged and Informed

As the law continues to evolve, so does your role as a citizen. Staying informed and proactive is key to everyday legal safety:

- Keep up with changes in local, state, and federal laws that may affect your daily routines.

- Participate in civic life, such as voting or public comment periods, to influence laws and policies.
- Seek trusted sources for legal updates, especially in areas like technology, health, and housing.

Remember, the law serves best when citizens are aware, engaged, and willing to advocate for their rights and responsibilities.

```
The U.S. legal system updates laws regularly to address new technologies and
social issues—your awareness is crucial for everyday legal safety.
```

The story of American law is one of continual adaptation. Laws change to reflect new realities, and your understanding of them is a vital tool for personal safety and empowerment. As we move forward, remember that the law's evolution is shaped not only by lawmakers and courts but by the everyday actions and voices of citizens like you.

With this understanding of how law adapts and protects, we're ready to step inside the courtroom. In the next chapter, you'll discover what happens during legal proceedings and how to navigate these pivotal moments with clarity and confidence.

Glossary

Acquittal

A legal judgment that officially and formally clears a defendant of criminal charges, declaring them "not guilty." An acquittal occurs when the prosecution fails to prove the defendant's guilt beyond a reasonable doubt. For example, if a jury finds insufficient evidence in a theft case, the accused may be acquitted. (See also: Burden of Proof, Conviction)

Arrest

The act of law enforcement taking a person into custody, typically because they are suspected of committing a crime. An arrest requires probable cause and often involves reading the suspect their rights (Miranda Rights). For example, a person caught shoplifting may be arrested on the spot. (See also: Detainment, Miranda Rights)

Burden of Proof

The obligation to present evidence to support one's claim in a legal dispute. In criminal cases, the prosecution bears the burden of proving the defendant's guilt "beyond a reasonable doubt." In civil cases, the standard is usually a "preponderance of the evidence." (See also: Burden of Persuasion, Acquittal)

Civil Law

The branch of law dealing with disputes between individuals, organizations, or between the two, in which compensation may be awarded to the victim. Examples include contract disputes, property disagreements, or family law matters like divorce. Civil cases differ from criminal cases, which involve offenses against the state. (See also: Criminal Law)

Common Law

A system of law based on precedents and judicial decisions rather than written statutes. Common law traditions, inherited from England, form a significant part of the U.S. legal system, especially in areas not covered by statutory law. For instance, tort law is largely governed by common law principles. (See also: Statutory Law, Precedent)

Contract

A legally binding agreement between two or more parties outlining obligations and rights. Contracts can be written or verbal, but certain agreements (such as real estate transactions) must be in writing. For example, a lease agreement between a landlord and tenant is a contract. (See also: Civil Law)

Conviction

A formal declaration by a court that someone is guilty of a criminal offense, typically following a trial or a plea of guilty. A conviction can result in penalties such as fines, community service, probation, or imprisonment. (See also: Acquittal, Sentencing)

Criminal Law

The body of law that deals with actions considered harmful to society as a whole and punishable by the state. Criminal law covers offenses such as theft, assault, and murder, and distinguishes between misdemeanors and felonies based on severity. (See also: Civil Law, Felony, Misdemeanor)

Defendant

The party in a legal case who is accused of wrongdoing or against whom a lawsuit is filed. In criminal cases, the defendant is the person charged with a crime; in civil cases, the defendant is the individual or entity being sued. (See also: Plaintiff, Prosecution)

Detainment

A temporary restriction of a person's freedom by law enforcement, often for questioning or investigation. Unlike arrest, detainment does not necessarily mean formal charges will follow. For example, police may detain someone briefly during a traffic stop. (See also: Arrest, Miranda Rights)

Due Process

The legal requirement that the government respect all legal rights owed to a person, ensuring fair treatment through the judicial system. This includes the right to a fair trial, to be heard, and to receive notice of proceedings. Due process is protected by the Fifth and Fourteenth Amendments. (See also: Miranda Rights)

Evidence

Any information presented in court to support or refute a claim. Evidence can be physical (like a weapon), documentary (like a contract), testimonial (statements by witnesses), or digital (emails, recordings). The rules of evidence determine what is admissible in court. (See also: Admissible Evidence, Hearsay)

Felony

A serious criminal offense punishable by more than one year in prison, or by death in extreme cases. Examples include murder, robbery, and arson. Felonies are distinguished from misdemeanors based on the severity of the crime and potential penalties. (See also: Misdemeanor, Sentencing)

First-Degree Crime

The most serious classification of a criminal offense, often involving intent, premeditation, or extreme harm. Examples include first-degree murder or armed robbery. Penalties are typically severe, including long prison sentences. (See also: Felony, Third-Degree Crime)

Hearsay

An out-of-court statement offered to prove the truth of the matter asserted, generally inadmissible as evidence due to reliability concerns. Exceptions exist, such as statements made under excited utterance. For example, "My friend told me she saw the crime" is usually hearsay. (See also: Evidence, Admissible Evidence)

Immigration Law

The set of federal laws and regulations governing who may enter, reside in, or become a citizen of the United States. Immigration law covers visas, green cards, asylum, and deportation processes. For example, applying for a work visa falls under immigration law. (See also: Due Process)

Jury

A group of citizens sworn to render a verdict in a legal case, based on evidence presented in court. Juries are typically used in criminal trials and some civil cases. The right to a trial by jury is guaranteed by the U.S. Constitution. (See also: Trial, Verdict)

Law Enforcement

Agencies and officers empowered by the government to enforce laws, maintain public order, and protect citizens. This includes police, sheriffs, federal agents, and others. Law enforcement plays a key role in investigating crimes, making arrests, and testifying in court. (See also: Arrest, Detainment)

Liability

Legal responsibility for one's actions or omissions, which may result in civil or criminal penalties. Liability can arise from breaching a contract, causing an accident, or violating regulations. For example, a driver who causes a car crash may be liable for damages. (See also: Civil Law, Negligence)

Misdemeanor

A less serious criminal offense, typically punishable by fines, probation, or jail time of less than one year. Examples include petty theft, disorderly conduct, or minor traffic violations. Misdemeanors are distinct from felonies in both severity and consequences. (See also: Felony)

Miranda Rights

The rights read to a suspect upon arrest, informing them of their right to remain silent and to have an attorney present during questioning. These rights stem from the Supreme Court case Miranda v. Arizona (1966), protecting individuals from self-incrimination. (See also: Arrest, Due Process)

Negligence

A failure to exercise reasonable care, resulting in harm or damage to another person or property. Negligence is a common basis for civil lawsuits, such as in car accidents or slip-and-fall cases. Plaintiffs must prove duty, breach, causation, and damages. (See also: Liability, Civil Law)

Plaintiff

The party who initiates a lawsuit, seeking relief or compensation for harm suffered. In civil cases, the plaintiff is the individual or entity alleging wrongdoing by the defendant. For example, a tenant suing a landlord over unsafe conditions is the plaintiff. (See also: Defendant)

Precedent

A previous court decision that guides future cases with similar facts or legal issues. Courts generally follow precedents to ensure consistency and predictability in the law. For example, the Supreme Court's interpretation of constitutional rights often sets precedents for lower courts. (See also: Common Law)

Prosecution

The legal party responsible for presenting the case against an individual accused of a crime. Prosecutors are government attorneys who represent the state or federal government in criminal trials. (See also: Defendant, Criminal Law)

Reasonable Doubt

The standard of proof required in criminal trials, meaning that if there is any reasonable uncertainty about the defendant's guilt, they must be acquitted. This high standard reflects the serious consequences of criminal conviction. (See also: Burden of Proof, Acquittal)

Regulation

A rule or directive made and maintained by an authority, typically a government agency, to control or govern conduct. Regulations cover areas such as business practices, environmental protection, and workplace safety. For example, the Environmental Protection Agency (EPA) issues regulations on air quality. (See also: Statutory Law)

Rights

Legal, social, or ethical principles of freedom or entitlement. In the U.S., rights such as free speech, due process, and equal protection are enshrined in the Constitution and enforced through courts. Rights protect individuals from government overreach and discrimination. (See also: Due Process, Miranda Rights)

Sentencing

The judicial determination of a punishment for someone convicted of a crime. Sentences can include fines, community service, probation, or imprisonment, and may depend on the severity of the offense and the defendant's criminal history. (See also: Conviction, Felony)

Statutory Law

Written laws enacted by legislative bodies, such as Congress or state legislatures. Statutory law contrasts with common law, which is developed through court decisions. For example, speed limits are set by statutes. (See also: Common Law, Regulation)

Third-Degree Crime

A classification for less severe felonies or offenses, often involving less harm or intent than first-degree crimes. Penalties are generally lighter, but third-degree crimes can still result in jail time or significant fines. For example, third-degree theft may involve property of lower value. (See also: Felony, First-Degree Crime)

Traffic Law

The body of law regulating vehicles, drivers, pedestrians, and road use. Traffic laws establish rules for speed limits, right-of-way, licensing, and driving under the influence. Violations can lead to fines, points on a license, or arrest for serious offenses. (See also: Regulation)

Trial

A formal judicial proceeding where evidence is presented, and arguments are made before a judge or jury to determine guilt, liability, or other legal questions. Trials are central to both civil and criminal justice systems. (See also: Jury, Verdict)

Verdict

The formal decision or finding made by a jury or judge on the matters presented in a trial. In criminal cases, the verdict is typically "guilty" or "not guilty"; in civil cases, it may determine liability and award damages. (See also: Trial, Acquittal)

This glossary provides foundational definitions to help readers navigate the U.S. legal system, understand their rights and responsibilities, and recognize the importance of key legal concepts in everyday life. By relating each term to real-life examples and related ideas, the glossary aims to make legal terminology accessible and relevant for all.

Annexure A: A Timeline of Key Milestones in U.S. Legal History

Understanding the U.S. legal system requires a sense of its evolution—how laws, institutions, and rights have developed over time. This timeline supplements the main narrative by tracing pivotal legal milestones, showing how historical moments shape the laws that govern everyday life. By highlighting landmark events, amendments, and court decisions, this annexure places today's legal realities in their broader historical context.

Timeline of Legal Milestones

Colonial Foundations (1607–1776)

- 1607: **Jamestown Settlement** begins, introducing English common law traditions to America.
- 1641: **Massachusetts Body of Liberties**—one of the first legal codes in the colonies, establishing rights for colonists and limitations on government power.

The Birth of a Nation (1776–1791)

- 1776: **Declaration of Independence** asserts inalienable rights.
- 1787: **U.S. Constitution** signed, creating the framework for federal government and law.
- 1791: **Bill of Rights** ratified, guaranteeing individual freedoms such as speech, religion, and due process.

Expanding Rights and Legal Systems (1800–1865)

- 1803: **Marbury v. Madison**—Supreme Court establishes judicial review, allowing courts to invalidate unconstitutional laws.
- 1865: **13th Amendment** abolishes slavery.

Civil Rights and Modernization (1865–1964)

- 1868: **14th Amendment** ensures equal protection under the law.
- 1920: **19th Amendment** grants women the right to vote.
- 1954: **Brown v. Board of Education**—Supreme Court rules school segregation unconstitutional.

- 1964: **Civil Rights Act** bans discrimination based on race, color, religion, sex, or national origin.

Contemporary Legal Developments (1965–Present)

- 1966: **Miranda v. Arizona**—Supreme Court requires police to inform suspects of their rights.
- 2001: **Patriot Act** expands government surveillance powers after 9/11.
- 2015: **Obergefell v. Hodges** legalizes same-sex marriage nationwide.

Examples and Applications

Example 1: From the Bill of Rights to Miranda Warnings

The **Fifth Amendment** (1791) established the right against self-incrimination—"no person... shall be compelled in any criminal case to be a witness against himself." Nearly two centuries later, **Miranda v. Arizona** (1966) transformed this right into a practical police procedure: officers must advise arrestees of their right to remain silent and to an attorney. This evolution illustrates how constitutional principles are interpreted and applied over time, directly affecting everyday law enforcement encounters.

Example 2: Civil Rights Legislation and Social Change

The **Civil Rights Act of 1964** didn't just change legal doctrine; it reshaped daily life for millions. By outlawing public segregation and employment discrimination, it forced businesses, schools, and governments to alter long-standing practices. Its effects are still felt today in anti-discrimination policies in workplaces, schools, and housing.

Tracing these milestones reveals how the American legal system is not static but responsive—shaped by social movements, judicial decisions, and constitutional amendments. Appreciating this history empowers citizens to understand not just what the law is, but why it exists and how it can continue to evolve.

Annexure B: Excerpts from Foundational Legal Documents

Primary sources offer unique insights into the language, intentions, and context behind U.S. law. This annexure brings readers closer to the words that anchor the legal system, fostering a deeper appreciation for the principles guiding everyday interactions with the law. Key excerpts are provided with explanations and real-world applications.

Excerpt 1: The Fourth Amendment to the U.S. Constitution

Text:

"The right of the people to be secure in their persons, houses, papers, and effects, against unreasonable searches and seizures, shall not be violated, and no Warrants shall issue, but upon probable cause, supported by Oath or affirmation, and particularly describing the place to be searched, and the persons or things to be seized."

Application:

This amendment is the cornerstone of privacy rights and protection from government intrusion. It underpins rules about police needing warrants to search homes or seize evidence. For example, if police want to search your car or home, they generally must have a warrant or a clearly defined exception (such as probable cause or consent).

Real-World Example:

In 2014's **Riley v. California**, the Supreme Court ruled that police generally cannot search a person's cellphone during an arrest without a warrant, applying the Fourth Amendment to modern digital privacy.

Excerpt 2: The Civil Rights Act of 1964, Title II

Text:

"All persons shall be entitled to the full and equal enjoyment of the goods, services, facilities, privileges, advantages, and accommodations of any place of public accommodation... without discrimination or segregation on the ground of race, color, religion, or national origin."

Application:

This provision directly affects hotels, restaurants, theaters, and other public spaces, making it illegal to refuse service based on race or other protected categories. It ensures equal participation in public life and remedies past injustices.

Real-World Example:

A restaurant cannot refuse to serve customers because of their ethnicity or religion. If they do, affected individuals can file a complaint with the Department of Justice or pursue a lawsuit.

Reading the actual language of foundational documents helps demystify the law and reveals the enduring power of phrases crafted centuries ago. These texts are not just historical artifacts—they are living instruments shaping personal rights and responsibilities every day.

Annexure C: Cultural Perspectives on Law—The U.S. and Beyond

While this book focuses on the U.S. legal system, laws do not exist in a vacuum. By comparing American legal principles with those from other cultures, readers gain insight into the values and priorities that shape different societies. This annexure offers a cross-cultural exploration, highlighting both contrasts and shared values.

Section 1: Due Process—A Universal Principle with Local Flavors

The U.S. Approach

Due process is enshrined in the Fifth and Fourteenth Amendments, requiring fair procedures before the government can deprive a person of life, liberty, or property. This includes the right to be heard, the right to notice, and the right to a fair trial.

Comparative Example: Germany

The German legal system also emphasizes due process but with different emphases. For instance, under the **Grundgesetz** (Basic Law), the right to a fair hearing and judicial review are fundamental. The German Constitutional Court actively reviews laws for fairness and constitutionality, sometimes even more assertively than U.S. courts.

Comparative Example: Japan

Japan's postwar constitution, influenced by American legal thought, guarantees due process rights. However, Japanese courts are generally less adversarial, and confessions play a larger role in criminal cases, reflecting cultural differences in conflict resolution and authority.

Section 2: Policing and Community Relations

The U.S. Context

American law enforcement is marked by the **Miranda warning** requirement and a strong emphasis on individual rights during police encounters. However, tensions sometimes arise over issues of racial profiling and use of force.

Comparative Example: United Kingdom

In the UK, police interact with the public under the **Police and Criminal Evidence Act (PACE)**, which outlines rules on searches, arrests, and detention. British policing emphasizes "policing by consent," with a greater focus on community trust and fewer armed officers compared to the U.S.

Comparative Example: South Africa

South Africa's post-apartheid constitution explicitly prohibits discrimination and brutality, addressing a legacy of police abuse. Laws require transparency and accountability, though challenges remain in practice.

Exploring global legal traditions highlights both the universal aspiration for justice and the variety of paths societies take to achieve it. Comparing systems can illuminate strengths and weaknesses in the U.S. approach, encouraging thoughtful engagement with legal reform and cultural understanding.

Annexure D: Everyday Encounters—Case Studies in Law and Life

To bridge the gap between abstract legal principles and real-life experience, this annexure presents case studies of common legal encounters. These stories illustrate how legal concepts play out in daily life, emphasizing rights, responsibilities, and possible outcomes.

Case Study 1: A Routine Traffic Stop

Scenario

Maria, a recent immigrant, is pulled over for a broken taillight. The officer asks for her license, registration, and proof of insurance. Maria is nervous and unsure of her rights.

Legal Issues at Play

Probable Cause: The officer must have a valid reason (the broken taillight) to initiate the stop.

Right to Remain Silent: Maria can answer questions about her identity and vehicle but is not required to answer unrelated questions.

Search and Seizure: The officer cannot search Maria's car without consent or probable cause of a separate crime.

Outcome

Maria provides her documents and politely declines to answer unrelated questions. The officer issues a warning and lets her go. Maria's knowledge of her rights helps ensure a respectful and lawful encounter.

Case Study 2: Tenant Rights and Eviction

Scenario

James, a tenant, receives a notice from his landlord demanding he leave within three days due to late rent. James has lived in the apartment for three years and believes the eviction is unfair.

Legal Issues at Play

Notice Requirements: State laws dictate how much notice must be given before eviction.

Right to a Hearing: In most states, tenants can contest an eviction in court.

Retaliation Protections: Landlords cannot evict tenants for complaining about unsafe conditions.

Outcome

James consults a legal aid organization, which helps him understand his rights. He appears in court and negotiates a payment plan, avoiding immediate eviction.

These case studies demonstrate that everyday legal situations often hinge on ordinary people understanding their rights and responsibilities. Being informed can make a significant difference, transforming potentially intimidating encounters into manageable, even empowering, experiences.

Bibliography

- Abrams, Norman, Sara Sun Beale, and Susan Riva Klein. *Federal Criminal Law and Its Enforcement*. 7th ed. St. Paul, MN: West Academic Publishing, 2020.
- American Bar Association. "Understanding the Legal System." Accessed March 15, 2024. https://www.americanbar.org/groups/public_education/resources/law_related_education network/how-courts-work/understanding-the-legal-system/.
- Bureau of Justice Statistics. "Criminal Justice System Flowchart." U.S. Department of Justice. Updated December 2023. https://bjs.ojp.gov/content/justsys.cfm.
- Carter, Lief H., and Thomas F. Burke. *Reason in Law*. 10th ed. Chicago: University of Chicago Press, 2019.
- Chemerinsky, Erwin. *The Case Against the Supreme Court*. New York: Penguin Books, 2014.
- Chew, Pat K., ed. *The Conflict and Culture Reader*. New York: New York University Press, 2001.
- Cornell Law School Legal Information Institute. "Legal Terms Glossary." Accessed March 10, 2024. https://www.law.cornell.edu/wex/category/legal_term_glossary.
- Dershowitz, Alan. *Rights From Wrongs: A Secular Theory of the Origins of Rights*. New York: Basic Books, 2006.
- Epps, Garrett. *American Justice 2019: The Shifting Supreme Court*. Baltimore: Johns Hopkins University Press, 2019.
- Epstein, Lee, and Thomas G. Walker. *Constitutional Law for a Changing America: Rights, Liberties, and Justice*. 11th ed. Thousand Oaks, CA: CQ Press, 2022.
- Friedman, Lawrence M. *American Law in the 21st Century*. New York: Oxford University Press, 2019.
- *Annotation: Friedman's work provides a comprehensive overview of how American law has evolved and how it functions in everyday life. The book's accessible style and coverage of legal institutions, rights, and responsibilities make it an invaluable resource for readers seeking to understand the practical impact of law on daily activities and citizenship.*
- Garner, Bryan A., ed. *Black's Law Dictionary*. 12th ed. St. Paul, MN: Thomson Reuters, 2023.
- *Annotation: As the definitive legal dictionary, this source is crucial for accurate definitions of legal terms and concepts. Its inclusion ensures the book's*

explanations of terminology such as "misdemeanor," "felony," and "burden of proof" are precise and authoritative.

- Gershman, Bennett L. *Prosecution Stories*. St. Paul, MN: West Academic Publishing, 2017.
- Gould, Jon B., and Scott Barclay. "Mind the Gap: The Place of Law in Everyday Life." *Law & Society Review* 49, no. 1 (2015): 5–27.
- *Annotation: This peer-reviewed article explores the intersection between legal institutions and daily experiences. It informs the book's narrative by emphasizing the often-overlooked role of law in routine interactions and decision-making, reinforcing the book's central theme of legal awareness in everyday contexts.*
- Grossman, Joanna L., and Lawrence M. Friedman. *Inside the Castle: Law and the Family in 20th Century America*. Princeton, NJ: Princeton University Press, 2011.
- Harr, J. Scott, and Karen M. Hess. *Constitutional Law and the Criminal Justice System*. 8th ed. Boston: Cengage Learning, 2023.
- Hobbes, Thomas. *Leviathan*. 1651. Edited by Richard Tuck. Cambridge: Cambridge University Press, 1991.
- Katz, Daniel Martin. "Quantitative Legal Prediction – Or – How I Learned to Stop Worrying and Start Preparing for the Data-Driven Future of the Legal Services Industry." *Emory Law Journal* 62, no. 4 (2013): 909–966.
- Kessler, Amalia D. *Inventing American Exceptionalism: The Origins of American Adversarial Legal Culture, 1800–1877*. New Haven: Yale University Press, 2017.
- Klein, Susan Riva, and Ingrid B. Grobey. "Criminal Law: Cases and Materials." 10th ed. St. Paul, MN: Foundation Press, 2021.
- Legal Services Corporation. "Your Legal Rights." Accessed March 12, 2024. https://www.lsc.gov/what-legal-aid/your-legal-rights.
- Lipman, Francine J. "The Taxation of Undocumented Immigrants: Separate, Unequal, and Without Representation." *Harvard Latino Law Review* 9 (2016): 1–58.
- National Immigration Law Center. "Know Your Rights." Accessed March 11, 2024. https://www.nilc.org/get-involved/community-education-resources/know-your-rights/.
- National Safety Council. *Traffic Safety Fact Book 2023*. Itasca, IL: National Safety Council, 2023.
- Neubauer, David W., and Stephen S. Meinhold. *Judicial Process: Law, Courts, and Politics in the United States*. 8th ed. Boston: Cengage Learning, 2022.
- Oyez Project. "Landmark Supreme Court Cases." Accessed March 14, 2024. https://www.oyez.org/cases.

- Sarat, Austin, and Thomas R. Kearns, eds. *Law in Everyday Life*. Ann Arbor: University of Michigan Press, 2009.
- *Annotation: This collection of essays provides varied perspectives on how law operates outside of courtrooms, focusing on its presence in social interactions, family life, and community norms. It supports the book's discussion of legal consciousness and the subtle ways law shapes behavior in diverse contexts.*
- Schulhofer, Stephen J. *More Essential Than Ever: The Fourth Amendment in the Twenty-First Century*. New York: Oxford University Press, 2017.
- Siegel, Reva B. "The Jurisprudence of Everyday Life." *Yale Law Journal* 124, no. 8 (2015): 2410–2443.
- Steiker, Carol S. "Capital Punishment and American Law." *Annual Review of Law and Social Science* 13 (2017): 147–164.
- U.S. Citizenship and Immigration Services. "Citizenship Rights and Responsibilities." Accessed March 13, 2024. https://www.uscis.gov/citizenship/learn-about-citizenship/citizenship-rights-and-responsibilities.
- U.S. Constitution. National Archives. Accessed March 10, 2024. https://www.archives.gov/founding-docs/constitution.
- Weiss, Deborah, and Kathy Hurley. *The Practical Guide to Legal Literacy: Strategies for Student Success in the Law School Classroom*. Durham, NC: Carolina Academic Press, 2019.
- *Annotation: Geared toward newcomers to legal studies, this guide addresses the foundational skills and concepts necessary for legal literacy. It directly supports the book's mission to make legal knowledge accessible to all readers, regardless of their background.*
- White, G. Edward. *Law in American History, Volume III: 1930–2000*. New York: Oxford University Press, 2019.
- Zimring, Franklin E., and Gordon Hawkins. *Crime Is Not the Problem: Lethal Violence in America*. New York: Oxford University Press, 2019.

These selected works offer foundational knowledge, practical frameworks, and in-depth analyses crucial to the book's themes. They collectively ensure the book is accurate, up-to-date, and accessible, blending comprehensive legal overviews, clear definitions, and real-life perspectives for readers seeking to navigate the U.S. legal system in everyday life.

Further Reading & Additional Resources

"The U.S. Constitution: A Reader" edited by Hillsdale College Politics Faculty

This comprehensive collection features the full text of the U.S. Constitution, landmark Supreme Court decisions, and key historical documents that have shaped American law. With accessible commentary and historical context, it's ideal for readers seeking to understand the legal foundations of everyday rights and responsibilities. The book's structured approach allows readers with little legal background to explore the evolution of the Constitution and its real-world impact, making it a foundational resource for anyone interested in U.S. law.

"Law 101: Everything You Need to Know About American Law" by Jay M. Feinman

Feinman's book is a celebrated introduction to the American legal system, covering essential topics such as civil rights, contracts, torts, criminal law, and the court system. Written in plain language, it demystifies legal concepts and addresses how laws affect daily life. Each chapter includes practical examples and case studies, helping readers relate legal theory to real-world scenarios. This is an excellent primer for those starting their exploration of law in everyday contexts.

Cornell Legal Information Institute (LII) – https://www.law.cornell.edu/

The Cornell LII is a free, reputable online resource offering accessible explanations of statutes, case law, and legal concepts. It includes a vast legal dictionary, guides on important legal topics, and up-to-date information on federal and state laws. For everyday legal questions or deeper research, LII is invaluable for both novices and those seeking more detailed legal information.

"Gideon's Trumpet" by Anthony Lewis

This narrative non-fiction classic recounts the landmark Supreme Court case Gideon v. Wainwright, which established the right to legal counsel for criminal defendants. Lewis's storytelling brings legal principles to life, illustrating the profound impact of the legal system on ordinary individuals. It's both an engaging read and a powerful example of how legal rights are won and maintained in the U.S.

"Street Law: A Course in Practical Law" by Lee P. Arbetman et al.

Designed originally for high school students, "Street Law" presents legal principles in a straightforward manner, focusing on issues most people encounter: housing, employment, consumer rights, and family law. Its practical orientation and relatable examples make it an excellent resource for anyone wanting to understand how the law affects everyday decisions and interactions.

The American Bar Association (ABA) – https://www.americanbar.org/groups/public_education/

The ABA provides a wealth of public legal education resources, including guides on criminal and civil law, interactive tools, and "Know Your Rights" materials. Their content is current, authoritative, and user-friendly, making it a trusted go-to for legal questions about rights, responsibilities, and navigating the justice system.

"A People's History of the Supreme Court" by Peter Irons

Irons offers a sweeping narrative of the U.S. Supreme Court's role in shaping American society, highlighting major cases that have influenced civil liberties, equality, and government power. By focusing on the people behind the cases, Irons gives readers a humanized view of how legal change occurs and why it matters for everyday life.

"Just Mercy: A Story of Justice and Redemption" by Bryan Stevenson

Stevenson's memoir details his work with the Equal Justice Initiative and the broader struggle for justice in the American legal system. Through real-life stories, he exposes the challenges of bias, inequality, and wrongful convictions, providing readers with a nuanced understanding of the stakes involved in legal proceedings, especially for marginalized communities.

Nolo: Legal Encyclopedia – https://www.nolo.com/legal-encyclopedia

Nolo's online legal encyclopedia is designed for non-lawyers and covers topics such as landlord-tenant law, family law, small business regulations, and more. Each entry breaks down complex legal issues into digestible, actionable advice. Nolo's guides are renowned for their clarity and reliability, making them perfect for readers seeking practical answers to everyday legal questions.

"The Legal Analyst: A Toolkit for Thinking About the Law" by Ward Farnsworth

Farnsworth introduces readers to the ways lawyers and judges analyze legal problems, offering tools and frameworks for understanding legal reasoning. This book bridges the gap between theory and practice, equipping readers to think critically about laws that affect their lives, from contracts to criminal justice.

"Evicted: Poverty and Profit in the American City" by Matthew Desmond

Desmond's Pulitzer Prize-winning book explores the intersection of housing, poverty, and law through the stories of tenants and landlords in Milwaukee. It sheds light on eviction proceedings, tenants' rights, and the legal challenges faced by vulnerable populations. "Evicted" is essential for understanding property rights and the social consequences of legal policies in daily life.

United States Courts – "Understanding the Federal Courts" – https://www.uscourts.gov/about-federal-courts/educational-resources/about-educational-outreach/activity-resources/about

This official site provides clear, concise explanations of the federal court system, including its structure, processes, and key terminology. With interactive materials and straightforward guides, it helps demystify court procedures and legal language for the general public, making it a valuable supplement to any study of U.S. law.

"The Color of Law: A Forgotten History of How Our Government Segregated America" by Richard Rothstein

Rothstein unpacks how laws and policies at federal, state, and local levels created and perpetuated racial segregation in housing. By connecting legal history to present-day realities, this book challenges readers to recognize the role of law in shaping social structures and everyday experiences.

PBS's "The Constitution: That Delicate Balance" (Documentary series)

This acclaimed PBS series explores constitutional issues through dramatized debates and expert commentary. It covers topics like freedom of speech, rights of the accused, and the balance of government powers, making constitutional principles accessible through engaging stories and real-life cases.

"The Nine: Inside the Secret World of the Supreme Court" by Jeffrey Toobin

Toobin's behind-the-scenes account of the modern Supreme Court reveals how personal dynamics, ideology, and landmark cases shape the nation's legal landscape. By focusing on the justices and their decision-making processes, the book offers insight into how high-level legal decisions trickle down to affect everyday American life.

ACLU "Know Your Rights" Guides – https://www.aclu.org/know-your-rights

The American Civil Liberties Union provides up-to-date guides on rights during police encounters, at protests, in the workplace, and more. These resources are particularly useful for immigrants, minorities, and anyone seeking to protect their civil liberties in everyday situations. The ACLU's clear, actionable advice is grounded in current law and policy.

"In Our Defense: The Bill of Rights In Action" by Ellen Alderman and Caroline Kennedy

This book examines each amendment of the Bill of Rights through real-world cases, illustrating how constitutional protections are applied and challenged in daily life. The accessible narratives help readers appreciate the continuing importance of fundamental rights in both ordinary and extraordinary circumstances.

United States Citizenship and Immigration Services (USCIS) – https://www.uscis.gov/citizenship/learn-about-citizenship

USCIS offers official guides and learning resources for new residents and citizens, including information on immigration law, citizenship requirements, and legal rights. The site's straightforward language and practical focus make it an essential resource for those navigating the complexities of U.S. immigration law.

"The Rule of Law" by Tom Bingham

Although focused primarily on the British legal system, Bingham's concise and readable book explores the universal principles underlying the rule of law. His insights are relevant to U.S. readers, offering a global perspective on why legal systems matter and how they function to protect everyday rights and order.

Harvard Law School's "Case Studies" – https://casestudies.law.harvard.edu/

Harvard Law's repository of case studies provides real-world scenarios and dilemmas to foster deeper understanding of legal processes and critical thinking. While some are designed for classroom use, many are accessible to general audiences and offer practical insights into how legal reasoning is applied to solve everyday problems.

These resources collectively offer a blend of foundational texts, practical guides, personal stories, and authoritative websites, ensuring readers gain both theoretical understanding and practical knowledge relevant to everyday legal questions and experiences.

Epilogue: Living the Law—A Journey Beyond the Courtroom

As we reach the end of our journey through the labyrinthine paths of the U.S. legal system, it is worth pausing to reflect on both the practical lessons and the deeper meanings that have emerged from these pages. The law, as we have seen, is not merely a set of rules etched into books or pronounced from high benches; it is a living, breathing force that shapes—and is shaped by—our daily actions, our shared values, and our collective dreams.

A Tapestry of Everyday Encounters

Throughout this book, we have explored the legal frameworks that underpin some of the most ordinary and extraordinary moments of life in the United States. From knowing your rights during a routine traffic stop, to understanding the intricacies of property ownership, business regulations, or immigration procedures, the law touches every facet of our experience. It is the silent architecture of our society, providing both the scaffolding for order and the guardrails that keep us safe.

Consider the story of Rosa Parks, whose quiet act of defiance in 1955—refusing to give up her seat on a Montgomery bus—became a catalyst for the Civil Rights Movement. Parks' simple, everyday decision thrust her into the heart of the legal system. Her arrest for violating segregation laws led to a legal battle that would ultimately test the constitutionality of Jim Crow statutes. Parks' courage, and the subsequent legal challenges, remind us that the law is not static; it evolves in response to the conscience of its people. Everyday acts, informed by legal awareness, can lead to seismic shifts in society.

The Law as a Mirror and a Map

The history of the U.S. legal system is filled with such transformative moments. In 1967, the Supreme Court case of **Loving v. Virginia** struck down laws banning interracial marriage. Mildred and Richard Loving, an interracial couple, were arrested simply for being married. Their fight for justice not only changed their own lives, but redefined the meaning of equality for millions. This case, like so many others, reflects the law's dual role as both a mirror—reflecting prevailing values and prejudices—and a map—charting the course toward a more just society.

Yet, the law's impact is not confined to high-profile cases. Every day, people across the country rely on small but crucial legal protections: a tenant contesting an unfair eviction notice, an employee advocating for fair wages, or a new immigrant navigating the pathway to citizenship. The stories of individuals like Dolores Huerta, who co-founded the United Farm Workers and used legal strategies to secure labor rights for agricultural workers, show how legal knowledge and advocacy can empower even the most marginalized voices.

Bridging Cultures and Building Understanding

The United States is far from alone in its legal journey. Around the world, societies grapple with the same fundamental questions: Who makes the laws? Who enforces them? How can justice be both fair and accessible? In Japan, for example, the concept of **wa** (harmony) is deeply embedded in both social norms and legal processes, emphasizing mediation and consensus-building over adversarial confrontation. In South Africa, the post-apartheid constitution enshrined a commitment to human dignity and equality, drawing on both Western legal traditions and indigenous principles of justice.

By comparing these global examples, we see that while legal systems may differ in form, their underlying purpose remains remarkably consistent: to balance individual rights with social responsibilities, to resolve conflicts peacefully, and to chart a path toward a more inclusive and harmonious society. The U.S. legal system, with its unique blend of common law tradition, constitutional guarantees, and dynamic pluralism, serves as a fascinating case study in this universal quest.

The Law in the Digital Age

As we look to the future, new challenges and opportunities arise. The digital revolution has transformed how we work, communicate, and even define community. Questions about privacy, digital speech, and cybersecurity now dominate legal discourse. The law must continually adapt to new realities—self-driving cars, artificial intelligence, global commerce—while still protecting the fundamental rights and freedoms that form its bedrock.

One recent example is the ongoing debate over data privacy in the United States. The **California Consumer Privacy Act (CCPA)**, passed in 2018, gave Californians unprecedented control over their personal data, inspiring similar legislation across the country. This shift reflects a growing awareness that, in a world where information is both currency and commodity, legal protections must evolve to keep pace with technological change.

Everyday Engagement: The Power of Informed Citizenship

Yet, for all its complexity, the law ultimately belongs to the people. It is shaped not just by lawyers, judges, or legislators, but by every citizen who pays attention, speaks up, and insists on fairness. The rights and responsibilities we have explored—whether about driving safely, starting a business, or knowing what to do when interacting with law enforcement—are tools for empowerment. They equip us to participate fully in civic life, to protect ourselves and those we love, and to contribute meaningfully to the greater good.

Reflect on the following:

The law is not just a shield, but a bridge—connecting us to one another and to the ideals we cherish.
Legal literacy is the foundation of effective citizenship. The more we understand our rights and duties, the more confidently we can navigate life's challenges.
Laws change when people demand change. The most powerful legal reforms often begin at the grassroots, with everyday people insisting that the law live up to its promises.

Toward a More Just and Compassionate Society

As we close this book, let us consider not only what the law is, but what it could become. The U.S. legal system, with all its imperfections, remains a work in progress—a grand experiment in democracy, fairness, and opportunity. Each generation is called to reimagine and renew it, drawing on the lessons of the past and the hopes of the future.

Your journey does not end here. Whether you are a student, a newcomer, or a lifelong resident, you have a role to play in shaping the law—by staying informed, asking questions, seeking justice, and speaking out against injustice. The law is not a distant abstraction; it is the sum of our choices, our courage, and our compassion.

A Call to Action

So, as you set this book aside, I invite you to carry its lessons into your everyday life:

- Ask questions. When you encounter a legal issue, seek out reliable information. Consult legal aid organizations, community resources, or trusted professionals.
- Share your knowledge. Help friends, family, and neighbors understand their rights and responsibilities. Legal literacy is a gift best shared.
- Get involved. Attend a town hall meeting, volunteer with a local advocacy group, or participate in jury duty when called. Democracy thrives when its citizens are engaged.

- Challenge injustice. If you witness unfairness or discrimination, speak up. The law's promise of justice depends on our collective vigilance.

In the words of Dr. Martin Luther King, Jr., *"Injustice anywhere is a threat to justice everywhere."* The legal system is only as strong—and as fair—as the people who sustain it. As you move forward, may you do so with confidence, curiosity, and a steadfast commitment to justice for all.

Let your understanding of the law be not just a shield, but a beacon, lighting the way to a more informed, equitable, and compassionate society. The story of law for everyday life is, in the end, the story of us all.

Afterword: Law as a Living Guide

As we reach the end of our exploration into the U.S. legal system and its profound role in shaping everyday life, it becomes clear that law is not merely a set of statutes or courtroom procedures—it is a living framework woven into the fabric of society. From the earliest colonial codes to today's complex regulations, the law has continuously evolved, adapting to new realities and reflecting the ever-changing values and aspirations of the people it serves.

The Historical Arc of Everyday Law

Looking back, the U.S. legal system's roots intertwine with English common law, yet its trajectory has been uniquely American. The founding documents—the Constitution and the Bill of Rights—established foundational protections and principles, but it was the lived experiences of diverse communities that gave these lofty ideals practical meaning. Over generations, landmark cases and legislative reforms—such as the Civil Rights Act of 1964 or the Americans with Disabilities Act—have expanded the promise of justice, making the law more accessible and inclusive.

One striking example of historical evolution is the expansion of **individual rights**. A century ago, everyday legal protections were much less robust; for instance, women's property rights and voting rights were sharply limited. Through advocacy and persistent reform, the legal system responded to societal demands, gradually advancing toward greater equality. This dynamic interplay between law and society continues today, reminding us that the legal system is never static, but always in conversation with its citizens.

Law in the Modern World: Emerging Trends

In recent years, we have witnessed new trends reshaping how the law functions in daily life. Two developments, in particular, illustrate the system's adaptability and its far-reaching impact.

1. The Rise of Digital Law

The digital revolution has introduced a host of novel legal questions. From privacy concerns in social media to the regulation of cryptocurrencies and artificial intelligence, the law now extends far beyond physical borders. For example, the debate over **data privacy**—highlighted by the passage of the California Consumer Privacy Act—signals a societal reckoning with how personal information is collected, stored, and used. As technology outpaces legislation, courts and lawmakers must constantly reinterpret existing statutes or craft entirely new rules, ensuring that digital innovation aligns with fundamental rights.

2. Access to Justice and Legal Empowerment

Another significant trend is the growing emphasis on **access to justice**. The traditional legal system, with its formal procedures and specialized language, can be daunting—even alienating—for ordinary people. In response, movements advocating for "legal empowerment" have emerged, championing clearer communication, simplified forms, and greater availability of affordable legal assistance. Online platforms now offer resources for individuals to navigate small claims, landlord-tenant disputes, or even immigration processes without the need for expensive litigation.

Globally, this trend echoes efforts in countries like India, where legal aid clinics and mobile courts bring justice to rural and underserved populations. The U.S. experience is part of a worldwide push to make law a tool for empowerment rather than exclusion.

The Law's Cultural Significance

Law is more than a set of rules; it is a reflection of a society's values, priorities, and sense of fairness. Everyday laws—traffic regulations, property rights, consumer protections—may at first seem mundane, but they shape our interactions, underpin order, and safeguard freedom. When citizens understand their rights and responsibilities, they are better equipped to participate meaningfully in civic life, resolve disputes peacefully, and hold authorities accountable.

This book has sought to demystify the legal system, making its principles accessible and relevant to all. By breaking down complex terms, illustrating concepts with real-world examples, and highlighting the human stories behind the rules, the aim has been to foster not just knowledge, but confidence—the confidence to advocate for oneself, to seek redress when wronged, and to contribute thoughtfully to public debates.

Looking Ahead: Law for the Next Generation

As we look to the future, the challenges facing the U.S. legal system are both daunting and inspiring. Issues such as climate change, cybercrime, and demographic shifts will test the boundaries of existing frameworks and demand innovative approaches. The law will need to reckon with advances in science, technology, and social organization, all while preserving bedrock principles of justice and equality.

At the same time, the growing diversity of American society offers the opportunity to reimagine law as more inclusive and responsive. Immigrants, young people, and historically marginalized groups are increasingly engaged in shaping the rules that govern daily life. Their perspectives, stories, and aspirations will continue to drive legal evolution—reminding us that, at its core, the law is a collective project.

The Book's Contribution and an Invitation

By equipping readers with a working knowledge of the legal system, this book contributes to a more informed, empowered populace. Understanding the law is not just the province of lawyers or judges; it is the right—and responsibility—of every resident. Whether you are navigating a landlord dispute, starting a business, or simply driving to work, the law is your companion, guide, and sometimes, your shield.

In closing, consider this book not as the end of your legal journey, but as a beginning. The legal landscape will continue to shift and expand in ways both predictable and surprising. Stay curious. Ask questions. Seek out resources and never hesitate to engage with the system that shapes so much of our collective experience.

The story of law in everyday life is, ultimately, the story of us all—constantly unfolding, perpetually renewed. May this knowledge inspire you to participate more fully, advocate more effectively, and imagine more boldly the future of justice in your community and beyond.

Made in United States
Troutdale, OR
11/03/2026

56845378R00148